Jane Austen and Philosophy

Great Authors and Philosophy

General Editor: Jacob Held,
editor of *Dr. Seuss and Philosophy*

The Great Authors and Philosophy series is for anyone who ever wondered about the deeper ideas in their favorite authors' books. Comprising entertaining, concise, and accessible takes on the philosophical ideas that classic and contemporary authors and their work convey, the books in this series bring together philosophical perspectives enhanced and illuminated by beloved stories from our culture.

Current and Forthcoming Titles in the Series

Jane Austen and Philosophy

Edited by Mimi Marinucci

ROWMAN & LITTLEFIELD
Lanham • Boulder • New York • London

Published by Rowman & Littlefield
A wholly owned subsidiary of The Rowman & Littlefield Publishing Group, Inc.
4501 Forbes Boulevard, Suite 200, Lanham, Maryland 20706
www.rowman.com

Unit A, Whitacre Mews, 26–34 Stannary Street, London SE11 4AB

Distributed by NATIONAL BOOK NETWORK

British Library Cataloguing in Publication Information Available

Library of Congress Cataloging-in-Publication Data

Names: Marinucci, Mimi, author.
Title: Jane Austen and philosophy / Mimi Marinucci.
Description: Lanham : Rowman & Littlefield, 2016. | Series: Great authors and
    philosophy | Includes bibliographical references and index.
Identifiers: LCCN 2016027114 (print) | LCCN 2016032213 (ebook) |
    ISBN 9781442257092 (pbk. : alk. paper) | ISBN 9781442257108 (Electronic)
Subjects: LCSH: Austen, Jane, 1775–1817—Criticism and interpretation. |
    Literature—Philosophy. | Literature and society—Great Britain—History—19th
    century.
Classification: LCC PR4038.P5 M37 2016 (print) | LCC PR4038.P5 (ebook) |
    DDC 823/.7—dc23
LC record available at https://lccn.loc.gov/2016027114

♾ ™ The paper used in this publication meets the minimum requirements of American National Standard for Information Sciences—Permanence of Paper for Printed Library Materials, ANSI/NISO Z39.48–1992.

Printed in the United States of America

Contents

PART II. MORALITY AND VIRTUE

PART III. WEALTH AND CLASS

PART IV. CONCEPTS AND CLARIFICATIONS

PART V. MONSTERS AND ZOMBIES

~

Acknowledgments

"There is nothing I would not do for those who are really my friends.
I have no notion of loving people by halves, it is not my nature."[1]

—Jane Austen, *Northanger Abby*

This collection is the result of the collaborative efforts of all the contributors. In addition to completing their own chapters, most of the authors read and responded to drafts of other chapters as well. The peer review process certainly strengthened the quality of the final manuscript, and I am extremely appreciative that I had the opportunity to work with this outstanding group of writers.

These writers would never have come together to produce this work at all, however, had it not been for Jacob Held. In addition to proposing the Great Authors and Philosophy series and encouraging me to serve as editor of the Jane Austen volume, he helped me at literally every stage of the process without ever making me feel bad about needing so much help. This was my first time editing this type of collaboration, and I am grateful that I had the support and assistance of such a professional and knowledgable mentor along the way.

I am also grateful that just about everyone involved in my personal and professional life was patient and understanding when my work on this and other projects led me to feel overwhelmed, distracted, absent, and sometimes worse. Their willingness to pick up the slack without complaint reinforces my belief that I have the best colleagues ever. Finally, I owe a special word of thanks to Melissa Rhoades, who helped with some last-minute copy editing at . . . well . . . the last minute.

Note

1. Jane Austen, *Northanger Abbey* (Chenango Forks, NY: Wild Jot Press, 2009), 129.

Introduction

"How Much Sooner One Tires of Anything" than of Jane Austen

Mimi Marinucci

This book is the second volume in the Great Authors and Philosophy series. Compared to Stephen King, who was the focus of the first volume, Jane Austen might not be characterized as a particularly prolific writer. Instead of referencing the familiar adage that what really counts is not quantity but quality, however, I will simply note that in consideration of her relatively short lifetime—she died when she was just forty-one years old—during a time when opportunities for women to publish were rather limited, the fact that she published six novels is quite remarkable—though two of them were published posthumously. Additionally, she was so prolific as a letter writer that much of her correspondence was eventually collected for publication— also posthumously.

What is perhaps even more noteworthy than the quantity of writing produced by Austen herself is the quantity of work produced in response to Austen's writing, of which this collection is just one of very many examples. First came *Sense and Sensibility* (1811), *Pride and Prejudice* (1813), *Mansfield Park* (1814), *Emma* (1815), *Northanger Abbey* (1817), and *Persuasion* (1817), which were initially published anonymously and for which Austen therefore enjoyed little personal recognition. Her work was popular, however, and its reception among scholars gradually gained momentum until she was securely situated within the western literary canon. Eventually came numerous film adaptations of Austen's novels, some of which are more faithful than others, beginning as early as 1938 with a television presentation based on *Pride and Prejudice*, and including, most recently, the 2016 motion picture *Pride and Prejudice and Zombies*, which is based on Seth Grahame-Smith's 2009 "mash-up" parody novel by the same name. In addition to film adaptations and literature mashups, there are also museums, societies, fan clubs, web archives, and blogs, as well as countless books, articles, college courses, and student theses, all dedicated to Jane Austen and her work. Indeed, there are even several Jane Austen board games! In other words, what began as a few novels has become a legacy about as large as they come for writers in general, let alone for a woman writing in Regency era England.

Just what it is that fascinates us about Jane Austen is difficult to pinpoint. To put it more accurately, there does not seem to be just one thing that fascinates us about Jane Austen. The variety of essays collected in this volume provides evidence of that fact. What follows is an overview of the structure and content of this book. Although it is inevitably too short to cover everything of philosophical interest about Jane Austen and her work, this collection highlights some themes that the contributors find particularly interesting.

Even on the most perfunctory reading, it is clear that love and marriage are of the utmost importance for Austen's characters. It is worth noting, however, that despite her apparent preoccupation with marriage, Austen never entered into that institution herself. She did have at least one brief romance, but when the relationship was ended by the family of her potential suitor, Austen seems to have followed her own advice, according to which "Anything is to be preferred or endured rather than marrying without affection."[1] Rather than marry for the sake of convenience, Austen opted to remain single and live with her family.

Given the prominence of romantic relationships throughout Austen's work, the first section of this book is organized around the intersecting themes of *Love and Marriage*. This section opens with the essay "Love in the Time of Epistemic Injustice," by Vittorio Bufacchi. Bufacchi uses examples from Austen to illustrate the concept of epistemic injustice, whereby social relations impact what an epistemic agent is able to know, in this case about love and relationships. In the next chapter, "Can there be Sense without Sensibility? The Middle Road to Love and Marriage in Jane Austen," Sally Winkle argues that Jane Austen employs a proto-feminist approach in her treatment of love and marriage, which renders her work especially attractive to contemporary readers, particularly many women. Next, in "Love, Marriage, and Dialectics in the Novels of Jane Austen," Suzie Gibson explores the dialectical tension within Austen's novels between marriages that are motivated by love, and marriages that are motivated by a desire for stability and security. The next chapter in this section, "Beyond Pride and Prejudice: Jane Austen and Friedrich Nietzsche on What Makes a Happy Marriage," by William Lindenmuth, explores connections between Austen and Nietzsche regarding marital relationships. The final chapter in the first section is "Marriage and Friendship in Jane Austen: Self-knowledge, Virtue, and the 'Second Self,'" by Kathleen Poorman Dougherty. In it, Dougherty establishes an analogy between the ideal form of romantic love advanced by Austen and the ideal form of friendship advanced by Aristotle.

Lindenmuth's chapter on marital happiness, though focused on Nietzsche rather than Aristotle, as well as Dougherty's chapter, which addresses Aristotle directly, lead nicely into the next section. The second section of this book, *Morality and Virtue*, begins with "Finding Happiness at Hartfield," in which Janelle Pötzsch examines Jane Austen's *Emma* as an account of happiness (eudaimonia) as addressed in Aristotle's *Nichomachean Ethics*. From here, David LaRocca's "The Last Great Representative of the Virtues: MacIntyre after Austen," also examines Austen's work through the lens of virtue ethics but shifts the focus from Aristotle to Alastair MacIntyre. This section ends with "Jane Austen and Moral Luck," in which Eva Dadlez argues that Austen's work offers a formative account of a phenomenon referred to within ethical theory as moral luck. Moral luck refers to situations in which people are regarded as morally responsible for their choices, even when the choices themselves are attributable, at least partly, to factors beyond their choosing.

The third section makes a close examination of Austen's depiction of *Wealth and Class*, which are more often matters of luck rather than of merit. Rita J. Dashwood's "Women Owning Property: The Great Lady in Jane Austen" addresses the role of women in managing economic decisions. Chris Ketcham's "Deconstructing Entailment" then offers a detailed analysis of the legal and financial details that underlie much of the drama in *Pride and Prejudice*. In "'Pictures of Perfection Make Me Sick and Wicked': Privilege and Parody in Emma," Nancy Marck Cantwell demonstrates some of the ways in which Austen's depictions of wealth and class interrogate class inequalities. In "'The Middle Classes at Play': Austen and Marx Go to Hollywood," Charles Bane offers a characterization of the 1940 film adaptation of *Pride and Prejudice* as a Marxist text.

The chapters included in the fourth section of this volume offer detailed analyses of concepts that are prominent features within Jane Austen's work. First, Elizabeth Olson and Charles Taliaferro examine Austen's treatment of the concept of secrecy in "Do You Want to Know a Secret? The Immorality and Morality of Secrets and the Subversive Jane Austen," ultimately suggesting that Austen's examples subvert the standard account by demonstrating that secrecy is actually virtuous in at least some cases. Similarly, Keith Dromm and Heather Salter examine Austen's treatment of the concept of "persuadability," or fickleness in "Persuasion, Influence, and Over-persuasion," ultimately suggesting that, again, Austen's examples subvert the standard account by demonstrating that "persuadability," or fickleness, is actually virtuous in at least some cases. In "The Language Games of Persuasion," Richard Gilmore differentiates two senses of "persuasion," as well as two corresponding senses of "marriage," and two corresponding senses of "constancy" at work in Austen's *Persuasion*.

The fifth and final section of this book turns attention away from Austen's original works and instead directs it onto the more recent genre of mashup literature. Mashups complicate, or perhaps trivialize, the plot of existing works by inserting incongruous and ostensibly absurd material into the original texts. The chapters in this section all address Seth Grahame-Smith's 2009 "collaboration" with Jane Austen, *Pride and Prejudice and Zombies*. In "Dead and Alive: Austen's Role in Mashup Literature," Amanda Riter argues that Grahame-Smith's stated goal of mocking the shallow and frivolous nature of Austen's original novel is undermined by some of the specific artistic choices he makes. In "Pride and Prejudice and Zombies: Regency, Repression, and Roundhouse Kicks," Andrea Zanin offers a more positive view of Grahame-Smith's project, reading the zombie plot as a glimpse into the repressed hostilities that must inevitably lurk within Elizabeth Bennet's subconscious. Finally, A. G. Holdier's " 'Till This Moment I Never Knew Myself': On Identities and Zombies" explores the identity relationship between characters from alternative versions of a story, thus asking whether Austen's Elizabeth Bennet and Grahame-Smith's Elizabeth Bennet can be meaningfully regarded as the same Elizabeth Bennet.

Pride and Prejudice and Zombies can be meaningfully understood as a collaborative project by both Seth Grahame-Smith and Jane Austen, and is often cited as such, despite the unwitting and posthumous nature of Austen's participation. Beyond the mashup literature, however, Austen is likewise responsible, at least partially, for a large and continually growing body of research and creative work that simply would not have come into existence without her. Assessed in this manner, Jane Austen is about as prolific as they come.

It was not without irony when Miss Bingley, apparently unable to take interest in the book she was holding, attempted to engage Mr. Darcy in conversation with the exclamation, "I declare after all there is no enjoyment like reading! How much sooner one tires of anything than of a book!"[2] When the books in question were written by Jane Austen, however, there is no irony in such a statement. There appears to be no likelihood of tiring of Jane Austen's books any time soon.

Notes

1. *Letters of Jane Austen—Brabourne Edition.* Letters to her niece, Fanny Knight, 1814–1816. Available online at http://www.pemberley.com/janeinfo/brablt15.html (accessed March 1, 2016).

2. Jane Austen, *Pride and Prejudice*, ch. 11. Available online at http://pemberley.com/janeinfo/ppv1n11.html (accessed March 1, 2016).

PART I

LOVE AND MARRIAGE

CHAPTER ONE

Love in the Time
of Epistemic Injustice

VITTORIO BUFACCHI

It is a truth universally acknowledged that society at the time of Jane Austen was profoundly unjust. In the first decades of the nineteenth century gross social and material inequalities based on gender, race, and social class were the norm, equality of opportunity was an alien notion, and class mobility was considered by those who held the reins of power as a threat to civilization, to be fought and resisted at all costs. At the turn of the nineteenth century in England, and throughout the Victorian era, for the vast majority of the population, and women in particular, life was determined by factors beyond their control to such an extent that their future was, at best, predictably bleak.[1]

This chapter focuses on a specific type of injustice that attracted much attention among philosophers in recent years, and was also pervasive during Jane Austen's time: epistemic injustice.[2] A close reading of five novels, *Persuasion* (hereafter P), *Emma* (E), *Northanger Abbey* (NA), *Pride and Prejudice* (PP) and *Sense and Sensibility* (SS) will show not only that the idea of epistemic injustice is accurate, compelling, and informative, but that thanks to Jane Austen we can perceive a dimension of epistemic injustice that has so far gone unnoticed in the philosophical literature.[3]

Jane Austen and Social Injustice

To her credit, albeit not always acknowledged, Jane Austen was not unaware of issues of social injustice around her, and perhaps keenly felt due to her own circumstances, indeed the narratives she writes about are all framed by such injustice, and a recurring theme in her novels is how the female characters, while very different in temperament and abilities, all share one common factor: they have to confront and overcome the social and economic unjust predicament they find themselves in. In general women in the nineteenth century had their destinies often dictated by the men in their lives, and as a result the opportunities to formulate and pursue their autonomously defined conception of the good life were severely curtailed.

One way to capture the institutional injustice at the heart of English society at the time is the precarious insecurity and vulnerability felt by many members of society, especially women. The heightened sense of vulnerability of women in Austen's work is a key theme in one of the best critical responses to Austen[4] by Mary Evans in *Jane Austen and the State*: "Jane Austen does not argue that women are helpless victims. . . . But what she does show is the vulnerability that leads to the paradox of both their inadequate protection (in the sense of real provision for their needs and those of their children) and their excessive restrictions (in terms of their inferior civil liberties and assumptions about female dependence)."[5]

Perhaps this is nowhere more obvious than in her best known work, *Pride and Prejudice*, where the future of the female members of the Bennet family is determined by the legal restriction, fully embraced by the dominant social norms of the day, that being women they would be barred from inheriting their family home, since (in most cases) estates were entailed on a male child.[6] In the story the laws pertaining to private property proved to be Mr. Collins's greatest asset and the source of desperation for Mrs. Bennet and her girls. Elizabeth Bennet is much more aware than her sisters of the economic vulnerability and material insecurity that define her life, and perhaps on this point she has something in common with her mother: like Elizabeth, Mrs. Bennet resents the profound injustice that women experience, which is what drives her to ensure that her daughters all marry well, since finding a rich husband is their only hope for long-term security. From this point of view Mrs. Bennet, far from being inept and inane, is in fact a paradigm of strategic rationality.

The rational, calculating, strategic reasoning of the characters in Austen's novels are carefully exposed and copiously analyzed in Michael Suk-Young Chwe's brilliant *Jane Austen, Game Theorist*.[7] Perhaps my only slight disagreement with Chwe is that he doesn't give Mrs. Bennet the credit she deserves, referring to her at one point as a "strategic sophomore," someone who thinks they know something they don't, taking pride in the trivial. I find Mary Evans's (1987) interpretation of Mrs. Bennet much more convincing: "Mrs Bennet in *Pride and Prejudice* is generally regarded as one of the absurd and comic figures of English fiction, and her preoccupation with marrying off her daughters as the mania of a somewhat inadequate intelligence. But in view of the economic exigencies facing the unmarried daughters of the eighteenth-century gentry, Mrs. Bennet's concerns do not seem entirely ridiculous. . . . Given that she has five daughters, it is little wonder that at times Mrs Bennet is less than rational."[8] The social injustice that pervaded English society in the early decades of the nineteenth century manifested itself in two ways: structural injustice (including economic injustice) and epistemic injustice.

Iris Marion Young[9] explains that structural injustice occurs whenever limitations unfairly constrain the opportunities of someone while granting privileges to others. The oppression which results from structural injustice often does not take the form of intentional coercion; instead it stems from the everyday practices of people who fail to question norms, habits, and the many hidden assumptions underlying institutional rules.[10]

Gender oppression is a clear example of structural injustice, as defined by Young. As Serena Parekh points out, "We can understand gender oppression as a form of structural injustice because it limits and shapes individual choices and circumstances, but is mostly sustained by the unintentional, unself-conscious actions of millions of people and in norms, habits, and institutions."[11] If that is the case today (and it is), it was even more so in Austen's time; it is not surprising therefore that the women in Jane Austen's novels are, in different ways and degrees, all victims and survivors of structural injustice.

It is the recognition of the institutional and cultural reality of the oppression of women in England throughout the eighteenth and nineteenth centuries that inspired authors as different as Mary Wollstonecraft, William Thompson, Harriet Taylor, and John Stuart Mill to denounce the injustice of society against women. But that was not the only injustice present at the time. Apart from structural injustice, there is another way to capture the oppression of women, then and now: epistemic injustice.

Jane Austen and Epistemic Injustice

The theory of epistemic injustice is one of the most recent, original, and influential contributions in philosophy to the way in which we theorize injustice. Miranda Fricker deserves much of the credit for drawing our attention to this phenomenon. In her groundbreaking book, *Epistemic Injustice*, she defines epistemic injustice in terms of the wrong done to someone specifically in their capacity as a knower. There are two types of epistemic injustice: testimonial injustice and hermeneutical injustice. Testimonial injustice manifests itself in patterns of incredulity, misinterpretation, silencing: "to be wronged in one's capacity as a knower is to be wronged in a capacity essential to human value. . . . The capacity to give knowledge to others is one side of the many-sided capacity so significant in human beings: namely, the capacity to reason."[12]

Fricker explains that testimonial injustice is closely associated with discrimination and prejudice, and it normally manifests itself as a credibility deficit—namely, when a speaker receives less credibility than she otherwise would have. In order to highlight the fact that the credibility deficit is usually tied to the notion of identity prejudice, Fricker uses two examples from twentieth-century films and novels. The first is taken from Anthony Minghella's screenplay of *The Talented Mr. Ripley*, where a young woman, Marge Sherwood, is silenced by an older man, Herbert Greenfield, who refuses to listen or give any credibility to her suspicions, and this only because she is a woman: "Marge, there's female intuition, and then there are facts."[13] Similarly in Harper Lee's *To Kill a Mockingbird* Tom Robinson is charged with raping a young girl. Tom Robinson is innocent, but because he is black while the girl is white, his testimony in court is not believed, and he is found guilty.

The two examples chosen by Fricker refer to particular individuals who are victims of identity prejudice, and are not believed in specific circumstances, the first relating to a murder, the second a rape. In the first case it is a young woman who is not believed, in the latter case a young black man. Testimonial injustice and identity prejudice are also present in Austen's novels, but in a different way. Virtually all the female characters in her novels are victims of testimonial injustice. The prejudice against the validity of epistemic claims by women is so widespread, so inculcated in the culture that it fails to shock us, or even register with the characters in Austen's novels. We almost come to expect it. Men had the monopoly over knowledge, and Austen knew it. In the early decades of the nineteenth century men simply had no respect for women as authentic sources of knowledge, or wisdom, and the assumption was that a man always knew more than a woman, hence he was by nature and nurture her superior. As Austen remarks in *Persuasion*: "Men have had every advantage of us in telling their own story. Education has been theirs in so much higher a degree; the pen has been in their hands."[14] Occasionally Austen highlights the comical absurdity of this state of affairs, as when in *Pride and Prejudice* Mr. Collins is so intoxicated by his sense of superiority that he is convinced that Elizabeth Bennet couldn't possibly refuse his proposal of marriage: "I am not now to learn. . . . That it is usual with young ladies to reject the addresses of the man whom they secretly mean to accept, when he first applies for their favour."[15] Clearly for Mr. Collins when a woman says "no" she means "yes." But more often than not the epistemic disadvantage women experience is portrayed by Austen in tragic terms. Perhaps this is most clear in her sixth and last novel, *Persuasion* (1818). Often referred to as Austen's most feminist novel, its main character, Anne Elliot, is arguably Austen's most complex creation. In the opening pages we are told that Anne Elliot is twenty-seven, yet she "was nobody with either father or sister; *her word had no weight*; her convenience was always to give way; she was only Anne" (emphasis added).[16] This description captures the essence of what Miranda Fricker refers to as epistemic injustice, in particular the claim that the heroine of this story, notwithstanding her astuteness and intelligence, is not given the epistemic credibility she deserves: no one listens to her, no one gives her any credit, no one is interested in what she has to say or contribute. The fact that at twenty-seven years of age Anne Elliot is the oldest of Austen's heroines is worth consideration. Women are victims of epistemic injustice not simply because they tend to attract the attentions of older and more experienced men; the issue is one of gender, not age.

What makes *Persuasion* particularly interesting is the fact that unlike the other heroines in Austen's previous novels, Anne Elliot is strong, independent, and confident. She is the only one to stand up against the pervasive epistemic injustice inflicted on all other members of her sex. In a pivotal scene it is Anne Elliot who has the confidence, and know-how, to step up and take control of the situation, not the men around her. This is when, during a seaside walk, in a misjudged attempt at flirting with a gentleman, young Louisa Musgrove jumps from a wall, falls on the pavement and is seriously injured: in Austen's words she lies "lifeless." Austen tells us that in this moment of crisis Anne Elliot takes charge of the situation, and while the other women who witnessed the accident are either insensible or hysterical, the men look to Anne for guidance: "Both [Charles Musgrove and Captain Wentworth] seemed to look to her for directions. 'Anne, Anne,'" cried Charles, "what is to be done next? What, in heaven's name, is to be done next?"[17] Anne is not a nurse, just a woman who deserves respect for her intellect and knowledge, and is not inferior to the men around her: in this scene gender roles are spectacularly turned upside down.

So far we have focused on one type of epistemic injustice, namely testimonial injustice. The other form of epistemic injustice is hermeneutical injustice. Hermeneutical injustice refers to instances when someone is not able to make sense of an experience due to prejudicial flaws in circumstances of shared resources for social interpretation, or in other words, when someone is harmed by a sort of gap in collective understanding which makes one's own experiences unintelligible: "Hermeneutical injustice is the injustice of having some significant area of one's social experience obscured from collective understanding owing to a structural identity prejudice in the collective hermeneutical resource."[18] Fricker points out that this definition brings out the discretionary character of epistemic injustice: "in both sorts of epistemic injustice, the subject suffers from one or another sort of prejudice against them *qua* social type."[19]

Fricker gives a number of examples of hermeneutical injustice, including sexual harassment in work places. According to Fricker, we can define this sort of hermeneutical injustice in the following way: "The injustice of having some significant area of one's social experience obscured from collective understanding owing to a structural identity prejudice in the collective hermeneutical resource."[20]

While there is nothing remotely resembling explicit physical sexual harassment in Austen's novels, this doesn't mean that hermeneutical injustice is not present. On the contrary, hermeneutical injustice is rife in her fictions. With a few notable exceptions, the female characters in Austen's novels seem to accept the oppressive norms that dictate every aspect of their lives, and are incapable of fully understanding what is happening in their world. In *Pride and Prejudice* Lydia Bennet is so intent to get one over her bigger sisters that she doesn't understand the risks and potential consequences of running away with Wickham. In *Northanger Abbey* Catherine Morland is unable to make sense of the fact that she is being sent home by General Tilney, unaccompanied by a servant and at an inconvenient (and potentially dangerous) time. In *Sense and Sensibility* Marianne's inability to understand Willoughby's abandonment of her has very serious consequences for her mental and physical health.

Whenever things don't work out as they should, or were hoped to, the women in Austen's novels always blame themselves first.

Epistemic injustice has attracted a great deal of attention in the philosophical literature on injustice since Fricker introduced this concept.[21] Building on Fricker's work, José Medina reminds us that testimonial injustice is problematic not only to the oppressed subjects, for all the reasons we are familiar with, but also to those who stand to gain from this injustice.[22] The problems that ensue from the epistemic excesses that privileged subjects enjoy is an under-researched issue. In particular, Medina reminds us that it is a vice to overestimate one's powers, epistemic or otherwise. Epistemic arrogance leads to cognitive immaturity, epistemic laziness (lack of curiosity), close-mindedness, and ultimately what Medina calls "active ignorance": the epistemic attitudes and habits that contribute to create and maintain bodies of ignorance. This is true of many male characters in Austen's novels, including Mr. Collins and Mr. Darcy in *Pride and Prejudice*,[23] Anne's father Sir Walter Elliot in *Persuasion*; Mr. Elton in *Emma*, and finally General Tilney in *Northanger Abbey*.

From Victim to Perpetrator

There are many reasons philosophers interested in gender issues could do worse than accumulate examples from Jane Austen's fiction. One reason, as we have seen so far, is to find confirmation and validation of *a priori* defined philosophical concepts, such as epistemic injustice. But there is also another reason: a close reading of her novels can reveal hidden dimensions and other subtle factors of philosophical concepts we are familiar with. I will discuss in this final section that there is a dimension of hermeneutical injustice that has not received the philosophical attention it deserves, but that comes out clearly thanks to the fine writing of Austen and the complexity of her characterizations. Namely, hermeneutical injustice does not only manifest itself when a victim of this injustice is incapable of making sense of her own experience, because she is hermeneutically marginalized. Instead it also reveals itself when the victim is unaware of the fact that she is instrumental in reproducing and propagating the same injustice in which she is a victim. This aspect of hermeneutical injustice will be referred to as the Perpetuating Force of Epistemic Injustice.

The Perpetuating Force of Epistemic Injustice can take two forms: it can be passive or active. In the passive form, the victim perpetuates the injustice when she fails to prevent the same injustice to be inflicted on others. Here we are treading on Judith Shklar's idea of passive injustice: "the refusal of both officials and of private citizens to prevent acts of wrongdoing when they could and should do so."[24] The character trait most closely associated with passive injustice is indifference: this is what makes social injustice not only pervasive, but also invasive and difficult to displace. There is a great deal of indifference in Austen's novels. In *Pride and Prejudice*, for all her cleverness even Elizabeth Bennet appears indifferent to the fate of her younger sisters, except when their actions have a potentially negative impact on her. Furthermore, she is blind to the even more serious injustice suffered by the women of social classes below her, starting from the maids and other servants at Longbourne,[25] and including her best friend, Charlotte Lucas.

But the Perpetuating Force of Epistemic Injustice can also take a more active or direct form. This is when the victims of epistemic injustice become the vehicles of more epistemic injustice, as they inflict the same type of injustice on other people around them, who happen to be more vulnerable and powerless than themselves. This is perhaps most obvious in *Emma*.

Emma Woodhouse, the twenty-one-year-old heroine is both the victim and perpetrator of epistemic injustice. In the opening sentence of the novel she is described as "handsome, clever, and rich"[26]; indeed later on we are told that "Emma is spoiled by being the cleverest of her family,"[27] but being clever is not enough for Emma to escape her predicament of being seen as socially and intellectually inferior to her male counterparts, so much so that Emma accepts her inferiority. But in an interesting twist to an otherwise recurring theme in Austen's novels whereby the female characters are always depicted as subordinate and subservient, we find that Emma passes from victim to perpetrator, and albeit involuntarily she becomes instrumental in perpetuating the type of epistemic injustice that is one of the sources of her oppression, and of social injustice more generally.

In the story, Emma amuses herself by playing matchmaker, and one of her projects is to find a respectable gentleman for seventeen-year-old Harriet Smith, an attractive but socially inferior young woman who she has decided to take under her wing. Harriet Smith was found as a baby abandoned outside a boarding school; as Austen explains, she "was the natural daughter of somebody."[28] The mysterious origins of Harriet Smith is indicative of the injustice of life in nineteenth-century England where someone's unknown parentage should not only be looked down upon but also treated as shameful and indecent, a sufficient reason to be excluded from certain circles. One can detect a certain sense of irony in Austen's writing when describing Harriet's parentage:

> She proved to be the daughter of a tradesman, rich enough to afford her the comfortable maintenance which had ever been hers, and decent enough to have always wished for concealment.—Such was the blood of gentility which Emma had for-

merly been so ready to vouch for!—It was likely to be as untainted, perhaps, as the blood of many a gentleman: but what a connexion had she been preparing for Mr. Knightley—or for the Churchills—or even for Mr Elton!—The stain of illegitimacy, unbleached by nobility or wealth, would have been a stain indeed.[29]

It is to Emma's credit that she takes an interest in Harriet, although her motivations for doing so are not always clear. Austen simply tells us: "Emma knew [Harriet] very well by sight and had long felt an interest in, on account of her beauty."[30] Nevertheless what soon becomes clear is the way Emma inflicts testimonial injustice on Harriet, perpetuating (no doubt involuntarily) the same epistemic injustice which she is the victim of. Harriet is in love with a young farmer, Mr. Martin, who by all accounts is a very decent, hard-working, and loving young man, but Emma will not have it. Harriet is Emma's personal project, and for her entertainment she is determined to find a better match for her. As a result, Emma appears to be incapable of listening to her friend in accepting that Harriet holds legitimate sentiments that ought to be acknowledged and respected. Instead Emma does her best to dissuade Harriet by piling on all the prejudices that people of Emma's class have against those of lower social standing. At first Emma tells Harriet that "Mr. Martin is now awkward and abrupt . . . he will be a completely gross, vulgar farmer—totally inattentive to appearances, and thinking of nothing but profit and loss,"[31] but when he makes a marriage proposal Emma is so afraid to lose her friend that she turns against Mr. Martin with renewed (undeserved) malice, telling Harriet that to marry Mr. Martin would mean to be "confined to the society of the illiterate and vulgar all your life,"[32] and that would be the end of their friendship as Emma would never visit her if she were to become Mrs. Martin.

Emma was published in December 1815, eighteen months before Jane Austen's death. This was followed by *Persuasion*, which Jane Austen finished in 1816 although it was only published posthumously in 1818. One could argue that while in her portrayal of women Austen was herself guilty of propagating the Perpetuation Force of Epistemic Injustice, especially in her earlier novels, this is not the case in her last novel. One recurring theme in earlier novels is the way a young woman's "epistemic awakening"[33] is triggered by a male character. Thus as Angela Ryan (2006) has pointed out, Elizabeth Bennet only acquires true "self-knowledge" upon reading Mr. Darcy's letter:

How humiliating this discovery!—Yet, how just a humiliation!—Had I been in love, I could not have been more wretchedly blind. But vanity, not love, has been my folly. Pleased with the preference of one, and offended by the neglect of the other, on the very beginning of our acquaintance, I have courted prepossession and ignorance and driven reason away. . . . Till this moment I never knew myself.[34]

It is disconcerting how Elizabeth Bennet needs Mr. Darcy to gain self-knowledge, which makes the contrast between her and Anne Elliot in *Persuasion* even greater, since Anne Elliot knows herself and doesn't need a man to acquire self-knowledge. The fact that there is no moment of "epistemic awakening" in Austen's more mature work is a testament to her wisdom, and perhaps feminist credentials.

Conclusion

Jane Austen was not a philosopher, but she had insights about social relations that have philosophical value. I have argued that Austen's novels add support to two types of epistemic injustice singled out by Miranda Fricker: testimonial and hermeneutical. Epistemic injustice is a powerful tool to explain gender oppression, past and present, and the validity of this philosophical concept finds corroboration in Austen's novels.

I have also argued that reading Austen can help philosophers interested in hermeneutical injustice to see an added dimension of this phenomenon. The aim was not only to highlight the extent to which Anne Elliot, Elizabeth Bennet, and many other female characters in Jane Austen's novels are the victims of both testimonial and hermeneutical injustice, but also how these characters give us a nuanced understanding of how epistemic injustice, once established, perpetuates itself. In Austen's novels the victims of epistemic injustice turn into being perpetrators of that same injustice; perhaps unintentionally and unwillingly, but always with devastating consequences for those even more vulnerable than themselves, we are reminded just how deeply ingrained and powerfully resilient epistemic injustice can be, and how difficult it is to overcome epistemic injustice once it is instituted.

Notes

1. I am grateful to Mary Edwards, Johanne Herlihy, and Clíona Ó Gallchoir for their comments and suggestions on an earlier draft of this chapter.

2. Injustice can be defined and measured in terms of three dominant factors: maldistribution, exclusion, and disempowerment. All three factors are present in abundance in

nineteenth-century Britain. For this three-dimensional analysis of social injustice, see V. Bufacchi (2012). Vittorio Bufacchi, *Social Injustice: Essays in Political Philosophy* (London: Palgrave, 2012).

3. Rogers (2006, xliii) would no doubt disapprove of my argument in this paper, and perhaps all the papers in this volume: "[Austen] was a novelist and we do her most serious art no service if we ask it to perform philosophic tasks in which she had little or no ascertainable interest." The point is not whether Jane Austen had an "interest" in philosophical problems; the fact remains that her work, whether she was aware of it or not, has philosophical value. There is no disservice in suggesting that Austen was an accidental philosopher.

4. There are of course many more recent feminist studies of Austen that focus precisely on issues of unequal power relations in the late eighteenth century, including Johnson (1988); Looser (1995); Bilger (1998); Greenfield (2002). I'm grateful to Clíona Ó Gallchoir for alerting me to this body of literature. Audrey Bilger, *Laughing Feminism: Subversive Comedy in Burney, Edgeworth and Austen* (Detroit, MI: Wayne State University Press, 1998); Susan C. Greenfield, *Mothering Daughters: Novels and the Politics of Family Romance in Burney and Austen* (Detroit, MI: Wayne State University Press, 2002); Claudia Johnson, *Jane Austen: Women, Politics and the Novel* (Chicago: University of Chicago Press, 1988); Devoney Looser (ed.), *Jane Austen and Discourses of Feminism* (Basingstoke: Palgrave, 1995).

5. Mary Evans, *Jane Austen and the State* (London: Tavistock Publications, 1987), x.

6. This is also the case in *Sense and Sensibility* with the Dashwood sisters, and their mother, who are forced to leave the family home at Norland when Mr. Henry Dashwood dies, since the estate passes to Mr. John Dashwood, son of Mr. Henry Dashwood from a previous marriage. In terms of women's vulnerability Miss Bates in *Emma* also comes to mind. I'm grateful to Johanne Herlihy for suggesting these references.

7. Michael Suk-Young Chwe, *Jane Austen, Game Theorist* (Princeton: Princeton University Press, 2013).

8. Mary Evans, *Jane Austen and the State*, 7.

9. Iris Marion Young, *Justice and the Politics of Difference* (Princeton, NJ: Princeton University Press, 1990); Iris Marion, *Inclusion and Democracy* (Oxford: Oxford University Press, 2002); Iris Marion, "Structural Injustice and the Politics of Difference," in T. Christiano and J. Christman (eds.), *Contemporary Debates in Political Philosophy* (Oxford: Blackwell, 2009).

10. Young singles out five categories of oppression that also double as categories of injustice: exploitation, marginalization, powerlessness, cultural imperialism, and violence. All of the above form the backdrop to Austen's novels.

11. Serena Parekh, "Getting to the Root of Gender Inequality: Structural Injustice and Political Responsibility," *Hypatia*, vol. 26, no. 4 (2011): 677.

12. Miranda Fricker, *Epistemic Injustice: Power & the Ethics of Knowing* (Oxford: Oxford University Press, 2007), 44.

13. Fricker, *Epistemic Injustice*, 9.

14. Jane Austen, *Persuasion* (Cambridge: Cambridge University Press, 2006), 335.

15. Jane Austen, *Pride and Prejudice* (Cambridge: Cambridge University Press, 2006), 120.

16. Austen, *Persuasion*, 6.

17. Austen, *Persuasion*, 120.

18. Fricker, *Epistemic Injustice*, 155.

19. Fricker, *Epistemic Injustice*, 155.

20. Fricker, *Epistemic Injustice*, 155.

21. See the forum of Fricker's book in *Theoria*, 2008, vol. 23/1, no. 61; the special issue on her book in *Social Epistemology* 2011, vol. 26, issue 2; and the symposia on her book in *Episteme*, 2010, vol. 7, issue 2. Fricker's work was also the subject of a two-day conference at the University of Bristol, "Understanding Epistemic Injustice," 26–27 June 2014.

22. José Medina, *The Epistemology of Resistance* (Oxford: Oxford University Press, 2013).

23. Mr. Darcy is guilty of epistemic arrogance in the first part of the book but seems to redeem himself by the time he makes the second proposal of marriage to Elizabeth Bennet.

24. Judith Shklar, *The Faces of Injustice* (New Haven, CT: Yale University Press, 1990), 5.

25. On this, although it isn't Jane Austen's work, Jo Baker, *Longbourn* (London: Doubleday, 2013) deserves to be praised. This novel tells the story of the servants in the Bennet's household, and the story unfolds simultaneously to the events described in *Pride and Prejudice*. The Bennet family is not only ignorant of their servants' troubles and tribulations but totally indifferent.

26. Jane Austen, *Emma* (London: Penguin, 1996), 7.

27. Austen, *Emma*, 36.

28. Austen, *Emma*, 23.

29. Austen, *Emma*, 450–51.

30. Austen, *Emma*, 23.

31. Austen, *Emma*, 33.

32. Austen, *Emma*, 53.

33. I am grateful to Mary Edwards for suggesting this idea, and for her views and suggestions around this topic.

34. Austen, *Pride and Prejudice*, 185. Angela Ryan, "Elizabeth's Missteps: hubris and hamartia in Pride and Prejudice", in *Pride and Prejudice: Le Roman de Jane Austen et le Film de Joe Wright* (New York: Ellipses Press, 2006).

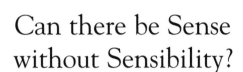

CHAPTER TWO

Can there be Sense without Sensibility?

The Middle Road to Love and Marriage in Jane Austen

SALLY WINKLE

Have you ever wondered why Jane Austen's novels resonate so deeply with twenty-first-century North American readers? Her novels are often read as romance fiction with fairy-tale endings. Austen's exploration of the kind of love and partnership that leads to a happy marriage is still relevant for many Americans and Europeans today, and seems to confirm many young women's fantasies of romantic love and marriage. Indeed, this narrow view of Austen as merely a romance author is quite common. However, I would argue that Austen is proto-feminist in her veneration of a love that is based on mutual respect, affection, intimacy, and common values, which seems to promote the equality of her male and female characters in their heterosexual relationships, despite and within the limitations of eighteenth-century patriarchal society. Her narratives offer much more than a simplistic concept of everlasting, passionate love and marital bliss.

Jane Austen's *Sense and Sensibility* is a complex representation of evolving concepts of love and marriage within late eighteenth-century upper-class British society. Her satirical portrayal of the conflicting philosophical trends of Rationality and Sentimentality as personified in her protagonists is present through witty dialogue, narration, and characterization; it also forms a foundation for her depiction of love, marriage, and social critique in this novel.

I maintain that Jane Austen's definition of love steers a middle passage between sense and sensibility. That is, her concept of love and marriage treads a path between pure rational practicality, marked by coldhearted calculation of what entails "a good match," on the one hand, and sentimental self-indulgence, based on a notion of eternal passion, undying devotion, and exultation in joy or misery on the other.

Both Rationality and Sentimentality influenced writers and philosophers throughout the eighteenth century in England, France, and Germany. Rationality stresses reason over emotion as well as development of the mind to improve character. In contrast, Sentimentality or Sensibility as a cultural movement encourages unchecked expression of feelings, primacy of ardent romantic love, and predilection for melancholy as well as love of nature and music.[1]

It is obvious from the beginning that of the two protagonists in *Sense and Sensibility*, Elinor represents "sense" while Marianne and their mother are very much immersed in a sentimental view of love, marriage, and nature. Happy endings depicting the relationships of Elinor and Edward or Marianne and Colonel Brandon in *Sense and Sensibility* suggest a tendency in Austen toward more rational views of love and marriage over unleashed passion and sentimental love without regard for future security. However, upon deeper reflection her narratives reveal a more complex concept of love and matrimony, an approach that negotiates a middle course between pure practicality and unchecked sentimentality. For example, Austen condemns marriage based solely on economic expedience as doomed to unhappiness in her novels, illustrated most clearly by the eventual match between John Willoughby and Miss Grey in *Sense and Sensibility*. Similarly, the marriage between Maria Bertram and Mr. Rushworth in *Mansfield Park* is a rational, socially advantageous union that ends in catastrophe because of the incompatibility of the bride and groom's characters.

Marriages founded only on male attraction to a beautiful young woman, thus focusing on the senses, with no thought to her education, character, intelligence, or temperament, are shown as recipes for discontent as well. Examples of unfortunate matches are abundant in *Sense and Sensibility*, including Sir John and Lady Middleton, Mr. and Mrs. Palmer, and Fanny and John Dashwood. In *Pride and Prejudice*, Elizabeth's parents, Mr. and Mrs. Bennet, provide a strong caution against unsuitable matches. Indeed, Jane

Austen's novels are as full of unhappy marriages as they are of vain, superficial, tedious characters of the British upper class.

A look at the early feminist ideas on rational education and gender expressed by eighteenth-century philosopher Mary Wollstonecraft can offer insight into Austen's depiction of women and their varied paths to love and marriage. Austen's narratives often ridicule shallow, uneducated, ignorant women and in this her descriptions coincide with the notions of Mary Wollstonecraft, as expressed in her pioneering work, A *Vindication of the Rights of Woman*, 1792. Wollstonecraft argues that women (read: middle-class women) often have little choice but to focus on their appearance, social status, and children because of their prescribed subordinate gender role in society.[2] In other words, instead of acquiring an education that will help them gain understanding and strong characters, girls and women are brought up to be beautiful, delicate, vain, and enchanting in order to please men and achieve an advantageous match.

To Wollstonecraft, when women embrace sentimentality they emphasize the senses, their feelings, and emotions to the detriment of reason or education. Relying solely on the senses is equated in her mind to a focus on pleasure, pleasing others, exalting frailty as virtue, and refusal to develop their reason.[3] This can lead women to a life of dependence on a man, since they regard their beauty and charm over men as their only power.[4] In many ways Austen's silly, frivolous female characters are exemplary of Wollstonecraft's arguments for reason and a rational, equal education for women, more physical exercise, and emphasis on rational thought to develop women's minds and hearts.

For readers who have wondered why so many of Jane Austen's wives and mothers are silly and irresponsible, while her unmarried young female protagonists are often smart, determined, and rational, this becomes more understandable upon reading Wollstonecraft, Austen's contemporary. Indeed, in Wollstonecraft's philosophical tract and in Austen's fiction, both authors observed and critiqued such uneducated women of their time as products of a patriarchal society determined by subordinate roles for women raised merely to be dependent on, and pleasing to, men. Wollstonecraft presents a critical framework for understanding and addressing the inequality experienced by middle- and upper-class women in eighteenth-century England, whereas Jane Austen colors in the picture with witty social critique and lively descriptions of ridiculous, superficial, and yet believable characters that illustrate many of the problems analyzed by the philosopher.

Austen introduces Mrs. Bennet, Elizabeth and Jane's mother, in the first chapter of *Pride and Prejudice* as "a woman of mean understanding, little information and uncertain temper. When she was discontented she fancied herself nervous. The business of her life was to get her daughters married; its solace was visiting and news."[5] As drawn by Austen, Mrs. Bennet is the epitome of a woman who attracted her husband through her youth and beauty, but whose "weak understanding and illiberal mind" had destroyed any respect or affection her husband had felt for her.[6] However, Austen does not place all the blame on Mrs. Bennet, as the novel focuses not only on Mrs. Bennet's folly, but also on Mr. Bennet's neglect as a husband. Instead of attempting to help his wife develop her character through reading and education, he exploits her ignorance as a source of his own amusement, to the mortification of his eldest daughter, Elizabeth. Indeed, Mrs. Bennet's lack of education can be interpreted as a product of a patriarchal society in which middle- and upper-class women's sole responsibility is to marry a man of suitable wealth and station and be a good wife and nurturing mother. Austen and Wollstonecraft both imply through their writings that women cannot be good wives and mothers or attain affectionate love and respect unless they are raised with sense and an emphasis on development of character and understanding. Mrs. Bennet's youngest daughters, Lydia and Kitty, reveal the inadequacies of their mother's parenting skills. Nonetheless, her single-minded goal to find husbands for her daughters demonstrates not only her reinforcement of social norms, but also her efforts to ensure her daughters' success within the narrow parameters of opportunities for middle- and upper-class women in patriarchal society.

Lucy Steele in *Sense and Sensibility* is typical of an instinctively clever young woman dedicated to pleasing those around her, especially if they can advance her prospects of a good match.

> Elinor saw, and pitied her for, the neglect of abilities which education might have rendered so respectable, but she saw, with less tenderness of feeling, the thorough want of delicacy, of rectitude, and integrity of mind, which her attentions, her assiduities, her flatteries . . . betrayed; and she could have no lasting satisfaction in the company of a person who joined insincerity with ignorance; . . .[7]

Jane Austen's critique of ignorant women is not limited to wives and mothers, as indicated in her depiction of a young woman who could have used her intelligence and talents to broaden and improve her mind and sentiments. Lucy, who is secretly engaged to Elinor's love interest, Edward, does not benefit from a comparison with Austen's sensible, honest heroine, and by the end of the novel after marrying for money, Lucy has become one of the tedious, obsequious married women appearing so frequently in Austen's fiction.

Jane Austen acknowledges repeatedly in her novels that marriage for middle- and upper-class women could not be separated from finances or economic survival. Women of these social classes in the eighteenth and nineteenth centuries were not allowed to work outside the home except in the direst circumstances; if they did not marry they were expected to live with their parents or at the home of a married brother or sister. For both men and women, and especially for women, marriage is a means of attaining financial security. The result in Austen's novels is often loveless marriages for both partners, as is the case with John Willoughby and Miss Grey in *Sense and Sensibility* and Charlotte Lucas and Mr. Collins in *Pride and Prejudice*.

Charlotte Lucas views marriage merely as a means to respectability and social acceptance; and her fate is marriage to the insufferable, pompous Mr. Collins, which her friend Elizabeth, Austen's major protagonist, cannot comprehend.

> Charlotte . . . was tolerably composed. She had gained her point and had time to consider it. Her reflections were in general satisfactory. Mr. Collins to be sure was neither sensible nor agreeable; his society was irksome and his attachment to her must be imaginary. But still he would be her husband.—Without thinking highly either of men or of matrimony, marriage had always been her object; it was the only honourable provision for well-educated young women of small fortune, and however uncertain of giving happiness, must be their pleasantest preservative from want.[8]

Charlotte's situation makes very plain the social expectations and narrow "choices" for middle- and upper-class women in England until the end of the nineteenth century. Austen calls attention to these restrictions throughout her narratives.[9] In the case of Charlotte, she condemns the social limitations on women without condemning the fictional character. As Elizabeth's close friend, Charlotte is a sympathetic, sensible, kind, and intelligent woman, yet she has accepted the extremely restrictive possibilities for her future as a twenty-seven-year-old upper-class British woman with limited fortune and lack of great beauty. She seeks the independence of her own household rather than remaining a dependent in her parents' home. She makes that choice, and although Elizabeth finds it hard to accept, Austen presents it as a rational, if unfortunate, decision. Jane Austen highlights the possibility of mutual love and choice of partners as a means of rendering the expected social institution of marriage for women more tolerable. As a rational thinker and social realist, Austen weaves narratives within a fictional society no less restrictive than her own. She gives her major protagonists the tools of sense, rational thought, education, and consciousness that enable them to develop their characters as they navigate the challenges of achieving financial comfort, contentment, mutual affection, respect, and a satisfying marriage to a partner of their choice.

In contrast to Mary Wollstonecraft's denouncement of sentimentality and sensibility as completely detrimental to the development of women's minds and characters, Austen's critique of sensibility consists of gentle mockery and narrative developments that establish a middle space between sentimental and rational love. In *Sense and Sensibility*, for example, Austen does not condemn Marianne or set her up as a superficial, static character. Instead, Marianne emerges as well educated and intelligent despite her inclination toward excessive sentimentality, and as willing to learn and grow from her experiences. Indeed, she must overcome her romantic fantasies of passionate first love in order to achieve contentment, peace, and lasting love with Colonel Brandon at the end of the novel.

Marianne's experience of falling in love with Willoughby in *Sense and Sensibility* is depicted as disastrous for herself, her family, and ultimately for Willoughby as well. At the beginning of the novel, Marianne is literally swept off her feet by the handsome, young, charming Mr. Willoughby as he carries her into the house after she sprained her ankle running down a hill in the rainy Devonshire countryside. Willoughby seems to share all her tastes, amusements, and passions, and sixteen-year-old Marianne is drawn to him with no thought of her future or the impact of her actions. She has fallen desperately in love, is caught up in the romance of her feelings. "When he was present she had no eyes for anyone else. Everything he did, was right. Everything he said, was clever. . . . If dancing formed the amusement of the night, they were partners for half the time; . . . Such conduct made them of course most exceedingly laughed at, but ridicule could not shame, and seemed hardly to provoke them."[10] Marianne sees nothing wrong with publicly demonstrating her affection for Willoughby, to the distress of Elinor, who wants her younger sister to act with more sense and less sensibility, as the latter results in complete disregard for propriety. Marianne is depicted as open and honest in her actions, but also as young, inexperienced, and impetuous. These are dangerous qualities for a young well-bred woman of modest means in the late eighteenth century, where future prospects for the middle-

and upper-class female population were restricted to a respectable marriage, with a compatible partner if she is lucky, and children, future heirs.

A twenty-first-century feminist reading of Austen's novels reveals connections between images of love in her fiction and bell hooks's concepts of love as articulated in her book *all about love: new visions*, which was written almost two hundred years later. African American feminist writer and scholar bell hooks critiques the romantic ideal of "falling in love" as giving up control, choice, and responsibility for one's actions.[11] She argues that the destructiveness of romantic love "resides in the notion that we come to love with no will and no capacity to choose. This illusion, perpetuated by so much romantic lore, stands in the way of our learning to love."[12] Hooks explains that we need to choose to love as an act of will and action, instead of allowing ourselves to "fall," that is, to relinquish our agency, our power, and control to another person.[13]

Keeping hooks's twenty-first-century concepts of love in mind, I would argue that in her fiction Austen critiques a fantasy of "falling in love" without thought of consequence, social expectations, or practical concerns such as income, status, or character. Marianne is a prime example of the risk for women giving up their power and control to a lover. Austen's novels are replete with young women falling in love with unworthy gentlemen who often abandon them, sometimes in untenable situations, such as Willoughby and the unfortunate Eliza in *Sense and Sensibility*. Indeed, Austen's allusion to desire in the context of love is extremely subtle and practically unmentionable except as a warning to vulnerable women who might give in to their fantasies and passions, as the immature, thoughtless younger sister Lydia did in eloping with Wickham in *Pride and Prejudice*. Marianne had violated strict rules of social propriety in allowing public demonstrations of affection with her suitor and more seriously, in secretly riding off with him one afternoon to tour Combe Magna, Willoughby's future estate, without a chaperone. These reckless acts proclaimed her attachment and led family and friends to assume there was a secret engagement, all of which contributed to her misery and despair when Willoughby rejected her.

Within the parameters of social expectations of her time, Austen's love relationships must be legitimated by marriage, and the woman is to remain a virgin until she enters matrimony. Despite these restrictions, as Austen's major protagonists follow this path, most are depicted as achieving deep affection, mutual respect, and contentment with their husbands in concluding passages of the novels. As a way of promoting their marital happiness, the author outfits her heroines with wit, education, and strong characters in order to hold their own in relationships with their male partners.

Austen's concept of desirable love within the social expectations of her time is conveyed through Elinor and Edward's feelings for one another in *Sense and Sensibility*. Elinor's love for Edward is founded on appreciation for his values, integrity, and understanding as well as their mutual respect and esteem for one another's characters. At the beginning of the novel she notes to her sister that "his mind is well-informed, his enjoyment of books exceedingly great, his imagination lively, his observation just and correct, and his taste delicate and pure."[14] Much to Marianne's chagrin, Elinor uses words such as "esteem" and "like" when expressing her feelings for Edward, partly because she is not certain he returns her affections. Elinor does not "fall in love" or relinquish control of her emotions as her sister Marianne does; her thoughts toward Edward are closer to bell hooks's definition of love as a choice, an act of will rather than Marianne's notion of once in a lifetime, absolute romantic love. As hooks proclaims, "How different things might be if, rather than saying 'I think I'm in love,' we were saying 'I've connected with someone in a way that makes me think I'm on the way to knowing love.'"[15] Jane Austen at the turn of the nineteenth century projects through her protagonist Elinor a woman who is on her "way to knowing love" within the context of British class culture and social expectations of the time.

Elinor's road to "knowing love" and the eventual happy ending of marriage to Edward is nonetheless a rocky one, as she must contend with Edward's secret engagement to Lucy Steele made four years earlier, divulged to her by Lucy, which she must conceal from her sisters and mother. Elinor's rational, composed behavior, fortitude, and strength of character are contrasted to Marianne's excessive self-indulgence in misery upon Willoughby's cruel rejection of her and his subsequent marriage to the very rich Miss Grey. Nonetheless, the narrator's insights into Elinor's thoughts reveal her intense feelings for Edward once she learns that he is lost to her, thus implying a degree of sensibility in her emotions toward him, despite her outward appearance of composure. Thus Elinor seems to combine both reason and deep feeling in her experience of love. Austen reminds us of Elinor's hidden emotions as she describes her protagonist's successful attempt to conceal her distress, "no one would have supposed . . . that Elinor was mourning in secret over obstacles which must divide her forever from the object of her love . . ." (141).

To Marianne's credit, once she learns of Elinor's quiet suffering for months while she was able to openly express her own grief and turmoil, she makes an effort to control the excesses of her sensibility in admiration of her older sister's sense. Nonetheless, Marianne's hopeless love for Willoughby and her dejection upon its demise practically kills her; her unchecked descent into despair compromises her health and results in a near-fatal illness, bringing her close to the fate of numerous heroines in eighteenth-century sentimental novels who died of grief over failed love relationships or cruel attacks upon their virtue.[16] Marianne later reflects on her own reckless behavior and recognizes that she brought illness on herself by neglecting her own health, proclaiming: "Had I died, it would have been self-destruction."[17]

The expression of love between Elinor and Edward is nonetheless tempered by practicality, especially considering his disinheritance. Despite the portrayal of their engagement as based on mutual esteem, real affection, deep feelings, and understanding, her thoughts as she accepts Edward's proposal indicate the power of economic reality in consideration of love and matrimony: "and they were neither of them quite enough in love to think that 350 pounds a-year would supply them with the comforts of life."[18] Through such satirical comments, Jane Austen constantly reminds the reader of the social expectations and financial obligations that limit women's decisions on what must be the most important step of their lives in a patriarchal society that vastly restricts their choices.

In her depiction of achievable, devoted, considerate love, the narrative of *Sense and Sensibility* manages to shift the reader's attention and approbation from the fantastic, unreal, potentially disastrous relationship between the unworthy, inconsiderate cad Willoughby and the naive, passionate Marianne to a more rational, more realizable and yet compelling match based on mutual affection and compatible characters as illustrated by Elinor and Edward. By constructing a narrative in which marriage between Elinor and Edward seems at first impossible, the reader is drawn into their dilemma with the hope that their quiet, tender love will be rewarded. Indeed, their relationship exemplifies Austen's middle ground between excessive sentimental love and purely practical pairings.

Jane Austen's depiction of satisfying love in *Sense and Sensibility* as treading a middle path between sense and sensibility is shown not only through Elinor and Edward's relationship, but also in Marianne's marriage to Colonel Brandon at the conclusion of the novel. In contrast to impetuously, hopelessly falling in love with the inconsiderate Willoughby, the final pages describe Marianne's increasing affection and gradual route to "knowing love" with Colonel Brandon, which was the ardent wish of her family and friends. "With such a confederacy against her—with the knowledge so intimate of his goodness—with a conviction of his fond attachment to herself, which at last, though long after it was observable to everybody else—burst on her—what could she do?"[19] She doesn't fall but slowly grows to love him over two years; yet her love is described as deep, combining both sensibility and sense. "Marianne could never love by halves; and her whole heart became, in time, as much devoted to her husband, as it had once been to Willoughby."[20] Marianne grows as a character and finds happiness in partnership and marriage with Colonel Brandon. I would argue that through this marriage Marianne has established a middle ground between sentimental and rational love.

To return to the question with which I began, what is it about Jane Austen's novels that draws audiences to her stories two hundred years after they were written? I believe that her proto-feminist approach to love and marriage as well as her emphasis on the education, intelligence, self-expression, and character development of her heroines appeal to a twenty-first-century female audience. Austen's novels provide twists to sentimental British and European novels of the eighteenth century in order to equip her female protagonists with power and agency as well as the hope for more equality in their relationships. Her happy ends are satisfying because they suggest partnerships that are achievable and sustainable, founded on practicality and also on compatibility, deep affection, intense feelings, and mutual respect between her characters, that is, a middle space between sense *and* sensibility.

Notes

1. Sally Winkle, *Woman as Bourgeois Ideal* (New York: Peter Lang, 1988), 34–37.

2. Mary Wollstonecraft, *A Vindication of the Rights of Women* (New York: W. W. Norton), 56–72.

3. Wollstonecraft, *Vindication*, 105–9.

4. Wollstonecraft, *Vindication*, 89–90. For more about the connections between Mary Wollstonecraft and Jane Austen, see Rachel Evans, "The Rationality and Femininity of Mary Wollstonecraft and Jane Austen," *Journal of International Women's Studies*, 7 (2006): 17–23; and Miriam Ascarelli, "A Feminist Connection: Jane Austen and Mary Wollstonecraft," *Persuasions on-line*, 25 (2004), accessed June 26, 2015, http://www.jasna.org/persuasions/on-line/vol25no1/ascarelli.html.

5. Jane Austen, *Pride and Prejudice*, reprint of *The Novels of Jane Austen: The Text based on Collation of the Early Editions* by R. W. Chapman, vol. 2, 3rd ed. (Oxford: Oxford University Press, 1933–1934), 5.

6. Jane Austen, *Pride and Prejudice*, 36.

7. Jane Austen, *Sense and Sensibility*, reprint of *The Novels of Jane Austen: The Text based on Collation of the Early Editions* by R. W. Chapman, vol. 1, 3rd ed. (Oxford: Oxford University Press, 1933–1934), 127.

8. Austen, *Pride and Prejudice*, 122.

9. Ascarelli, "A Feminist Connection: Jane Austen and Mary Wollstonecraft," 4–5.

10. Austen, *Sense and Sensibility*, 53–54.

11. bell hooks, *all about love: new visions* (New York: HarperCollins, 2000), 170–72.

12. hooks, *all about love*, 170.

13. hooks, *all about love*, 170–77.

14. Austen *Sense and Sensibility*, 20.

15. hooks, *all about love*, 177.

16. Prominent examples are Samuel Richardson, *Clarissa, or, The history of a young lady: comprehending the most important concerns of private life*, 3rd ed. Originally published London: S. Richardson, 1751 (New York: AMS Press, 1990); and Jean Jacques Rousseau, *Eloisa, or, A series of original letters*. Reprint. Originally published: London: Printed for Vernor and Hood, Longman and Rees, Cuthel and Martin, J. Walker, Lane and Newman, B. Crosby, J. Hookham, and J. Harding, 1803 (Oxford: Woodstock Books, 1989).

17. Austen, *Sense and Sensibility*, 345.

18. Austen, *Sense and Sensibility*, 369.

19. Austen, *Sense and Sensibility*, 378.

20. Austen, *Sense and Sensibility*, 379.

CHAPTER THREE

Love, Marriage, and Dialectics in the Novels of Jane Austen

Suzie Gibson

Jane Austen's major novels—*Sense and Sensibility*, *Pride and Prejudice*, *Emma*, *Mansfield Park*, and *Persuasion*—are propelled and sustained by dialectical forces that are in part reconciled through the marriage bond. Dialectical reasoning involves debate, argument, and conflict, also key factors in providing narrative drama and suspense. Originally a Platonic device,[1] dialectics involves the struggle of contrary positions that are ideally resolved or reconciled. Significantly, it is through the struggle of oppositions that Austen's heroines showcase their skills in conversation, intelligence, and wit. Elizabeth Bennet is particularly adept at this, making her very attractive to Mr. Darcy in *Pride and Prejudice*. The ability to successfully negotiate Austen's complex social worlds through reasoning, good humor, and intelligence is what makes each of her heroines likable, marriageable, and moreover, lovable.

Significantly, love in her fiction operates as the most potent antidote to conflict. However, attaining it is very difficult. Austen honors only a small portion of heroines who enjoy the pleasures of being loved. Loving their suitors and being loved in return distinguish the sisters Marianne and Elinor Dashwood in *Sense and Sensibility*, as well as Elizabeth Bennet in *Pride and Prejudice*, Fanny Price in *Mansfield Park*, and Anne Elliot in *Persuasion*. Yet because the institution of marriage in Austen's world is based upon securing and/or bettering one's material wealth and social position, love can be overlooked or even made redundant. The economic and social moorings of marriage are potentially disrupted by love in representing something far more profound or even transcendent. In this way, love could be thought of as a true gift in exceeding the calculation of economic and socially sanctioned marriages.[2] Not operating within a system of economic gains and losses, love has the potential to disturb Austen's carefully mannered and manicured worlds. Certainly its lack of materiality bequeaths upon it an otherworldliness that promises to deliver Austen's heroines from the ordinariness of marriage's financial and class-conscious origins.

Narrative and Dialectics

The structural logic of Austen's fictions is deeply indebted to dialectical reasoning, as the titles *Pride and Prejudice* and *Sense and Sensibility* clearly demonstrate. In the case of *Pride and Prejudice* the challenge is to reconcile these negative attributes. Standard interpretations associate the disagreeable trait of pride with the egotism of Mr. Darcy, while the other unsavory characteristic of prejudice is associated with Elizabeth's misjudgment of him.

However, complicating this ostensibly neat opposition is the idea that each character has more than his or her fair share of both pride and prejudice. This is well illustrated in a dramatic scene of confrontation when Darcy first proposes marriage to Elizabeth. Both his pride and prejudice are put on show through conflicting emotions that involve expressing his love for Elizabeth while also demeaning her family. The awkwardness and turmoil of his proposal is well conveyed through stilted words that betray the agony of a kind of love that is prepared to tolerate what he believes are embarrassing in-laws. In this scene, Austen also gives keen insight into Elizabeth's thinking as she takes in the full horror of Darcy's words. Clearly doing a terrible job at wooing, we learn of Elizabeth's pain in being informed of her family's supposed "inferiority" and the kind of "degradation" involved in being related to them.[3] Very aware of Darcy's discomfort, she is nonetheless unfazed in retorting with force and intelligence. Her retaliation assumes a position of pride in reflecting Darcy's self-regard. What is also impressive about her rejection is the extraordinary control she exerts in maintaining composure. Her dignified refusal turns the tables on the original opposition between her prejudice and Darcy's pride:

> In such cases as this, it is, I believe the established mode to express a sense of obligation for the sentiments avowed, however unequally they may be returned. It is natural that obligation should be felt, and if I could *feel* gratitude, I would now

thank you. But I cannot—I have never desired your good opinion, and you have certainly bestowed it unwillingly. (PP 125)

Elizabeth's astonishingly well-phrased rejection elicits in Darcy great surprise as well as resentment. He tries to settle the score by responding in a manner equal to her dignity in preserving some kind of pride. What their intense exchange enacts is the intermingling and overlapping of pride and prejudice. Such confusion and misunderstanding provides the stuff of drama. And in romance fiction it operates as an essential ingredient in creating obstacles that are necessary to testing love's strength. Moreover, Elizabeth's initial misreading of Darcy needs to be corrected, and this involves an important coming of wisdom where her eyes are opened to his great capacity for compassion. Harold Bloom's fine analysis of *Pride and Prejudice* mentions its dialectical structure in arguing that the "wills of both lovers" and by this he means that Elizabeth and Darcy "work by similar dialectics" involving a shared and not "wholly illegitimate pride."[4] He elaborates:

> They come to see their wills are naturally allied, since they have no differences upon the will. The will to what? Their will, Austen's, is neither the will to live nor the will to power. They wish to be esteemed precisely where they estimate value to be high, and neither can afford to make a fundamental error, which is both the anxiety and the comedy of the first proposal scene.[5]

Bloom ultimately argues that Lizzy and Darcy are very similar, which is why they complement each other in making what he believes to be the perfect coupling. This is very interesting in thinking again about dialectics and how their opposition is really only about their misunderstanding of one another since they are, at least according to Bloom, immensely suited because they are extremely similar.

In the novel's later stages Elizabeth's growing self-awareness comes to be a rite of passage that involves developing strong feelings for Darcy. Her process of loving him is experienced as an introspective movement. Notably after visiting Darcy's magnificent mansion of Pemberley, and seeing him contextualized within his astonishingly grand home and gardens, her feelings are all the more intensified. Elizabeth's coming of wisdom enacts an important narrative action that goes beyond the petty feelings of pride and prejudice to reach a more transcendent sphere of feeling that leads to love and forgiveness. Love's generosity awakens much beauty of feeling in this novel, leaving a lasting impression of happiness.

In Austen's fictions generally, love has the power to dispel conflict and opposition, enabling lovers to enjoy happy unions. It must be noted, however, that Elizabeth's experience of grand love also involves attaining epic wealth. It seems that her newfound wisdom and humility are greatly rewarded. It also cannot be forgotten that her visit to Pemberley was a crucial factor in giving her the opportunity to experience the grandeur and magnificence of a life with Darcy that she earlier rebuffed. Imagining herself as the first lady of Pemberley inspires feelings of deep regret and sorrow. But like a romance fairy tale, all that is wrong is eventually righted as Lizzy and Darcy come together in mutual love and forgiveness.

Sense and Sensibility also dramatizes the tension and collision of competing forces and emotions. The lead characters, sisters Elinor and Marianne Dashwood represent the oppositional drives of reason and emotion. Elinor, the sensible older sister, thinks of others before herself. Marianne on the other hand is a romantic who can be easily carried away and hurt. It is implied that Marianne's sensibility has the capacity to be self-centered while Elinor's reason comes across as cold and remote. There is then no hierarchical value given to each position as both sense and sensibility have their shortcomings. Yet there are also many positives: sensibility embraces a vivacious and spontaneous way of being, while sensibleness affirms the value of logic and reasoning. It is unclear which sentiment Austen values the most, but it is evident that balance needs to be struck between these conflicting positions.

Significantly, it is the character of Marianne who changes the most in learning the value of reason. Her character undergoes a great transformation after much heartbreak, suffering, and illness. Being unkindly manipulated and misled by her first beloved, she comes to acknowledge the value of thinking beyond herself. Through her ordeal, Marianne grows into a much calmer and wiser heroine. Also, being loved by Colonel Brandon—a kind, sensible, and moreover wealthy older gentleman—helps her process of maturation along. In this novel, her sister Elinor too undergoes a transformation as she learns to value the delight of living in the moment that leaves her open enough to fall in love with Edward Ferrars. Again, love operates as the crucial balancing principle, enabling oppositions to coexist and even unify.

Although love heals conflict in Austen's novels, once it is contained and settled within the institution of marriage, the question of whether it will continue to operate as a curative agent remains uncertain. One can never underestimate the efficacy of Austen's artificial social spheres that contextualize and, in many respects, determine the thoughts, actions, and decisions of her protagonists. The resplendent force of love might have the potential to disrupt convention and rule, but by the same token it could also be extinguished by society's hypocrisies and affectations. For example, Elizabeth Bennet's parents, clearly ill-matched, represent the majority of marriages that might have begun with love but which ultimately end up being unhappy.

Love might initially free individuals, yet its social articulation through or as marriage potentially enslaves it. What we have here is another opposition between love and marriage where the former represents liberation and the latter imprisonment. The demonization of marriage is nothing new since it has long been disparaged. As a legally binding agreement it certainly puts into place laws that are designed to compel individuals in either keeping or breaking their promises and vows. The question remains: can love trump the material and economic moorings of marriage? Perhaps Austen's later novels *Mansfield Park* and *Persuasion* can provide some insight here.

The Power of Persuasion

There is a dramatic shift in tone in Austen's *Mansfield Park* and particularly in her last work of fiction, the posthumously published *Persuasion*. The overwhelming pressures to accumulate wealth, marry into money, and sustain or even better one's social position threaten to overshadow the prospects of her heroines Fanny Price and Anne Elliot. Even though all of Austen's protagonists are developed and mediated through the rules and conventions of society, in these two fictions there is a significant darkness threatening to outweigh the levity of her ironic observations. The third-person narration in *Persuasion* is also extremely critical of the social hypocrisies of high society, and it is also through the lead heroine's very accommodating and humble attitudes that the vanities of others are highlighted.

Compared to *Persuasion*, *Pride and Prejudice* and *Sense and Sensibility* come across as giddy, even buoyant tales about love's initial blindness and eventual wisdom. In *Persuasion*, Austen does not hold back in providing a scathing account of the vanities and superficialities of a world whose variety of characters lack self-awareness and genuine kindness. The opening sentence, which reads like a lengthy paragraph, sets a scorching tone:

> Sir Walter Elliot, of Kellynch-hall, in Somersetshire, was a man who, for his own amusement, never took up any book but the Baronetage; there he found occupation for an idle hour, consolation in a distressed one; there his faculties were roused into admiration and respect, by contemplating the limited remnant of the earliest patents; there any unwelcome sensations, arising from domestic affairs, changed

naturally into pity and contempt as he turned over the almost endless creations of the last century—and there, if every other leaf were powerless, he could read his own history with an interest which never failed—this was the page at which his favourite volume always opened.[6]

We are made immediately aware of an extremely pompous and narcissistic patriarch whose only interest in life is tracing the lineage of his aristocratic origins. The *Baronetage* volume that Austen refers to operates as a mirror through which he gazes admiringly into his past. Cleverly, Austen introduces the Elliot family, with which her narrative is concerned, through a father who is extravagantly self-absorbed. On the second page we are emphatically informed that

> Vanity was the beginning and the end of Sir Walter Elliot's character; vanity of person and of situation. He had been remarkably handsome in his youth; and, at fifty-four, he was still a very fine man. Few women could think more of their personal appearance than he did; nor could the valet of any new made lord be more delighted with the place he held in society.[7]

Austen does not hold back here! Her outright denunciation of Sir Walter makes Elizabeth's judgment of Darcy's seem comparatively mild. What Austen achieves through focusing on Sir Walter's many flaws and failings is to create a difficult situation through which her heroine, Anne Elliot—his daughter—must somehow navigate. Significantly, we also learn in this scathing introduction that Sir Walter is a widower who never remarries, intensifying the picture of Anne's hardship in being motherless. Single life also means that her father's whims, fancies, and indulgences remain unchecked as we learn that his deceased wife used to humor, soften, or at the very least conceal his failings.[8] Anne though is not completely isolated, as we are informed that she is valued by a mother-replacement in the character of Lady Russell, who is also widowed and of independent means. She operates as Anne's confidant and ally.

What is another crucial piece of information in these opening pages is the revelation that at the tender age of nineteen Anne fell madly in love with (and was once engaged to) a handsome naval officer, only to be forced to break it off by family pressure (due to his lack of money and social position). Theorist Gillian Beer argues that the title *Persuasion* is extremely important in revealing Austen's concerns about the levels and intensities of society's coercions and oppressions.[9] Anne is certainly victim of the heavy-handed persuasions and tactics of her social and familial context as her vain father and his socially savvy companion, Lady Russell, force her to renege on a promise to a man she loves. This leaves her scarred for many years until she is miraculously given the opportunity to meet Captain Wentworth seven years later in enabling their reunion under very different circumstances.

Not unlike Elizabeth in *Pride and Prejudice*, *Persuasion*'s lead heroine also undergoes a getting of wisdom, where she comes to learn more about herself through understanding the depth of her love for Captain Wentworth. The rekindling of their passion is made possible by her father's economic irresponsibility since he is forced to rent out his beloved Kellynch Hall to Captain Wentworth's sister and brother-in-law. Once Anne crosses paths with him many years later, she is given the rare opportunity to rediscover the youthful joys of falling in love. Significantly over a seven-year period, Captain Wentworth accumulates great wealth and social status. He is thus thrust back into Anne's life as a very worthy catch.

The social duress of marrying for economic and social gain alone is further poignantly dramatized in *Pride and Prejudice* when we learn of Charlotte Lucas's attachment to the buffoonish Mr. Collins. In a telling scene, she reveals her engagement to her best friend, Lizzy, who we know thinks he is a fool. The conversation is difficult and uncomfortable because Charlotte is unaware of Lizzie's attitude:

> 'Engaged to Mr. Collins! My dear Charlotte,—impossible!'
>
> The steady countenance which Miss Lucas commanded in telling her story, gave way to a momentary confusion here on receiving so direct a reproach [. . .]
>
> 'I see what you are feeling,' replied Charlotte,—you must be surprised, very much surprised [. . .] I am not a romantic you know. I never was. I ask only a comfortable home [. . .][10]

Charlotte is very conscious of the economic practicalities of marriage, which means that Mr. Collins's proposal spares her from the shame and financial hardship of being a spinster. In fact, she openly admits to Elizabeth that she has compromised herself. She does not believe in the fairy tale of love. Not being born into a rich family, as well as no longer being considered young and described as being plain, means that Charlotte has limited options. In many ways, she is hard done by in this novel because she compromises herself in fulfilling the social mores and values of her day.[11] This is unsettling to say the least since it requires sacrificing one's self for the good of one's family in also securing their place in society. It is evident that her friend Elizabeth knows this and shows concern, but once made aware of Charlotte's feelings and vulnerability, she is quick to soften her judgment.

One could argue that Charlotte's loveless marriage does not reconcile conflict as there is a lingering bitter taste of self-sacrifice. In this instance marriage may not resolve tension even though it spares Charlotte from experiencing the social humiliation of spinsterhood. There nonetheless exists an overshadowing sense of disquiet and incompletion haunting her compromise. In Charlotte's case, marriage is not necessarily about preserving or bettering one's social position but is a far more desperate measure in surviving a ruthlessly superficial world. This is unsettling to say the least.

Persuasion's narrative is also organized around the anxiety of marriage. The fact that Anne Elliot remains unmarried in her late twenties is worrying for Lady Russell, who does have her best interests at heart, even though she cannot think outside society's conventional wisdom. The theme of persuasion is subtly evoked throughout a narrative whose point of view is channeled through the delicate intelligence of its morally enlightened heroine. Through the wise consciousness of Anne Elliot, we are persuaded that love just might have a chance even if it is only ever sanctioned because of social and economic advantage.

The conclusion of *Persuasion* is deeply moving as both readers and the heroine Anne come to learn of Captain Wentworth's enduring love when he softly takes her hand exclaiming, "Anne, my own dear Anne!"; we are told in this beautiful passage that

> Bursting forth in the fullness of exquisite feeling—and all the suspense and indecision were over. They were reunited. They were restored to all that had been lost. They were carried back to the past with only an increase of attachment and confidence [. . .][12]

Persuasion's finale suggests that the resilience of Anne's and Captain Wentworth's affection conquers the obstacles of vain patriarchs and social observances, yet what must never be forgotten is that it is only after Wentworth makes his name and fortune that he is able to express his love for Anne, and this in turn allows her to reciprocate. Love alone cannot claim total victory as social mores still have the power to determine what is possible and impossible.

Unlike *Pride and Prejudice*, *Persuasion* does not foreground the witty repartee between jousting lovers, but rather provides an extremely subtle morality tale whose charm, like its sensitive heroine, Anne, is extremely heartfelt and profound. It is also worth keeping in mind that Anne marries into seafaring life, which means that her future with Captain Wentworth will not necessarily be anchored within the frivolities of Bath's landlocked community. There is then a real chance that love will prevail in their marriage if it is able to flourish outside the frontiers of fashionable society.

Social and Familial Prisons and Prisms

In Austen's world, one's social class and family name determine, to the point of even dictating, what characters can and cannot do. In the case of Fanny Price and Anne Elliot, their social and familial circumstances operate as psychological and economic prisons. These characters are very much underdogs who must navigate with great care and caution the egos, whims, and vanities of their friends and relatives. However, in *Persuasion* it is not only society that operates as psychological prison; it is also the powerful bonds of family, and its capacity to limit one's choices. Society then is not the only institution that contextualizes and to some degree controls the individual, but also the old-fashioned blood bonds of a pedigreed family.

A family's lack of wealth and social standing also has a huge impact on Austen's heroines. Fanny Price for instance in *Mansfield Park* strikes a particularly poignant figure in her material poverty. Fanny, the eldest of a poor and socially disadvantaged family, comes to be a charity case for her mother's rich sister Lady Bertram. At the young age of ten she is adopted into the Bertram family and is made to feel at every opportunity of her social inferiority. Sir Thomas Bertram pompously declares to his wife and her sister Mrs. Norris that in adopting Fanny Price she will enjoy the comforts and privileges in his home, Mansfield Park, but he will never let his daughters forget their class superiority for in every way they differ in "rank, fortune, rights, and expectations."[13] His devastating words express the extraordinary snobbery of a father who cannot see beyond his family's social importance. Sir Thomas's speech reveals Austen's growing anger toward a false world of arrogant patriarchs who come to represent the society's greater failings. Even more than Charlotte Lucas, Fanny is extremely disadvantaged by the disastrous effects of her family's poverty. For most of the novel, she is made to feel like an outsider, even an interloper to the grand world of Mansfield Park. Austen's heroine may be shy and unassuming, yet she proves to have great inner strength by surviving a nasty world of arrogant patriarchs, would-be lovers, and cruel and manipulative aunts.

Very much like Anne Elliot in *Persuasion*, Fanny operates as the novel's moral center. She has a pure heart; and after much humiliation, pain, and disapproval her goodness and consistency throughout her long years of living at Mansfield Park are rewarded. Sir Bertram's esteemed daughters prove to be utter disappointments in their narcissism and lack of respect. Their ill-matched marriages and scandals prove that integrity and goodness have nothing to do with a family name. Fanny also proves herself to be a worthy surrogate daughter by remaining true and loyal, and this in turn yields her uncle's respect. Importantly, her virtuosity gains the love of her cousin Edmund, whom she had always adored as a child. After much complication and misunderstanding he finally comes to realize that he cannot live without Fanny, and so once again love triumphs over adversity, as cousins become lovers:

> With so much true merit and true love, and no want of fortune or friends, the happiness of the married cousins must appear as secure as earthly happiness can be. Equally formed for domestic life, and attached to country pleasures, their home was the home of affection and comfort; and to complete the picture of good, the acquisition of Mansfield living by the death of Dr. Grant, occurred just after they had been married long enough to begin to want an increase of income [. . .][14]

Fanny Price's story is a rags to riches saga. She is remunerated for her unpretentiousness, loyalty, and kindness. She and Anne Elliot are very much softer, shyer heroines compared to the feistiness of Elizabeth Bennet. Anne and Fanny also share many earthy qualities that promise to deliver them from the false mirrors of high society. Their decision to repose in rural and seaside landscapes reflects their sincere, introspective personalities that just might save their marriages from the frivolities and debasements of high society.

As is evident in Austen's novels, marriage functions as a stabilizing agent in not only providing economic and social security, but also narrative and psychological closure. In the case of Elizabeth's marriage to Darcy, Marianne's to Colonel Brandon, Anne's to Captain Wentworth, and finally Fanny's to Edmund Bertram, love is also crucial to this end. Love operates as a transcendent principle in that it has the power to trump the economic and social moorings of marriage. Except that in all of these marriages, economics and social status are still very much in place.

Even though all of Austen's lead heroines marry for love, they never miss out on the material benefits of economic security and social prominence.

Love might elevate Austen's protagonists above the fray of ordinary existence, but the realities of needing a roof over one's head can never be underestimated. Those who misuse their wealth and social standing ultimately come undone. Austen is very much a pragmatist whose romances never lose sight of the need to have a solid financial foundation. Even though love always promises so much more, it is nonetheless only ever successful between those of good fortune and social standing.

Love then can never be extracted from the social prisons and prisms of Austen's artificial worlds. It may deliver her favored heroines from the compromises and humiliations of marrying only for social and economic reasons, but it can never transcend the very contexts and spheres in which it is felt and articulated. As a linguistic phenomenon, love is anchored within the very conversations and silences of Austen's fashionable society. Transcending or abolishing dialectical structures is yet to be achieved. Love certainly enables astonishing moments of profound ecstasy to be experienced where characters are temporarily suspended beyond the ordinariness of life, but once translated and contained within the institution of marriage, it is subsumed within very neat and precise worlds of Austen's society.

Notes

1. Plato, *Early Socratic Dialogues*, trans. Trevor J. Saunders (Penguin Classics, 2005).

2. Jacques Derrida, *Given Time: I. Counterfeit Money*, trans. Peggy Kamuf (Chicago: University of Chicago Press, 1992), 4.

3. Jane Austen, *Pride and Prejudice*, ed. Donald Grey (Norton Critical Edition: Indiana University, 2001), 125.

4. Harold Bloom, "Jane Austen," *Novelists and Novels* (New York: Chelsea House Publishers, 2005), 55–56.

5. Bloom, "Jane Austen," 55.

6. Jane Austen, *Persuasion*, ed. D. W. Harding (London: Penguin Books, 1965), 35.

7. Austen, *Persuasion*, 36.

8. Austen, *Persuasion*, 36.

9. Gillian Beer, "Introduction," *Persuasion* (London: Penguin Classics, 1998).

10. Austen, *Pride and Prejudice*, 85.

11. Joshua Rothman, "On Charlotte Lucas's Choice," *The New Yorker*, February 7, 2013, accessed September 18, 2015, http://www.newyorker.com/books/page-turner/on-charlotte-lucass-choice.

12. Austen, *Persuasion*, 260.

13. Jane Austen, *Mansfield Park* (London: Penguin Books, 1966), 47.

14. Austen, *Mansfield Park*, 456–57.

~

CHAPTER FOUR

Beyond Pride and Prejudice

Jane Austen and Friedrich Nietzsche on What Makes a Happy Marriage

WILLIAM A. LINDENMUTH

In Jane Austen's works, the female characters are often obsessed with marriage, but not necessarily for romantic reasons. This is because of "entailment," a nineteenth-century law mandating that certain properties could not be broken up, and therefore would continue down only to male heirs. Because of this, daughters who were cared for by their fathers were left without much recourse if the father were to pass away before the daughters had secured a husband. The Bennet family of *Pride and Prejudice* consists of a father, a mother, and five sisters. Fearing the untimely death of her spouse, Mrs. Bennet is in a tizzy over getting them hitched, and has all of them, aged twenty-two to fifteen, "out" in society, hunting for husbands.

"One of Us Will Have to Marry Very Well"[1]

While we can be amused with Mrs. Bennet's agitation and Mr. Bennet's seeming indifference, the quandary of attaining security was a real concern for nineteenth-century women. Most had to put quite an effort into finding an appropriate suitor. Just what "appropriate" means, though, is up for debate. Does this mean they both occupy the same social class? Are in love? Are matched in attractiveness? Are the same age? Will benefit their families

39

best through this match? And who should decide this: the family, or only the individuals involved? Modern Western readers usually regard marriage to anyone other than a perceived soulmate as anathema. Getting to choose a romantic partner is seen as one of the most important freedoms we have. Yet today, the majority of unarranged marriages end in divorce, and some see this as evidence that we are doing something wrong. If this is the case, we need to reevaluate what kinds of marriages are ideal ones. In doing so, we must also ask and answer the question, "If someone says that they are happy, should anyone else be able to tell them that they are wrong?" Jane Austen and the philosopher Friedrich Nietzsche (1844–1900), both products of the nineteenth century, can provide modern readers guidance on this issue.

"Happiness in Marriage is Entirely a Matter of Chance"[2]

The plot of *Pride and Prejudice* centers on the two eldest Bennet daughters, Jane and Elizabeth (Lizzy), and their potential romantic prospects. The first man to propose to Lizzy is Mr. Collins, a clergyman who is next in line to inherit the estate. As Mr. Bennet morbidly reminds the family, Mr. Collins is the man who "may turn you all out of this house as soon as"[3] Mr. Bennet has died. Mr. Collins, while certainly embodying his description as "a mixture of pride and obsequiousness, self-importance and humility,"[4] is actually doing the Bennets a favor: he promises to try and marry one of the sisters, so they are not turned out of their home. As the mother tells him that Jane is most likely spoken for, he turns his attention to Lizzy. Depictions of Mr. Collins present him as awkward, foolish, and a complete boor, and as we are sympathetic to Lizzy, we know there is no chance of her accepting him. Mr. Collins proposes, and Lizzy thanks but denies him, justifying it by saying, "You could not make *me* happy, and I am convinced that I am the last woman in the world who could make you so."[5] Lizzy acknowledges his feelings regarding the family and situation but assures him that he "may take possession of Longbourn estate whenever it falls, without any self-reproach."[6]

Our romantic feelings may be satisfied here, but is this the proper ethical decision? In his proposal, Mr. Collins reminds Lizzy that "it is by no means certain that another offer of marriage may ever be made you."[7] As with other Jane Austen works, everything works out for the best in the end. It might have gone much worse. Is Lizzy being *irresponsible* in that she is not being practical, *selfish* in not thinking of the welfare of her mother (who desperately wants this union) and sisters, and naive in thinking she will get better proposals or that everything will be fine if she does not? She explains to Mr. Collins "I thank you . . . for the honour you have done me in your proposals, but to accept them is absolutely impossible. My feelings in every respect forbid it."[8] Are feelings the only reason to get married?

We can speculate as to what Jane Austen herself thinks, but we do know that other characters in the novel believe otherwise. Charlotte Lucas, the best friend of Lizzy, marries Mr. Collins the second she realizes Lizzy won't. Lizzy is shocked and disappointed, but Charlotte calmly spells out her position:

> You must be surprised, very much surprised—so lately as Mr. Collins was wishing to marry you. But when you have had time to think it over, I hope you will be satisfied with what I have done. I am not romantic, you know; I never was. I ask only a comfortable home; and considering Mr. Collins's character, connection, and situation in life, I am convinced that my chance of happiness with him is as fair as most people can boast on entering the marriage state.

It certainly doesn't seem as if Charlotte is a paragon model for behavior, here, and one could argue that Austen is giving us this example to show that the social institution of marriage doesn't encourage good relationships because of the way that property ownership works. However, there must be some provision for the fact that not all people have the same constitution. How we feel about this will also depend on how closely we ally our feelings and prejudices with Lizzy's. While mulling over this the narrator reports that Lizzy "had always felt that Charlotte's opinion of matrimony was not exactly like her own, but she had not supposed it to be possible that, when called into action, she would have sacrificed every better feeling to worldly advantage."[9] Charlotte cites "character, connection, and situation" as reasons, but according to Lizzy, these are not the "better feelings" she speaks of. Clearly one's name and connections have an *enormous* effect on how one experiences the world and how much of the world is even accessible in the first place. Is there something unethical, then, in refusing advantageous matches for the families connected simply because one finds the potential spouse to be uninteresting?

"Miss Bennet, Do You Know Who I Am?"[10]

The most notorious example of marital intercession in all of Jane Austen begins when Lizzy Bennet draws the attention of an extremely wealthy man,

Mr. Darcy. Socially, marriage between them would be seen as "advantageous" for her and a poor choice for him. Mr. Darcy was proud and initially uninterested in Lizzy, but grew to love her through her principles, personality, and countenance. Lizzy, however, is prejudiced and rejects this second marriage proposal, believing Darcy arrogant and uncivil.

The noblewoman Lady Catherine de Bourgh is the "nearest relation" Mr. Darcy "has in the world" and believes she is "entitled to know all his dearest concerns."[11] When Lady Catherine hears of the proposal, she is disgusted. Her daughter has been arranged to be married to Mr. Darcy, although the two are incompatible. She sees Lizzy as a cunning usurper, an upstart without "family, connections, or fortune"[12] who is simply trying to worm her way into an arrangement that is far above her. Lady Catherine insists that "This match, to which you have the presumption to aspire, can never take place."[13] She thinks people should not "quit the sphere in which [they] have been brought up," and that elders and "superiors" should generally guide the decisions and affairs of the younger and "inferiors."[14] She also has no problem telling Lizzy as much to her face, and treats the Bennets with severe disregard. Lady Catherine is indignant and almost mystified that someone she views as so decidedly beneath her could act in this way. She interrogates Lizzy:

> While in their cradles, we planned the union: and now, at the moment when the wishes of both sisters would be accomplished in their marriage, to be prevented by a young woman of inferior birth, of no importance in the world, and wholly unallied to the family! Do you pay no regard to the wishes of his friends? To his tacit engagement with Miss de Bourgh? Are you lost to every feeling of propriety and delicacy?[15]

Lizzy, on the other hand, believes that people should make their own decisions, and that *social* station should have little *moral* effect on how one ought to behave or treat others. She acknowledges that Darcy's elders wanted him to marry Lady Catherine's daughter, but asks what bearing that should have on her, or on him, for that matter. She replies:

> Allow me to say, Lady Catherine, that the arguments with which you have supported this extraordinary application have been as frivolous as the application was ill-judged. You have widely mistaken my character, if you think I can be worked on by such persuasions as these. How far your nephew might approve of your interference in his affairs, I cannot tell; but you have certainly no right to concern yourself in mine.[16]

Miss Bennet and Lady Catherine clearly disagree on not only what marriage should be, but also on how much personal decisions should be determined by others. Lizzy summarizes her feelings on the matter by stating, "I am only resolved to act in that manner, which will, in my own opinion, constitute my happiness, without reference to you, or to any person so wholly unconnected with me."[17]

"We Shall Have to Be Philosophers, Mary"[18]

Clearly we are meant to identify and sympathize with the independent Lizzy, but can nothing be said for Lady Catherine's position? Is Austen taking the position that each person is uniquely suited to knowing what is best for him? In short, no. There is not a consistent result on either side, as a comparison of various instances of characters in *Pride and Prejudice* interfering on the behalf of others will show.

In some instances, paternalism has negative results, as when Mr. Darcy impedes the relationship between Bingley and Jane, erroneously believing Jane an unaffectionate opportunist. He boasts, "I have no wish of denying that I did everything in my power to separate my friend from your sister, or that I rejoice in my success."[19] He later regrets his interference and relents. But Darcy's other two intrusions, both involving the rake Mr. Wickham, are portrayed as positive. Darcy stops him from seducing and marrying his fifteen-year-old sister, Georgiana, and then later influences him to marry Lizzy's fifteen-year-old sister, Lydia, after he has seduced her.[20] We laugh at the contriving yet artless efforts of the single-minded Mrs. Bennet to avail upon every opportunity to accrue wedding proposals for her daughters, but sometimes they work, as when she forces everyone out of the room to give Jane and Bingley privacy.

Of course, this objective view toward happiness all follows the perspective the novel wishes to take. It is not difficult to see that because of his track record, Wickham is a serial philanderer and dishonest person. We can also somewhat dismiss the perspectives of Lydia and Georgiana because of their youth and inexperience, but we cannot say that *every* individual knows best as to what will make them happy. Lydia in particular seems to be quite pleased with her decision to run off with Wickham.

In the chaste 1995 BBC mini-series of *Pride and Prejudice*, the most ribald it gets is when Lydia delivers the line "Lord, it makes me want to burst out laughing, when I think that I have done what none of my sisters has [sic]."[21] Lydia wants attention, sex, and a handsome, charming husband, and she gets that. "I can't wait to see my mother's face," she exclaims in the film, "And my sisters! Kitty will be *so envious*." If Desire Satisfaction Theory—the idea that life is good only as long as people get what they want—is true, then Lydia is doing very well.[22] If, however, we have some conception of an objective theory of human welfare, then we have to say that there is a standard of what a good life must be, and the presence or absence of certain things will place us squarely on the side of happy or unhappy. This film adaptation of Austen certainly seems to reflect the "good life" interpretation, ending the story with a double wedding of the Bennet sisters while the vicar tells us the meaning of marriage, reading from *The Book of Common Prayer*, and providing text which is not in the novel. As he delivers his sermon, the camera passes over couples as if showing examples of the vicar's words, and to approve or reprove them:

> An honorable estate . . . signifying to us the mystical union between Christ and His Church, and therefore is not by any to be enterprised lightly [camera shows us the elder Bennet couple], or wantonly, to satisfy man's carnal lusts and appetites, but reverently [cue the puritanical Mary], discreetly, wisely, soberly, and in the fear of God, duly considering the causes for which matrimony was ordained. First . . . for the procreation of children [Lady Catherine and the sickly daughter Anne, coughing in their large, lonely room], secondly, as a remedy against sin [Wickham drinking in a rumpled bed with Lydia], and to avoid fornication. Thirdly, [finally showing the "proper" couples to be married] for the mutual society, help, and comfort that one ought to have of the other. . . .

If we agree that this film is a good interpretation of Austen—I certainly do—and that throughout the novel she is making claims toward an objective view of happiness, then this places Austen much closer to a philosopher like Aristotle (384–322 BC), who believes happiness to be a sort of reward for getting things right. So, if one is intelligent, has good friendships, is healthy, lives comfortably, and shows moderation in most things, one is objectively happy. It's a resultant condition of things, rather than a state of mind. Of course, we could tell Lydia all this, and she might just laugh in our faces.

"The Very Rich Can Afford to Give Offense Wherever They Go"[23]

Two other Austen novels provide good examples with which to compare Lizzy's situation. For example, in *Emma* much of the narrative is devoted to our "handsome, clever, and rich"[24] title character playing the matchmaker. Notably, she encourages her new friend Harriet Smith toward Mr. Elton, who actually has his eyes on Emma, and discourages the favorable proposal of Robert Martin, thinking him beneath Harriet. Emma's path to becoming a wise and virtuous person mostly stems from her learning humility from her matchmaking mistakes and what it actually means to be a good friend.

Mansfield Park involves another case of a wealthy, older landlord ordering a younger person whom to marry. The protagonist of this story is Fanny Price, a young and beleaguered girl who—because of poverty—must be raised by her uncle, Sir Thomas Bertram, and his family, who mostly treat her like a servant. Regardless, she becomes a bright, beautiful, and virtuous woman and gains the affections of an ostensibly great match. She doesn't think him trustworthy (he isn't), though, and refuses the offer. Sir Thomas insists that regardless of her affection or sensibilities she marry the man. The dialogue in the 1999 film adaptation presents this relationship bluntly:

> Sir Thomas: Do you trust me?
> Fanny: I trust that my future is entirely dependent upon you, sir.
> Sir Thomas: Let me repeat: do you trust *me*?
> Fanny: Yes, sir.
> Sir Thomas: Well, I trust him. You *will* marry him.
> Fanny: I will not . . . Sir.[25]

However, in the novel, Sir Thomas details exactly what he thinks is wrong with not just her, but every young woman who thinks independently:

> I had thought you peculiarly free from wilfulness of temper, self-conceit, and every tendency to that independence of spirit which prevails so much in modern days, even in young women, and which in young women is offensive and disgusting beyond all common offence. But you have now shewn me that you can be wilful and perverse; that you can and will decide for yourself, without any consideration or deference for those who have surely some right to guide you, without even asking their advice. You have shewn yourself very, very different from anything that I had imagined. The advantage or disadvantage of your family, of your parents, your brothers and sisters, never seems to have had a moment's share in your thoughts on this occasion. How *they* might be benefited, how *they* must rejoice in such an establishment for you, is nothing to *you*. You think only of yourself. . . .[26]

Sir Thomas, like *Pride and Prejudice*'s Lady Catherine, presents the case that "aristocrats" (literally "power of the best") should decide for their inferiors, and sometimes limit their freedom, knowing what is right for them better than they know themselves. Sir Thomas is mistaken in his trust of the suitor, but thinks it a good match for Fanny. However, Lady Catherine isn't trying to benefit Lizzy at all. Marriage between Darcy and Lady Catherine's daughter would benefit *her* family. She can dress it up as the wishes of his mother all she wants, but Darcy has shown no interest in Anne, nor Anne in him. Even if Lizzy were guilty of being as predatory as she is accused, there is nothing in Lady Catherine's argument to tempt her.

Lady Catherine's displeasure at the sisters seeking to be "most advantageously married" is based solely in a fear of losing influence. She struggles to use it to limit Lizzy's will, but Lizzy has no constraint to support the dominance of Lady Catherine's family. As Lady Catherine repeatedly reminds Lizzy, she is unaccustomed to this treatment and to not getting her way. But how does that obligate Lizzy? After being reminded of Mr. Darcy's engagement to Anne, she replies:

> But what is that to me? If there is no other objection to my marrying your nephew, I shall certainly not be kept from it by knowing that his mother and aunt wished him to marry Miss de Bourgh. You both did as much as you could in planning the marriage. Its completion depended on others. If Mr. Darcy is neither by honour nor inclination confined to his cousin, why is not he to make another choice? And if I am that choice, why may not I accept him?[27]

We must ask if Lady Catherine's demands are sound. Or are they simply like scaffolding for an old building that should be torn down?

Philosophizing with a Hammer

A habitual concern of the nineteenth-century philosopher Friedrich Nietzsche was tradition. In his essay "The Use and Abuse of History for Life," he argues that sometimes traditions are just that, simply things we do because that's how they were done before. He considers that when necessary, they should be abandoned for something better, something new, especially when these traditions no longer work for us. In his book *Twilight of the Idols*, Nietzsche has the subtitle of "How to Philosophize With a Hammer," and he encourages us to "philosophize with a hammer." Consider what a hammer is for. First, it "sounds out" (i.e., we rap it against something to see if it is hollow). Second, if it is hollow, we smash it. Third, and most difficultly, we build something in its place.

This is precisely what Austen is doing with entailment, the aristocracy, and arranged marriage. The whole of *Pride and Prejudice* can be seen as an examination of relationships, and the various reasons people wed each other. Some are bad (e.g., the rash, ill-conceived, and impetuous marriage of Wickham and Lydia). This relationship seems to be based on fleeting, ephemeral things. Some relationships seem lasting, but are not full of love. For example, Charlotte and Mr. Collins; Charlotte might be "content," but she's not "happy." In addition, the relationship between the elder Bennets is often portrayed as them simply annoyed with one another. We are given the impression that they married young and for superficial reasons, and now the mother spends her day fretting over the daughters' romantic entanglements and money, while the father hides and drinks in his study, "not to be disturbed."

Then we have the purportedly ideal marriages of Lizzy and Darcy, and Jane and Bingley, that are based on mutual love and affection as well as solid and reliable financial support. These relationships have feeling, but the support comes from the bottom and not the top. With the exception of a few counterexamples such as Darcy's friend Colonel Fitzwilliam, Bingley and Darcy's peers and family are not supportive of the relationship. Austen shows us that while Darcy and Bingley are worthy gentlemen, the rest of their society is full of self-important prigs. It seems that as far as Austen is concerned, these relationships are to be admired and imitated.

"I Should So Like to Marry for Love"[28]

Let us examine just what makes a good marriage. According to Nietzsche, "The best friend will probably get the best wife, because a good marriage is based on a talent for friendship."[29] While never marrying himself, Nietzsche showed some great insights into what made relationships work. With this proclamation he is saying that, contrary to the prevailing ideas about looks or money, marriage is really about the sorts of things that friends help each other through. What do you *really* spend most of the time doing with your partner? Talking. To wit: "When entering a marriage, one should ask the question: do you think you will be able to have good conversations with this woman right into old age? Everything else in marriage is transitory, but most of the time in interaction is spent in conversation."[30] This should be obvious, but no one ever says this. It's not *romantic*, but it's true. In fact, Nietzsche regards romantic passion with some suspicion, especially for the young and inexperienced: "Sensuality often makes love grow too quickly, so that the root remains weak and is easy to pull out."[31] If this is true, then Wickham and Lydia do not have the best prospects for a long relationship. Perhaps this also mean that the Bingleys and the Darcys have better chances because it took them a while to get married, and they all had to fight for it.

Passion can also never be promised, but we do it all the time. Nietzsche explains, "One can promise actions but not feelings, for the latter are involuntary. . . . To promise to love someone therefore means: For as long as I love you I shall render to you the actions of love; if I cease to love you, you will continue to receive the same actions from me, though from other motives."[32] This, then, means that a good relationship is one where both involved have respect for the institution of marriage, and not just the often transitory experience of attraction. Again, this is a mark against Wickham and Lydia, but not against the elder Bennets, as we get the sense that they are no longer romantically interested in one another but believe in upholding their relationship for the family and society.

Jane and Lizzy's relationships seem to share these things, but only Jane remarks that it will benefit her family as well. After she elatedly accepts the proposal of Mr. Bingley, she says "to know that what I have to relate will give such pleasure to all my dear family! How shall [I] bear so much happiness!"[33] Lizzy doesn't speak to this at all, which is an interesting decision on Austen's part. Is she saying that this shouldn't be on our minds, and that, like Lizzy, we "should be only resolved to act in a manner which will constitute [our] own happiness without reference to" anything else? Perhaps this is the one realm of life where we should not be asked to sacrifice.

"Are the Shades of Pemberley to Be Thus Polluted?"[34]

In Darcy's first proposal to Lizzy he almost seems to do it against his will. After some nervous chit-chat, he erupts with, "In vain I have struggled. It will not do. My feelings will not be repressed. You must allow me to tell you how ardently I admire and love you."[35] The text does not elaborate on his proposal,[36] but her response tells us enough: "Why with so evident a desire of offending and insulting me, you chose to tell me that you liked me against your will, against your reason, and even against your character?"[37] Lizzy clearly feels that *who an individual is* stems significantly less from family or social class, but is this because this is *true*, or because she measures less in comparison?

Likewise, Lady Catherine presents a laundry list of issues ("honor, decorum, prudence," etc.) as to why the Bennet/Darcy union should not take place. "Justice originates among approximately equal powers,"[38] says Nietzsche, and from Lady Catherine's perspective, Lizzy is not an equal. She remarks that people should remain in the spheres in which they are raised and sees no reason to question her way of viewing or doing things. When Lizzy claims to compete with her—"In marrying your nephew, I should not consider myself as quitting that sphere. He is a gentleman; I am a gentleman's daughter; so far we are equal," Lady Catherine raises the stakes: "True. You *are* a gentleman's daughter. But who was your mother? Who are your uncles and aunts? Do not imagine me ignorant of their condition."[39] Lady Catherine is embodying the Nietzschean master morality, the idea that "It is the powerful who *understand* how to honor,"[40] and that those beneath are simply grasping at straws. "The ruling group determines what is good,"[41] says Nietzsche, and Lady Catherine is a ruling group. Or was, rather, for she *loses* this fight.

Nietzsche argues that when aristocrats lack fine manners they get overthrown: "For at bottom the masses are willing to submit to slavery of any kind, if only the higher-ups constantly legitimize themselves as higher, as *born* to command—by having noble manners."[42] Lady Catherine's downfall of influence is a result of this, and throughout the first half of the book, so goes Darcy. Lizzy initially refuses him in a way that haunts and reforms him, saying, "had you behaved in a more gentlemanlike manner."[43]

Her words and method of rejection hold a mirror up to him and are the catalyst that changes him and his ways. He was unhappy and disdainful toward most and didn't know why. He realizes that he wants to be the kind of person deserving of a relationship based on mutual affection and respect. The irony is, if Lady Catherine was right about Lizzy, she would have accepted the very advantageous match to Mr. Darcy in the first place. But because she is not, because she is genuine, and smart, and kind, and caring, she refuses Darcy in all of his wealthy, proud arrogance. Little did he know that this devastating loss would lead to his greatest triumph: to be loved by someone like Elizabeth Bennet.

Notes

1. *Pride and Prejudice* (United Kingdom: British Broadcasting Company [BBC] miniseries, 1995).

2. Jane Austen, *Pride and Prejudice* (Project Gutenberg EBook, 2008), http://www.gutenberg.org/files/1342/1342-pdf.pdf.

3. Austen, *Pride and Prejudice*, 39.

4. Austen, *Pride and Prejudice*, 44.

5. Austen, *Pride and Prejudice*, 66.

6. Austen, *Pride and Prejudice*, 66.

7. Austen, *Pride and Prejudice*, 66.

8. Austen, *Pride and Prejudice*, 66.

9. Austen, *Pride and Prejudice*, 66.

10. Austen, *Pride and Prejudice*, 205

11. Austen, *Pride and Prejudice*, 205.

12. Austen, *Pride and Prejudice*, 206.

13. Austen, *Pride and Prejudice*, 205.

14. Austen, *Pride and Prejudice*, 206.

15. Austen, *Pride and Prejudice*, 206.

16. Austen, *Pride and Prejudice*, 207.

17. Austen, *Pride and Prejudice*, 208.

18. *Pride and Prejudice*, BBC.

19. Austen, *Pride and Prejudice*, 113.

20. This is *not* desirable, from a modern perspective, but they saw it as the best possible solution to keep as much familial and Christian dignity intact as possible.

21. *Pride and Prejudice*, BBC.

22. Russ Shafer-Landau defines it as "Something is good for you *if* it satisfies your desires, *only if* it satisfies your desires, and *because* it satisfies your desires." Russ Shafer-Landau, *The Fundamentals of Ethics* (Oxford: Oxford University Press, 2015), 44–45.

23. *Pride and Prejudice*, BBC.

24. Jane Austen, *Emma* (Project Gutenberg EBook, 2008), 2, https://www.gutenberg.org/files/158/158-pdf.

25. *Mansfield Park* (United Kingdom: Miramax Films, 1999).

26. Jane Austen, *Mansfield Park* (Project Gutenberg EBook, 2008), 164–65, https://www.gutenberg.org/files/141/141-pdf.

27. Austen, *Pride and Prejudice*, 206.

28. *Pride and Prejudice*, BBC.

29. Friedrich Nietzsche, *Human, All Too Human*, trans. by Marion Faber, with Stephan Lehmann (Lincoln: University of Nebraska Press, 1984), #378.

30. Nietzsche, *Human, All Too Human*, #406.

31. Friedrich Nietzsche, *Beyond Good and Evil*, trans. by Walter Kaufmann (New York: Random House, 1966), #120.

32. Friedrich Nietzsche, *Human, All Too Human*, #58.

33. Austen, *Pride and Prejudice*, 200.

34. Austen, *Pride and Prejudice*, 205.

35. Austen, *Pride and Prejudice*, 112.

36. The 1995 BBC version has him say, "I am fully aware that I will be going expressly against the wishes of my family, my friends, and I hardly need add, my own better judgment."

37. Austen, *Pride and Prejudice*, 113.

38. Friedrich Nietzsche, *Human, All Too Human*, #92.

39. Austen, *Pride and Prejudice*, 206–7.

40. Friedrich Nietzsche, *Beyond Good and Evil*, #260.

41. Friedrich Nietzsche, *Beyond Good and Evil*, #260.

42. Friedrich Nietzsche, *The Gay Science*, trans. by Walter Kaufmann (New York: Random House, 1974), #40.

43. Austen, *Pride and Prejudice*, 114.

~

CHAPTER FIVE

Marriage and Friendship in Jane Austen

Self-knowledge, Virtue, and the "Second Self"

KATHLEEN POORMAN DOUGHERTY

Early in *Pride and Prejudice*, Charlotte Lucas explains to Elizabeth Bennet that a woman must be practical, but not too choosy, in matters of marriage. In discussing Jane Bennet's affection for Mr. Bingley, Charlotte explains to Elizabeth that taking more time to get to know Mr. Bingley better will do little to ensure that Jane would be happy with him:

> I should think she has as good a chance of happiness as if she were to be studying his character for a twelvemonth. Happiness in marriage is entirely a matter of chance. If the dispositions of the parties are ever so well known to each other or ever so similar beforehand, it does not advance their felicity in the least. They always continue to grow sufficiently unlike afterwards to have their share of vexation; and it is better to know as little as possible of the defects of the person with whom you are to pass your life.[1]

Though this surely seems to be the approach that Charlotte takes in her own life, as she readily marries the obsequious Mr. Collins after knowing him only briefly, it is advice absolutely contrary to this that Jane Austen gives her readers regarding marriage and happiness throughout her novels. In fact, the marriages that Austen's novels present as the most promising are between two persons of similarly admirable character who have come to know one another intimately well before tying themselves together in marriage. Consider, for example, the marriages of Jane Bennet and Charles Bingley, Elizabeth Bennet and Fitzwilliam Darcy, and Emma Woodhouse and George Knightley.

In Austen's world, those who choose well choose for virtue and compatibility, not merely status or security. And a seeming lack of status can even be overcome if one's character is thought to be good enough. For example, by the end of *Pride and Prejudice*, Mr. Darcy finds Elizabeth Bennet to be his equal and ever so much more beautiful as he also begins to see her for who she is and for her virtue, independent of her family or her position in society. Though these marriages noted above are not all "practical" marriages, in each case the characters perceive their compatibility, they gain greater self-knowledge, and they are made morally better by their relationships with one another. In these ways, Austen's portrayal of the ideal marriage bears a striking resemblance to Aristotle's notion of complete friendship, where the friend is valued for who she is, and becomes almost a "second self." This paper will explore more fully the similarities between Austen's view of the ideal marriage and Aristotle's understanding of complete friendship, distinguishing complete friendship from its inferior forms, considering the role of good character in friendship, and finally, reflecting upon the ways in which friendship is thought to make us morally better by improving our self-knowledge, and thus, our character.

Inferior Friendships

Aristotle devotes two of ten chapters in his *Nicomachean Ethics* to a discussion of the nature of friendship, highlighting his understanding of the centrality of friendship to the moral life. Aristotle delineates three distinct types of friendships, with the types distinguished by what motivates them, or the object of love. The first two, friendships of utility and friendships of pleasure, are thought to be inferior to the most complete type of friendship, where the friend is loved "for who he is."[2] The claim is not that any of the three types of friendship are bad or undesirable, but simply that complete or perfect friendship is far superior to the other two types. In fact, we might have friends of each of the different sorts quite regularly in full and rewarding human lives.

Friendships of utility are based in the usefulness of the parties to each other; likewise, friendships of pleasure are based in the pleasure that the parties bring to one another. These friendships, Aristotle describes as "coincidental," that is, they are dependent upon circumstances.[3] A friendship of utility can be rather inconsistent and will last only so long as the parties remain useful to one another, for, "What is useful does not remain the same, but is different at different times."[4] In many ways, we might think of these as relationships of convenience. Austen's novels are full of friendships of utility, for these kinds of friends might be neighbors with whom one has mutually beneficial relationships, they might be acquaintances who provide social status, or they might be relationships that are maintained because of social roles.

In *Emma*, Emma Woodhouse and Mrs. Elton provide a prime example of a friendship of utility. Once Emma declines Mr. Elton's proposal of marriage, he is very quickly engaged to a Miss Augusta Hawkins, who soon becomes Mrs. Elton. Because Mr. Elton is the local reverend, and Emma's status in the village is of the utmost importance, Emma has little choice but to befriend the new Mrs. Elton. It is readily apparent to the reader that Mrs. Elton is almost insufferable; her self-centeredness and all too familiar tone are simply the first cues. We soon learn that further acquaintance with Mrs. Elton has not prompted Emma to rethink her judgment, for she still deems Mrs. Elton "self-important, presuming, familiar, ignorant, and ill-bred."[5] Even so, because of their positions, Emma must befriend Mrs. Elton, carrying through with all the appropriate social graces, such as hosting a dinner in her honor, socializing with her regularly, and acquiescing to allow Mrs. Elton the position of honor at the Weston's ball. We can imagine that Mrs. Elton does not think much more highly of Emma. Their relationship remains one simply of utility, for they are socially useful to one another. For either to attempt to reject the other would result in a tremendous breach in the social order, thus they are friendly to one another out of their own self-interest; likewise, we can imagine that were something to change making the friendship no longer useful, that the relationship would promptly end.

Charlotte's marriage to Mr. Collins might also be seen as a friendship of utility. Charlotte seems to have no illusions about the kind of arrangement to which she is agreeing, though her dear friend Elizabeth Bennet can make no sense of it. Elizabeth describes Mr. Collins as a "conceited, pompous, narrow-minded, silly man" and believes that "the woman who marries him cannot have a proper way of thinking."[6] However, Mr. Collins has a stable living and needs a proper wife, and Charlotte needs a husband. At age twenty-seven, Charlotte is plain, lacking in good prospects, and increasingly becoming a burden to her family. She defends her decision to marry him, saying, "I am not romantic, you know; I never was. I ask only a comfortable home; and considering Mr. Collins's character, connections, and situation in life, I am convinced that my chance of happiness with him is as fair as most people can boast on entering the marriage state."[7] Charlotte thus has very modest expectations of her marriage, and assumes not that it will be particularly satisfying, but that it will provide her with what she needs. Marriage to Charlotte also provides Mr. Collins with increased status and greater respect in his role as a member of the clergy. Thus, their relationship is one of mutual utility.

Friendships of pleasure function much like friendships of utility but are sustained because the parties find one another pleasurable. Aristotle suggests that young people most often experience friendships of pleasure and that these friendships are not easily sustained, for young people quickly change their minds, finding one thing pleasurable today and another tomorrow. Similarly, young people are prone to fleeting passions, and are thus in and out of love quickly.[8] *Pride and Prejudice*'s Mr. Wickham and Lydia are surely an obvious case of friendship of pleasure. Lydia especially seems to be caught up in the pleasure of it all. In running off with Wickham, she gives no thought to anything but her own immediate satisfaction: she thinks nothing of the burden she has placed on her family with respect to money, honor, or emotional distress. It never seems to occur to her that anyone else was impacted by her decision, and she seems utterly happy with the initial pleasure and status of being married, having given no real thought to what will happen once the pleasure wears off. Austen encourages us to imagine that once the initial thrill of their relationship has faded, Lydia and Wickham may eventually find one another quite burdensome, if not entirely distasteful.

Relationships of pleasure need not end in distaste; rather, they can simply dissipate. This is what seems to happen with Emma's relationship to Harriet Smith. Emma rejects what might be thought a more suitable friendship with Jane Fairfax, most likely because Emma is rather threatened by Jane, in lieu of a friendship with Harriet Smith, a woman of unknown lineage and with no real status and a flighty and ill-formed character. Emma's interest in Harriet seems to be that she is pretty, pleasant enough, and in need of a good husband, which allows Emma to make her a project. Once it is finally determined, however, that Harriet will marry Mr. Martin, a farmer, and that she is not descended from a gentleman as Emma hoped, their relationship simply fades away. The pleasure Emma found in making Harriet a project has ended, as has the intrigue of Harriet's unknown background. As a means of letting the friendship go, Emma arranges for her sister Isabella to have Harriet for an extended visit, easing the transition. The diminishing of the friendship is neither cruel nor callous, but the pleasure to be gained from it has come to an end.

Perfect Friendship

Perfect or complete friendship, on Aristotle's account, differs dramatically from friendships of utility and pleasure, and is described in contrast to these more incomplete relationships: "But complete friendship is the friendship of good people similar in virtue; for they wish goods in the same way to each other insofar as they are good, and they are good in their own right."[9] In a complete friendship, the friends love one another for who they are, rather than some benefit that they bring to one another. As Aristotle puts it, "Now those who wish good to their friend for the friend's own sake are friends most of all; for they have this attitude because of the friend himself, not coincidentally."[10] Moreover, the most perfect friendships are those formed between two people of equally good character; genuine friendship is impossible for those lacking virtue, and it is good character that must be the foundation of the relationship. So, in loving each other for who they are, what the friends love most of all about one another is their mutual good character.

Not just any two people of good character must be friends, for good character will not fit one obvious and straightforward model, even if there is agreement about how the virtues should be conceived. Aristotle provides a comprehensive list of the virtues including the moral virtues of generosity, courage, temperance, wit, friendliness, and good temper, among others, as well as numerous intellectual virtues. But the ways in which these virtues might manifest themselves would be dependent on a host of other individual factors, including temperament, personality, and individual interests and experiences. For example, Austen surely gives us the impression that both Jane Bennet and Elizabeth Bennet have good characters, even if not perfectly good characters, yet they seem to be very different sorts of people. Even if they are both properly thought of as having good character, certain virtues stand out as more salient in one sister or the other. Jane's calmer, more reserved temperament makes us think that she is likely friendlier or perhaps more temperate, whereas Elizabeth's more vibrant personality makes it likely that she is more courageous and wittier. Though Elizabeth, too, is surely capable of being friendly or temperate, her character tends to lend itself more readily to the development of other traits; thus, friendliness or temperance might manifest themselves differently in Elizabeth than in Jane.

Given the myriad ways in which good character can arise, the friend is beloved for all of the particular manifestations of character that make this friend a distinct, particular individual. Friendship is then grounded in a love for the "unique, irreplaceable individual" that the friend is.[11] People of good character may come in many varieties reflecting the tremendous diversity among people and experiences, making friendship even more about finding all the particularities in the individual friend admirable and worthy of love.

Aristotle tells us that complete friendships are "likely to be rare" as those who are truly virtuous are also quite rare.[12] However, he cannot mean that only perfectly virtuous people can have friendships based on their good character. Rather, it is likely that there will be degrees of virtue, and so our friendships will only approximate the ideal. Even so, basing a relationship in mutual good character, even if that character is only striving toward the ideal, is preferable to the alternatives. As one scholar puts it: "clearly enough, there are few or no paragons of virtue in the world, and if only such paragons can have friendships of the basic kind, then most people, including virtually all of Aristotle's readers will be declared incapable of anything but thoroughly self-centered associations."[13]

Because complete friendship must be grounded in the character of the friend, it cannot be acquired quickly and takes time to develop. It takes time to "become accustomed to each other" and "to gain the other's confidence," for another's character cannot be fully known quickly.[14] There can be glimpses and positive indicators of a good character, but a good character is much more than charm or a becoming presence. "Those who are quick to treat each other in friendly ways wish to be friends, but are not friends, unless they are also lovable, and know this. For though the wish for friendship comes quickly, friendship does not."[15] This is precisely the sort of lesson that the Mr. Wickhams of the world are supposed to teach; though Mr. Wickham is particularly engaging and pleasant to be around, his character turns out to be altogether lacking and downright deplorable. While Elizabeth initially found him quite pleasing with his gallant air and his engaging manner, it was only over time that his true character became apparent. In the end it is impossible for a woman such as Elizabeth Bennet to befriend a man of such indignity and indiscretion as Mr. Wickham, for no amount of charm can overcome a bad character.

The view that perfect friendship takes time to develop, and perhaps more importantly, that confirmation of good character takes time to emerge, justifies Jane Bennet's hesitation in showing her affection for Mr. Bingley too readily. By the time their engagement is secured, it is easily apparent to all that they are suited to one another and are of equally good characters; most importantly, it is clear to both Jane and Mr. Bingley. From Elizabeth's perspective "they had for basis the excellent understanding and super-excellent disposition of Jane, and a general similarity of feeling and taste between her and himself."[16] Over time, Jane and Mr. Bingley have learned that they not only have equally good characters, but also similar temperaments. As Mr. Bennet puts it, "I have not a doubt of your doing very well together. Your tempers are by no means unlike. You are each so complying, that nothing will ever be resolved on; so easy, that every servant will cheat you; and so generous, that you will always exceed your income."[17] Jane rather takes affront to this, suggesting that it would be unforgivable for her to demonstrate "imprudence or thoughtlessness" regarding money, and we hope that her good sense will carry them through, but Mr. Bennet's claim is a fair observation about their shared weaknesses.[18]

Friendship and Self-knowledge

Friendship is more than a pleasant addition to the moral life; in the Aristotelian realm, it is essential. The virtuous person not only desires friends, but needs them. Aristotle provides a long list of the ways and times we might need friends: the wealthy need friends to be the beneficiaries of their generosity, while for the poor, friends are the only refuge. The young need friends to guide them; the old need friends to support them in times of need.[19] Friendship, however, is good for more than just external benefits. A brief exploration of the Aristotelian virtues shows an understanding of virtue that is inherently social. Among Aristotle's virtues are generosity, wit, and good temper. It is difficult to imagine the need for generosity without others to benefit from that generosity, or the ability to be witty without someone else to find humor in our jokes. Aristotle is providing for us a conception of the virtuous person that is premised on the idea that virtue is social. Though we should find pleasure in our own virtue, the need for virtue is partly to help build a just society. Without community and relationships, virtue could be superfluous. Though the virtuous person should be self-sufficient, that is not the same as being entirely solitary. The virtues that Aristotle is espousing are a set of virtues and a theory of morality appropriate for those expected to play an important public role and invested in the sustaining of a society, for his audience is generally young Athenian gentlemen of property.[20] In many ways this might not seem all that different than the world of the landed gentry that we find in Jane Austen!

Though friendship serves a broader social purpose, it is important in ways more central to our individual character. We need friends to be the objects of our virtuous actions, but we also need friends to help us improve our own character. It is partly through the sharing of our lives with another virtuous person that we can become better, for "good people's life together allows the cultivation of virtue."[21] Besides enhancing the richness of our human lives, helping to improve our character is the most important moral role for friendship: having friends actually serves to make us better people. The complete friend is more than another person of good character, for Aristotle describes the friend as "another yourself" who "supplies what your own efforts cannot supply."[22] This is a strong claim and holds a special significance for Aristotle. In suggesting that the friend is a "second self," Aristotle tells us that the friend helps make self-knowledge, and thus greater virtue, possible. We cannot observe our own actions, and cannot have an objective view of ourselves, but good actions can be observed in the friend: "As then when we wish to see our own face, we do so by looking into the mirror, in the same way when we wish to know ourselves we can obtain that knowledge by looking at our friend. For the friend is, as we assert, a second self."[23] The friend, then, functions rather like a mirror, so that those traits I cannot see in myself, I can see in my friend. From this, I can learn to see myself and understand myself more fully. Aristotle helps us along a bit in making sense of this when he explains that "it is a most difficult thing . . . to attain a knowledge of oneself."[24] This difficulty is made apparent, he tells us, by the ways in which we criticize others for having the same traits that we possess ourselves, only because we are blinded by our own perspective. Thus we need the perspective of the friend to help us see aright, which might occur by seeing similarities, but also by making contrasts.[25] Elizabeth Bennet and Mr. Darcy can help us understand just how this can be the case.

Near the beginning of *Pride and Prejudice*, Elizabeth Bennet has decided that Mr. Darcy is pompous, inconsiderate, and self-important. His refusal to dance at the ball, even when numerous young women do not have partners, leads Elizabeth to write him off as entirely lacking in character. He is "haughty, reserved, and fastidious, and his manners, though well-bred, were not inviting."[26] This interpretation is only exacerbated when she overhears him dismiss her as "tolerable, but not handsome enough to tempt *me*."[27] His apparent pride leaves her all too willing to engage any possible evidence to corroborate her view, for she is so certain of her interpretation of Mr. Darcy that she resists all evidence to the contrary. Elizabeth is more typically thoughtful and perceptive, but her vanity has gotten the better of her. As soon as she feels rejected by Mr. Darcy, she is altogether unwilling to see him in any charitable light. Mr. Darcy, however, softens to Elizabeth more readily. Though he finds her to be from an unsuitable family, it is clear that he finds her to have admirable traits, well beyond her lovely eyes. Initially he notices the "easy playfulness" of her manners and the "uncommon intelligence" of her face.[28] More time together at Rosings Park results in Mr. Darcy proposing to Elizabeth, but with an admission that it is against his better judgment. Though Elizabeth rejects him forcefully, this is the turning point in their relationship, and the point at which Elizabeth begins to see Mr. Darcy more charitably. This is also, however, the point at which both Mr. Darcy and Elizabeth begin to see themselves more clearly. Upon receiving a letter from Mr. Darcy explaining his behavior, regarding both her and Mr. Wickham, Elizabeth is mortified to realize how mistaken she has been, acting out of vanity and poor judgment: "How despicably I have acted!" She cried; "I, who have prided myself on my discernment! I, who have valued myself on my abilities! . . . Till this moment I never knew myself."[29] Realizing her terrible errors in judgment, Elizabeth soon shifts her judgment, little by little, with each new piece of evidence that she allows herself to see. As Mr. Darcy's character becomes more known to her, she finally is able to see him as he is:

> to comprehend that he was exactly the man who, in disposition and talents, would most suit her. His understanding and temper, though unlike her own, would have answered all her wishes. It was an union that must have been to the advantage of both: by her ease and liveliness, his mind might have been softened, his manners improved; and from his judgment, information, and knowledge of the world, she must have received benefit of greater importance.[30]

Austen makes clear to us that not only is Elizabeth's character improved by Mr. Darcy, but his will be by her as well. Only when Elizabeth points out to Darcy his behavior does he begin to fully understand the way in which she has experienced him. Each of them reflects back to the other a picture they would not have been able to see of themselves in any other way, and thus they help one another to become better. By the end of the novel, they appear both to themselves, and to the reader, as perfectly complementary to one another, and Austen leaves us confident in their long-term happiness and virtue.

Emma and Mr. Knightley provide another example of the ways in which friends can help to make us better, even if a somewhat less clear-cut case. Though Emma and Mr. Knightley have been longtime companions, Emma does not realize her love for Mr. Knightley until she seriously considers the possibility that he would marry Harriet. When Harriet confesses her affection for Mr. Knightley, mistakenly believing that he has demonstrated feelings for her, Emma's response is almost visceral. Only then does Emma fully come to know her own feelings. Though Mr. Knightley has long been a fixture in her life, Emma had never considered or acknowledged her real feelings for him: "A few minutes were sufficient for making her acquainted with her own heart. A mind like hers, once opening to suspicion, made rapid progress; she touched, she admitted, she acknowledged the whole truth. . . . It darted through her with the speed of an arrow that Mr. Knightley must marry no one but herself!"[31]

What makes Emma's relationship with Mr. Knightley fit the Aristotelian mold less easily is that their relationship has been long characterized by Mr. Knightley's admonishment and encouragement of Emma to be better. As she meddles in Harriet Smith's affairs, encouraging her to hope for a better match than Robert Martin, Mr. Knightley tells Emma: "She was as happy as possible with the Martins in the summer. She had no sense of superiority then. If she has it now, you have given it. You have been no friend to Harriet Smith, Emma."[32] Emma often does not want to hear what Mr. Knightley has to say. Even when she has made him angry enough that he stays away longer than usual, "She was sorry, but could not repent."[33] On a similar theme, Mr. Knightley suggests that Emma would do well to be a better friend to Jane Fairfax, that Jane is a more suitable and appropriate friend, partly because of her good character. Perhaps the most famous scene is the one in which Mr. Knightley admonishes for her abominable behavior in mocking Miss Bates: "Emma, I must once more speak to you as I have been used to do; a privilege rather endured than allowed, perhaps, but I must still use it. I cannot see you acting wrong, without a remonstrance. How could you be so unfeeling to Miss Bates? How could you be so insolent in your wit to a woman of her character, age, and situation? Emma, I had not thought it possible."[34] Emma recognizes immediately her guilt, even if she does not readily admit it to Mr. Knightley, presumably out of embarrassment. She knows immediately upon being chastised how very wrong she had been. In this situation, Emma sees herself reflected in Mr. Knightley's judgment, which is effective only because of the strong bond they already share. Without their friendship, his opinion could not be given so easily or accepted, even if with some resistance.

Mr. Knightley, too, learns to know himself better in his relationship with Emma, even if the shift is more subtle. When Mr. Knightley finally confesses his love for Emma, we learn that his realization of his feelings has also been somewhat surprising. In his profession of love, we see one frustrated by his lack of eloquence, and recognizing that he has been hard on Emma, not always demonstrating well his affection for her: "If I loved you less, I might be able to talk about it more. But you know what I am. You hear nothing but truth from me. I have blamed you, and lectured you, and you have borne it as no other woman in England would have borne it. . . . God knows I have been a very indifferent lover. But you understand me."[35] Moreover, we come to understand that Mr. Knightley, too, has had a hard time making sense of his feelings. It turns out that Mr. Knightley had felt intimidated by the easy charm of Frank Churchill, and expected Emma to be crushed at the announcement of his engagement to Jane Fairfax. In fact, his jealousy of Frank Churchill often confused his feelings for Emma. "He had been in love with Emma, and jealous of Frank Churchill, from about the same period, one sentiment having probably enlightened him as to the other."[36] In his effort to escape, Mr. Knightley flees to his brother's house only to be confronted with a happy family setting and coming face to face more fully with his own desires. Only when Emma is completely nonplussed at Frank Churchill's engagement does Mr. Knightley come to realize the depth of his affection for her. Fortunately, Emma was all too willing to hear his profession of love and to return it readily. As Austen tells us, "Mr. Knightley could not impute to Emma a more relenting heart than she possessed, or a heart more disposed to accept of his."[37] For all of his correction, it is clear that Mr. Knightley admires Emma and loves her for who she is, and that she wants to be worthy of his love. She is not only his equal in status and charm, but also is growing to be his equal in character. Thus, Austen leads us to believe that they will make the perfect and ideal match.

Like the ideal marriages that Austen presents, complete friendship is to be long lasting. As it is grounded in good character, which no one would willingly sacrifice, there is nothing to fade away. Austen's works prompt us to believe that these ideal marriages are happy because the characters are compatible, good, and deserving of one another. If, as Aristotle suggests, this kind of relationship can not only improve self-knowledge but also virtue, then the most important relationships must never be left to chance, as Charlotte Lucas suggests, for not only one's happiness, but also one's future character is at stake.

Notes

1. Jane Austen, *Pride and Prejudice* in *Jane Austen: Her Complete Novels* (New York: Avenel Books, 1981), 188.

2. Aristotle, *Nicomachean Ethics*, 2nd ed., trans. Terence Irwin (Indianapolis: Hackett, 1999), 1156a17.

3. Aristotle, *Nicomachean Ethics*, 1156a17.

4. Aristotle, *Nicomachean Ethics*, 1156a23.

5. Jane Austen, *Emma* in *Jane Austen: Her Complete Novels* (New York: Avenel Books, 1981), 716.

6. Austen, *Pride and Prejudice*, 236

7. Austen, *Pride and Prejudice*, 237.

8. Aristotle, *Nicomachean Ethics*, 1156a32–1156b5.

9. Aristotle, *Nicomachean Ethics*, 1156b7–8.

10. Aristotle, *Nicomachean Ethics*, 1156b10–12.

11. Neera Badhwar, "Friends as Ends in Themselves," in *Philosophy and Phenomenological Research*, 48 (September 1987), 5.

12. Aristotle, *Nicomachean Ethics*, 1156b25–27.

13. John M. Cooper, "Aristotle on Friendship" in *Essays on Aristotle's Ethics*, ed. Amélie Oksenberg Rorty (Berkeley: University of California Press, 1980), 305.

14. Aristotle, *Nicomachean Ethics*, 1156b26–30.

15. Aristotle, *Nicomachean Ethics*, 1156b30–33.

16. Austen, *Pride and Prejudice*, 340.

17. Austen, *Pride and Prejudice*, 340.

18. Jane Austen, *Pride and Prejudice*, 340.

19. Aristotle, *Nicomachean Ethics*, 1155a1–15.

20. Aristotle's ethical works are often thought to be the lecture notes for his teaching at his Athenian school, the Lyceum. For further discussion, see D. S. Hutchinson, "Ethics" in *The Cambridge Companion to Aristotle*, ed. Jonathan Barnes (Cambridge: Cambridge University Press, 1995), 197–99.

21. Aristotle, *Nicomachean Ethics*, 1170a12.

22. Aristotle, *Nicomachean Ethics*, 1169b5–7.

23. Aristotle, *Magna Moralia*, 1213a, as cited and translated by John M. Cooper, "Friendship and the Good in Aristotle," *The Philosophical Review*, 86 (July 1977), 296. Cooper here gives a much fuller analysis of the relationship between friendship and self-knowledge.

24. Aristotle, *Magna Moralia*, 1213a.

25. Nancy Sherman, "Aristotle on Friendship and the Shared Life," *Philosophy and Phenomenological Research*, 47 (June 1987), 611.

26. Austen, *Pride and Prejudice*, 185.

27. Austen, *Pride and Prejudice*, 183.

28. Austen, *Pride and Prejudice*, 188.

29. Austen, *Pride and Prejudice*, 275–76.

30. Austen, *Pride and Prejudice*, 322.

31. Austen, *Emma*, 776.

32. Austen, *Emma*, 614.

33. Austen, *Emma*, 617.
34. Austen, *Emma*, 760.
35. Austen, *Emma*, 786.
36. Austen, *Emma*, 787.
37. Austen, *Emma*, 787.

PART II

MORALITY AND VIRTUE

CHAPTER SIX

Finding Happiness at Hartfield

JANELLE PÖTZSCH

If happiness were indeed all about "being well deceived,"[1] handsome, clever, and rich Miss Woodhouse could just continue to lead her sheltered life at sleepy Highbury. Her tasks were limited to arranging dinner parties and finding ways to escape that chatterbox Miss Bates. There were signs which implied just that: at the beginning of the novel, we learn that our heroine has "too much her own way" and is prone to "think a little too well of herself"—two characteristics Austen dubs Emma's "real evils."[2] This telling choice of words sets the stage for one of the most delightful novels of formation English literature has to offer. Much to Emma's distress, and against all her expectations, she soon learns that her outlook on the world requires serious adjustment. That it takes more than a comfortable home and an indulgent father to order around to be truly content dawns only very gradually on her.

The development Emma experiences in the course of the novel is all the more astounding given the fact she's actually quite unwilling to "submit to anything requiring industry and patience," as a conscientious Mr. George Knightley tells us. And why should she? There's general agreement that Emma's "the cleverest of her family";[3] and given her crowd of admirers, from her father to Mr. and Mrs. Weston and, above all, Harriet Smith, she's in the pleasurable state of perpetual self-affirmation. Only the moral compass of the novel, George Knightley, understands that Emma's friendship with Harriet promises more harm than good. He considers Harriet Smith "the very worst sort of companion that Emma could possibly have" for the simple reason that her shortcomings boost Emma's vanity: "How can Emma imagine she has anything to learn herself, while Harriet is presenting such a delightful inferiority?"[4] Put differently, the people around Emma offer her no incentive whatsoever for personal change—instead, she's given to understand that she's just perfect the way she is. At first sight, this doesn't seem too much of a problem: receiving approval from those around us is a decisive component for flourishing and well-being.

Alas, it all depends on the dose: it is one thing to give your child the kind of emotional support it takes to become a confident and level-headed adult and quite another one to indulge her such as to become as smug and haughty as Miss Woodhouse. What such an upbringing, if not averted, could lead to is nicely illustrated by Mrs. Elton, aka Augusta Hawkins, a character who reads like a parody of Emma. We learn that Mrs. Elton is "extremely well satisfied with herself,"[5] even though she's a woman of only "a little beauty and a little accomplishment, but so little judgment that she thought herself coming with superior knowledge of the world."[6]

"A Little Learning Is a Dangerous Thing"[7]

Emma's own artistic and scholarly endeavors haven't yielded much either, even though she "had always wanted to do everything." But as Mr. Knightley has already pointed out, "steadiness had always been wanting." As a result, Emma remained clearly below her possibilities and never "approached the degree of excellence which she would have been glad to command, and ought not to have failed of." Nevertheless, Emma likes people to have a different, more flattering picture of her: "She was not much deceived as to her own skill either as an artist or a musician, but she was not . . . sorry to know her reputation for accomplishment often higher than it deserved."[8]

Emma's tendency to self-deception doesn't stop here. Her enthusiastic plans to educate herself have led to little more than the writing of impressive reading lists,[9] and she also lets slide her ambitious attempts to school Harriet: "Her views of improving her little friend's mind, by a great deal of useful reading and conversation, had never yet led to more than a few first chapters, and the intention of going on to-morrow."[10]

To make matters worse, Emma and Mrs. Elton have not only little learning in common, but also poor judgment. And thanks to their remarkable self-confidence, this doesn't keep either of them from meddling with other people's lives.[11] All this is highly entertaining, but only for the reader. Sadly, Emma isn't just a conceited, spoiled brat; she's a conceited, spoiled brat with a lot of influence. As the other characters of the novel find out the hard way, her behavior has far-reaching consequences. She spoils the advances of Robert Martin, drives a wedge between Frank Churchill and Jane Fairfax, and puts weird ideas in the simple mind of Harriet Smith.

In other words, Emma's misled views make her behave in a way which causes much conflict and pain in drowsy Highbury. This is all the more troubling given her high social rank and the communal duties which come with it. Emma won't be able to meet the moral requirements her position entails unless she lets go of her misconceptions. That's what Austen meant by calling Emma's character traits "real evils."[12] Although the term "evil" may sound a bit too harsh for a moody twenty-one-year-old, it's not completely unfounded since Emma's shortcomings hinder her from meeting the moral demands of her social role. What's more, Emma's disposition is harmful not only for the other characters, but first and foremost for her. For one, her misjudgments prevent her from truly befriending other people—take her reserved attitude toward Jane Fairfax, the only young woman in Highbury who had "been given an excellent education"[13] and whose "decided superiority both in beauty and acquirements"[14] make her a far more suitable companion for Emma than that natural daughter of somebody named Harriet Smith.[15] In this regard, it's also worth asking whether the relation between Emma and Harriet deserves to be called a friendship at all, since Emma sought Harriet's acquaintance mainly for selfish reasons—and petty ones at that: "As a walking companion, Emma had very early foreseen how useful she might find her.[16] Moreover, Emma delights in the prospects of patronizing Harriet. When weighing the pros and cons of Harriet's companionship, comparing it to the friendship with her former governess, she ponders that "Harriet would be loved as one to whom she could be useful. For Mrs Weston there was nothing to be done; for Harriet every thing."[17]

Things are disappointingly different for Emma when it comes to Jane Fairfax: Here, all the advantages of a friendship must be on Emma's side, given Jane's first-class education and understanding (to make matters even worse for Emma, Jane is also of breathtaking beauty).[18] Precisely this seems to be the problem: Jane is so superior that Emma feels insignificant in her presence and hence meets her with reserve. Even though Emma herself can't give a reason for her aversion toward Jane, George Knightley voices the suspicion that "it was because she saw in her the really accomplished young woman, which she wanted to be thought of herself."[19]

Moreover, Emma's distorted worldview is a serious stumbling block for her own happiness. It's only after Harriet's confession of having a crush on George Knightley that she, the avowed spinster who at the beginning of the novel declared to "have very little intention of ever marrying at all,"[20] becomes aware of her own feelings: "Why was the evil so dreadfully increased by Harriet's having some hope of a return? It darted through her, with the speed of an arrow, that Mr. Knightley must marry no one but herself!"[21] Emma's self-deception hindered her from acknowledging her emotions and made her act against her own interests—not only when it comes to her unconscious love of George Knightley, but also as regards her flirtatious behavior toward Frank Churchill, a man who actually couldn't mean any less to her. These and numerous other episodes demonstrate that Emma is quite oblivious of her actual desires. She was well-deceived but far from being happy.

This would come as no surprise to ancient Greek philosopher Aristotle (384–322 BC). In his *Nicomachean Ethics*, Aristotle tried nothing less than to show that man strives first and foremost for happiness, or *eudaimonia*. The ancient idea of happiness differs from our modern understanding of being happy insofar as it's not about being effusive or exalted. Rather, what Aristotle has in mind is a lasting frame of mind of contentment, which results from leading a certain way of life. Specifically, happiness is claimed to be some sort of activity.

On the face of it, the claim that people want to be happy may sound trivial: All of Austen's characters, not to mention ourselves, are employed in the pursuit of happiness. Harriet Smith is on the lookout for a husband, Frank Churchill can't wait to finally propose to Jane, and Augusta Elton is wrapped up in bragging. Yet, Aristotle's account of happiness is quite different from, not to say aloft of, these mundane targets. The aims of Harriet and Frank, for instance, are founded in pleasure, or lust. In Aristotle's view, this attitude doesn't do much justice to human nature, even though it's widely shared: "[T]he generality of men and the most vulgar identify the Good with pleasure, and accordingly are content with the Life of Enjoyment." The problem with this stance is that they thereby "show themselves to be utterly slavish, by preferring what is only a life for cattle."[22]

Equally doubtful is the mind-set of people like Mr. and Mrs. Elton, who are so eager for other people's esteem. Aristotle thinks the pursuit of honor too superficial. It's almost as if he had the Eltons in mind when writing that "men's motive in pursuing honor seems to be to assure themselves of their own merit."[23] The problem here is twofold: For one, honor depends on those who confer it, that is, other people need to be able to understand why honor is or is not due to someone. This implies that honor is nothing inherent to a person, but something which is being granted. Second, people are being honored for a reason, which means that honor is the result of something. Jane Fairfax isn't admired just for the sake of it, but for her demeanor and accomplishments. Put differently: we don't become good or happy because we receive honor, but we receive honor because we're good. It's a bit like in the "Euthyphro dilemma" Aristotle's teacher Plato gives us in his *Euthyphro*, a dialogue on what it means to be pious: "Is that which is holy loved by the gods because it is holy, or is it holy because it is loved by the gods?"[24]

Honor and piety hence offer no reliable guidelines for establishing whether a person can be deemed happy or not.

How else then can we tell who leads a good and happy life? According to Aristotle, we may find that out "by ascertaining what is man's function."[25] This claim sounds more preposterous to modern ears than it actually is. To begin with, we have to ask ourselves which feature distinguishes man from all other living beings, a feature which moreover should be shared by people as different as Mr. Woodhouse and Mr. Knightley. Mere living is something which even plants do, whereas growth and pleasure are things we share with animals. Aristotle therefore concludes that the decisive characteristic which sets a human being apart from any other living being is its capability to reason: "[T]he function of man is the active exercise of the soul's faculties in conformity with rational principle."[26] Only a human being who acts according to his innate "function" of reasoning can be both good and happy.

But besides such conduct, Aristotle underlines that happiness also depends on so-called external goods like wealth, beauty, and good friends: "[A] man of very ugly appearance or low birth, or childless and alone in the world, is not our idea of a happy man, and still less so perhaps is one who has children or friends that are worthless, or who has had good ones but lost them by death."[27] Take noble but poor Jane Fairfax, who has such a hard time being happy for the simple reason of her uncertain prospects. The same goes for her aunt, Miss Bates, as is discernible in Mr. Knightley's harsh criticism of Emma after she insulted Miss Bates on Box Hill:

> Were she a woman of fortune, I would [. . .] not quarrel with you for any liberties of manner. Were she your equal in situation—but, Emma, consider how far this is from being the case. She is poor; she has sunk from the comforts she was born to; and, if she live to old age, must probably sink more. Her situation should secure your compassion.[28]

Very much in accordance with Aristotle, Mr. Knightley senses that the respect and goodwill of others are most likely the only sources of contentment a person as deprived as Miss Bates has. Truly happy she probably can no longer be, which is why Knightley appeals to Emma's pity.

But even if we keep this criterion in mind, the claim that we're happy only if we take the pains to be reasonable still needs some clarification. After all, people can do a lot of harm when acting on their reason—just think of Emma's matchmaking. Her schemes are quite thought out, but they have no real-world foundation. Emma's conclusions are correct, but she acts (and thinks) on flawed premises. To rip off the lacing of one's boot to give two potential lovers some time together is a promising endeavor only if these two people are actually interested in each other. It obviously takes something more than reason to attain happiness and to become a good person. That's why Aristotle holds that the exercise of the soul mentioned above should be carried out not only in conformity with reason, but also with *virtue*.

Something's Greek to You?

For the contemporary reader, the term "virtue" might sound rather prudish, laden as it is with sexual connotations. In ancient Greek thought, however, "virtue" covers far more than that. It denotes the disposition to strive for something good and laudable. This isn't restricted to sex: Aristotle distinguishes between virtues of the mind, or intellectual virtues (like wisdom and prudence) and moral virtues (like temperance). In Aristotle's terms, virtues are "praiseworthy dispositions."[29] Intellectual virtues take time and experience to develop. Recall the banter between Emma and Knightley in chapter 12, where they come to speak of the age difference between them. Emma concedes that sixteen years are indeed a "material difference," which explains Knightley's superior judgment. But still, "does not the lapse of one-and-twenty years bring our understandings a good deal nearer?" Knightley, however, isn't inclined to succumb and (teasingly?) replies: "Yes—a good deal *nearer*."[30] Emma might have become more mature in the meantime, but Knightley still has the advantage of sixteen years over her.

Things are different, and much more complicated, when it comes to moral virtues. According to Aristotle, we obtain these only by performing them. Put differently, we have to practise virtues until they have become our second nature, or habit. This is also in accordance with the origin of the term "ethics": it stems from the Greek "ethos," which stands for "habit," or "custom."

In this regard, to acquire moral virtues is a bit like acquiring musical skills: Emma will become an accomplished piano player only by regular practice. We learn to play Chopin only by performing his pieces, and we become just only by performing just acts. Aristotle declares that "our moral dispositions are formed as a result of the corresponding activities. Hence it is incumbent on us to control the character of our activities, since on the quality of these depends the quality of our dispositions."[31] This illustrates why Emma's behavior on Box Hill is so severely criticized by Knightley. As long as she's willing to waive basic decorum for the sake of a bad joke, Emma's far from meeting the moral standards her privileged position implies. In a way, she's refusing to act upon people's social expectations, especially those of Knightley.

Fortunately, though, Emma is no hopeless case, as becomes evident in her reaction to Knightley's reproach: "She was vexed beyond what could have been expressed—almost beyond what she could conceal. Never had she felt so agitated, mortified, grieved at any circumstance in her life."[32] Emma real-izes very quickly that Knightley is right in scolding her and feels sincere remorse about her conduct toward Miss Bates. She hence seems to have a good grasp of which kind of behavior is appropriate and which is not. Still, as we learn shortly before her taunting remark at the expense of Miss Bates: "Emma could not resist."[33] So she did have a hunch that her comment prom-ises no good. That she made it nonetheless makes her a prime example of unrestraint, or moral weakness. According to Aristotle, an "unrestrained man does things that he knows to be evil, under the influence of passion."[34]

But how can people act against their better knowledge? Why did Emma say what she did even though she sensed it to be wrong? Aristotle declares that unrestraint is either impetuousness or weakness: "The weak deliberate, but then are prevented by passion from keeping to their resolution; the impetuous are led by passion because they do not stop to deliberate."[35] Emma clearly belongs to the first category. Both the weak and the impetuous display a specific lack of knowledge. Unrestrained people who get carried away by their passion are like drunken people: they may know certain things, from poetry to correct behavior, but they're unable to truly act upon it. Their passion (or drunkenness) suspends their knowledge. Intoxicated or infuriated people may recall some lines of a charade or *The Vicar of Wakefield* or what else they've once learned, but like actors in a play, they just *impersonate*; what they say has nothing to do with their authentic self. Unrestrained people face the problem that their moral knowledge hasn't yet "become part of the tissue of the mind," as Aristotle puts it.[36]

As mentioned above, virtues need to become our second nature. If we can still be overpowered by passion (or, as in Emma's case, by the desire to shine as a wit), this means that we are quite familiar with moral guidelines, but these aren't yet sufficiently rooted in our mind—which is why Emma can so lightheartedly disregard them at Box Hill. Like the above-mentioned actor, she likes to change roles (and rules . . .). But as her reaction to Knightley's rebuke indicates, she's not really wicked: For one, she feels deep regret over what she's done, and second, her moral flaws show up only now and then, that is, they're temporary. What's more, Emma doesn't harm others deliberately. In Aristotle's words, that's why an unrestrained person is like "a state which passes all the proper enactments, and has good laws, but which never keeps its laws."[37] (This characterization is also pretty much in accord with Emma's good intentions of educating herself and Harriet.)

The Importance of Being Earnest

Obviously, then, a change of heart (and mind) in Emma would benefit not only the people of Highbury, but first and foremost Emma herself. Her self-deception is a serious hindrance to her attainment of happiness for it prevents her from making full use of her capacities, that is, "the active exercise of the soul's faculties" which according to Aristotle is so decisive for being happy. In Aristotle's view, we as human beings can become happy only if we live in accordance with our specific human "function," or virtue: We need to develop and use our reason. Sadly, Emma seems to have only little opportunity to accomplish this. There are several indications that Emma simply isn't challenged enough. She's not only "the cleverest of her family,"[38] but also of the whole bunch of Highbury (with the likely exception of George Knightley)—a constellation which makes Emma quite smug about herself.[39] Unsurprisingly, such tremendous lack of intellectual stimulation does sooner or later result in languor. Tediousness overcomes Emma time and again in the novel, most notably shortly after the first visit of Frank Churchill. The sudden departure of one of the very few sharp people in Highbury makes Emma aware of how dull her surroundings actually are. But as usual, her conclusion is completely amiss: "This sensation of listlessness, weariness, stupidity, this disinclination to sit down and employ myself, this feeling of every thing's being dull and insipid about the house!—I must be in love."[40]

Luckily enough, Emma was never in danger of becoming Mrs. Churchill, since Frank Churchill was secretly engaged to Jane Fairfax long before his visit to Highbury. And if she were, she and Frank would surely send the Eltons off to second place in the competition of "most annoying couple in Austen." Both would mutually intensify their faults, which are actually quite similar: As explained above in connection with the Box Hill incident,

Emma's flaw as an unrestrained person is that the moral virtues she needs to develop in order to be happy haven't yet become her second nature—she's willing to disregard them at leisure. This makes her behavior rather unreliable and erratic. But according to Aristotle, a virtuous person always acts predictably for the simple reason that the moral virtues (which, naturally, always require a very specific way of acting in order to be both attained and acted upon) have become part of her character. That's the idea behind Mrs. Weston's remark that "Mr. Knightley does nothing mysteriously."[41]

Compare this to Frank Churchill, toward whom Knightley feels a deep and immediate distrust even before their meeting in person. The style of Frank's letters as well as his somewhat thin excuses of why he has to repeatedly postpone his trip to Highbury to visit his father are enough to make him suspicious of this young man. And Frank's secrecy and playfulness do indeed pose a threat to the social fabric of Highbury. Like the unrestrained Emma, lighthearted Frank doesn't show his authentic self, as becomes obvious in his penchant for games, which he uses to lead people (especially Emma) astray—just recall his conversation with Emma about who might have given Jane the expensive piano. Apart from this talk, where he manages to dupe in fact both Emma as well as his secret fiancée (for both women think the other being ridiculed), there is the far-too-open flirtation with Emma, another kind of game he uses to misinform the others about his true attachment. The problem with games is that people are no longer bound by the ordinary rules of social discourse while playing, as poor Miss Bates learns at Box Hill.

In fact, Frank's games prepared the ground for Emma's conduct at Box Hill. At the beginning of the chapter, we learn that there was a "deficiency" among the group, "a want of union,"[42] which caused them to separate into parties. The immature conduct of Emma and Frank, which is rooted in their lack of Aristotelian virtue, dissolves social ties. Eventually, though, both characters become aware of their social duties and change for the better. This development is not only in accordance with Aristotle's ideas on true virtue, but also hints at an even more profound discussion of his *Nicomachean Ethics*: the question of which lifestyle is the happiest and hence the most desirable one. For Aristotle, only two candidates qualify for this enquiry: the *bios politikos* and the *bios theôrêtikos*, the political and the theoretical life. Regarding this issue, Aristotle proves himself almost as snobbish as Miss Woodhouse when he declares that it's the theoretical life of the scientist/philosopher which promises the most in terms of contentment. But some of his arguments are worth considering: For one, the theoretical or contemplating life is in accordance with the best part of us, our intellect. Second, contemplation is something we can carry on most continuously, so apparently it's something we are very apt to do. And finally, contemplation is quite self-sufficient:

> For while it is true that the wise man equally with the just man and the rest requires the necessaries of life, yet, these being adequately supplied, whereas the just man needs other persons towards whom or with whose aid he may act justly [. . .], the wise man on the contrary can also contemplate by himself, and the more the wiser he is.[43]

Yet, this self-sufficiency of the philosopher who spends his time pondering "theoretical," that is, rather useless things with no applicability whatsoever actually isn't that self-sufficient. Rather, the existence of the philosopher (or of a high daughter like Emma Woodhouse, for that matter) depends on a high cultural and economic stage of development. That's where the *bios politikos*, the political life, comes in, which, after all, ranks second as regards the desirability of different lifestyles. It's the life of people like George Knightley, who take seriously the social duties their high rank demands. Nevertheless, we shouldn't strive for the political life in order to gain public esteem. In this regard, Knightley is remarkably different from the Eltons, and also from Emma: although superior in both wealth and education, he never shows off or uses the usual status symbols like carriages, but prefers to walk.

In contrast to him, Emma and Mrs. Elton act nice in order to impress and boast—like when Mrs. Elton exclaims at the Crown, "What a pleasure it is to send one's carriage to a friend!" to let people know that it was *her* carriage which brought Jane and Miss Bates to the ball.[44] Similarly, Emma's visit to the Bates in chapter 44 is meant as atonement for her behavior at Box Hill. But according to Aristotle, it is one thing to act morally because others expect you to do (or because you want to impress), and another one because you really want to act morally. Put differently, we're virtuous only if we delight in acting virtuously: "[A]cts done in conformity with the virtues are not done justly or temperately if they themselves are of a certain sort, but only if the agent also is in a certain state of mind when he does them." Specifically, we need to "act with knowledge," "deliberately choose the act, and choose it for its own sake," and the act we perform "must spring from a fixed and permanent disposition of character."[45] Recall how Knightley leads Harriet to the set at the Crown after Mr. Elton declines to dance with her—despite a few minutes earlier, Emma spotted Knightley "among the standers-by, where he ought not to be; he ought to be dancing—not classing himself with the husbands, and fathers, and whist-players."[46] Apparently, Knightley is a reluctant dancer. Yet, he changes his mind to make Harriet forget the rude behavior of her former heartthrob.

Unfortunately, Emma still seems far from meeting the moral standards of her future husband, let alone Aristotle, as her rather unkind conduct toward Harriet in the last few chapters of the novel indicate. Whether Miss Woodhouse will ever succeed in truly overcoming her egocentricity must be left to be guessed.

Notes

1. Jonathan Swift, *The Writings of Jonathan Swift*, ed. Robert A. Greenberg and William B. Piper (New York: Norton, 1973), 351. For Swift's influence on Austen, see Claude Rawson, *Swift and Others* (Cambridge: Cambridge University Press, 2015), 205–26.

2. Jane Austen, *Emma* (London: Penguin, 1994), 5.

3. Austen, *Emma*, 29.

4. Austen, *Emma*, 30.

5. Austen, *Emma*, 205.

6. Austen, *Emma*, 211.

7. Alexander Pope, "An Essay on Criticism," in *Alexander Pope. The Major Works, including "The Rape of the Lock" and "The Dunciad,"* ed. Pat Rogers (Oxford: Oxford University Press 2008), 24.

8. Austen, *Emma*, 35.

9. Austen, *Emma*, 29.

10. Austen, *Emma*, 54.

11. For example, Emma's schemes of finding whom she considers a desirable husband for Harriet is mirrored in Mrs. Elton's endeavors to set up Jane Fairfax as a high-class governess. In both cases, their plans are far from meeting the preferences of the people concerned: Harriet prefers Robert Martin to Mr. Elton, and Jane would rather work at an ordinary school than in an affluent household.

12. Austen, *Emma*, 5.

13. Austen, *Emma*, 123.

14. Austen, *Emma*, 124.

15. For more on justice existing only when powers are equal, see the chapter in this volume by William A. Lindenmuth.

16. Austen, *Emma*, 20.

17. Austen, *Emma*, 21.

18. Austen, *Emma*, 126.

19. Austen, *Emma*, 125. Just one sentence after this quote, we learn that "though the

accusation had been eagerly refuted at the time, there were moments of self-examination in which [Emma's] conscience could not quite acquit her."

20. Austen, *Emma*, 66.

21. Austen, *Emma*, 308.

22. Aristotle, *Nicomachean Ethics* (London: Heinemann, 1962), 14f.

23. Aristotle, *Nicomachean Ethics*, 15.

24. "Plato, *Euthyphro*," http://www.perseus.tufts.edu/hopper/text?doc = Perseus%3A text%3A1999.01.0170%3Atext%3DEuthyph.%3Asection%3D10a.

25. Aristotle, *Nicomachean Ethics*, 31.

26. Aristotle, *Nicomachean Ethics*, 33.

27. Aristotle, *Nicomachean Ethics*, 43.

28. Austen, *Emma*, 283f.

29. Aristotle, *Nicomachean Ethics*, 69.

30. Austen, *Emma*, 77 (emphasis in the text).

31. Aristotle, *Nicomachean Ethics*, 75.

32. Austen, *Emma*, 284.

33. Austen, *Emma*, 280.

34. Aristotle, *Nicomachean Ethics*, 377f.

35. Aristotle, *Nicomachean Ethics*, 417.

36. Aristotle, *Nicomachean Ethics*, 391.

37. Aristotle, *Nicomachean Ethics*, 427f.

38. Austen, *Emma*, 29.

39. Jane Fairfax is very educated, but since we receive hardly any other information regarding her person (she has only little direct speech, and Austen gives no stream-of-consciousness narration for this character), we can't know for sure how intelligent she is (and her secretiveness about her attachment to Frank Churchill doesn't count!).

40. Austen, *Emma*, 198.

41. Austen, *Emma*, 171.

42. Austen, *Emma*, 277.

43. Aristotle, *Nicomachean Ethics*, 615.

44. Austen, *Emma*, 242.

45. Aristotle, *Nicomachean Ethics*, 85.

46. Austen, *Emma*, 245.

CHAPTER SEVEN

⌇

The Last Great Representative
of the Virtues

MacIntyre after Austen

David LaRocca

In a celebrated edition of *Thug Notes*, Sparky Sweets offers a critical analysis of Jane Austen's *Pride and Prejudice* that illuminates her qualities as a novelist and, we are meant to believe, as a moralist and social critic: "You might be thankin': is dis real talk right here, or is it Jane Austen just playin' when she tho' out big ass terms like 'universal truth.' . . . [S]he says 'Fuck the 'stablishment and be actin' strong-willed, indepennent, and don't take no lip from that Darcy. Now that's some kinda' woman."[1] Dr. Sweets emphasizes that Austen "[be] slingin' her own special kind of irony dat schola's been geekin' out 'bout for years."[2] To be sure, the present volume represents just such "schola's geekin' out," and I hope to join in.

In another landmark work of philosophical interpretation, *After Virtue: A Study in Moral Theory* (1981), Alasdair MacIntyre discusses with probing insight the sorts of philosophers and figures you would expect to read about in a book about the most prominent contributions to Western moral theory: Homer, Plato, Aristotle, Jesus, Nietzsche, and . . . Jane Austen?—Do you mean J. L. Austin? No, *Jane Austen*. Without a wink, or a tongue anywhere near his cheek, and pushing his estimation of Austen even further than Dr. Sweets's analysis, MacIntyre writes that Austen is "the last great representative of the classical tradition of the virtues."[3] Such an unqualified and effusive claim may be welcome by Austen readers and fans (and may even seem immediately plausible to them), but what are philosophers to make of it? MacIntyre is keenly aware that it is in large measure due to her status as a writer, that is, as a novelist, that her work may have escaped the serious attention of philosophers: "It has proved easy for later generations not to understand her importance as a moralist because she is after all a novelist."[4] Of course, MacIntyre proves himself to be an exception to the rule, as he is a philosopher who takes Austen very seriously as a moralist "even though" she is a novelist (revealing in the process, like Stanley Cavell, that there is much that philosophy can—and should—learn from literature in all its manifestations, whether they come to us as poetry, novels, plays, operas, or films).

I will leave aside the broader project of discussing philosophy's fraught relationship with the literary arts—something that famously commences with Plato—so I may turn instead, and more specifically, to how MacIntyre understands Austen's role in the history of moral philosophy (focusing especially on the kinds of virtues she depicts, heralds, and defends). As a hint of the riches within MacIntyre's book—as well as the nuance of his subject— it's worth briefly dwelling on the fecund double entendre of its title, After Virtue: at once capturing the sense of living in the wake of virtue's cultural dominance (a time that C. S. Lewis suggests terminated with Austen), and of pursuing (a theory or theories of) virtue. The subtitle of the present essay means to parallel this pun by directing attention not just to the fact that MacIntyre follows Austen in time and space, but that he also follows after her thought as well—to sort it, to situate it anew. Through a close reading of MacIntyre's remarks in After Virtue, the following interrelated questions will be addressed: What is it that draws MacIntyre's attention to Austen in particular? How does her work connect to the prominent moral contributions of Homer, Aristotle, and the New Testament on the role of virtue in Western thought? And why should we feel remiss, as philosophers, for overlooking her signal and signature contribution to ethical thinking? In a book devoted to Jane Austen and Philosophy, in a series devoted to great authors and philosophy, it would seem there are few better places to dwell than on MacIntyre's remarkably bold, incisive, and fortified praise of Austen's striking contribution to—and continuation of—a hallmark tradition in Western philosophical thinking.

"So, da truth is," as Dr. Sweets remarks, "my girl Jane Austen don't play it straight. She be slingin' irony all day, 'ryday, makin' this book loud before all kinds of opposing interpretations." MacIntyre, almost alone among professional philosophers, has vaunted just one such theory—namely, that Austen should be spoken of with equal respect and esteem when it comes to discerning the legacy of Western moral thought. Millennia after Homer, Plato, and the New Testament, we have Jane Austen, and we ought to accord her contributions to ethical thinking with similar merit.

Conceiving the Virtues in Philosophy, Literature, and Religion

One of the conundrums that MacIntyre sets his sights upon is the question of whether the long history of Western thought exhibits anything like a coherent conception of the virtues. He worries that perhaps there are "just too many different and incompatible conceptions of a virtue for there to be any real unity to the concept or indeed to the history."[5] He reaches out to the usual suspects: "Homer, Sophocles, Aristotle, the New Testament and medieval thinkers differ from each other in too many ways." Thus, it may be that we are not in a position to decipher or delineate anything like a "single core conception" of virtue. If this is the case, then the Western moral tradition may appear hopelessly fractured, and the hope that we might find a modern interpreter to consolidate some of the West's extensive and diverse contributions to moral thought, a dream deferred.

With MacIntyre's broad erudition in the works of Greek antiquity and especially millennia of moral philosophy, it's not surprising that he can manage to reduce much of Homer, Aristotle, and the New Testament to a set of specific and prominent traits—admitting, as he must, that they are often in conflict, or simply contradictory. If Homer heralds physical strength as an *arête* (virtue), we'll not be surprised to find Aristotle, a few centuries later, championing friendship.[6] Aristotle's love of "practical intelligence" (*phronêsis*) puts him not only at a distance from Homer, but from us as well.[7] As MacIntyre parses it: "The mind receives from Aristotle the kind of tribute which the body receives from Homer."[8] When we turn to the relationship of the virtues to the social order, our distance from ancient Greece seems even more pronounced: "according to Aristotle certain virtues are only available to those of great riches and of high social status; there are virtues which are unavailable to the poor man, even if he is a free man."[9] The significance of the social order for thinking about Austen's contribution may already be dawning (since the retention or acquisition of wealth is such a preoccupation of her novels), but I'll return to this crucial aspect in more detail below.

By the time we reach the New Testament, about as far in time from Aristotle as Aristotle was from Homer, the virtues have shifted again. As MacIntyre sees it: "the New Testament not only praises virtues of which Aristotle
knows nothing—faith, hope, love—and says nothing about virtues such as
phronêsis which are crucial for Aristotle, but it praises at least one quality
as a virtue which Aristotle seems to count as one of the vices relative to
magnanimity, namely, humility."[10] The comedy inherent in this class of
Aristotelian and New Testament thinking reaches a zenith when MacIntyre
confirms that "Aristotle would certainly not have admired Jesus Christ and
he would have been horrified by St. Paul."[11] The comedy is funny only until
it is tragedy, which is to say that the conflict discernible between Aristotle
and Christian thinking needs attention and even remediation if we're going
to get anything like a coherent sense of the virtues through time.

"A virtue," MacIntyre tells us, "is a quality the exercise of which leads to
the achievement of the human *telos* [or end]."[12] And since Aristotle and
Christians *agree* that the "relationship of means to end is internal and not
external . . . , this parallelism [. . .] allows Aquinas to synthesize Aristotle
and the New Testament."[13] Aquinas' spirit of rapprochement between two
distinctive traditions of virtue stands as a medieval model for the kind of
moral harmonizing—across traditions—we ought to see at work, MacIntyre
argues, in the novels of Jane Austen.

MacIntyre on Austen's Virtues

One of the signature virtues in Austen's work—especially her six major novels: *Sense and Sensibility* (1811), *Pride and Prejudice* (1813), *Mansfield Park*
(1814), *Emma* (1815), *Northanger Abbey* (1818, posthumous), and *Persuasion*
(1818, posthumous)—is constancy. MacIntyre might be treated as a modern-
day Aquinas, since he makes the argument—as Aquinas did for a blending
of Aristotelian and Christian virtues—that Austen's ideas are highly compatible with Aristotle's, and MacIntyre emphasizes, lest we lose track: "It
matters here that Jane Austen is a Christian."[14] When Austen's characters
speak of "constancy," they are surely alluding to what we mean by the term:
loyalty, fidelity, faith, and in the broader context of the concern with marriage through her major novels, love (even and especially romantic love).
MacIntyre, again in the role of interpreter between traditions, time periods,
literary forms, and languages, pauses to illuminate moments of overlap and
agreement, for example: "In some ways constancy plays a role in Jane Austen
analogous to that of *phronêsis* in Aristotle; it is a virtue the possession of

which is a prerequisite for the possession of other virtues."[15] In short, constancy is a condition for the possibility of acquiring or exercising other virtues.

To make sure we don't suspect Austen's Aristotelianism—as channeled and transformed by her Christianity—is a one-off, MacIntyre argues that Austen issues forth a refinement of Aristotelian categories. Not easy! Especially as Aristotle seemingly invented categories as such. For instance, where Aristotle acknowledges "agreeableness" as a virtue, Austen begs to differ: "she treats it as only the simulacrum of a genuine virtue," namely, amiability; she is "deeply suspicious of an agreeableness that conceals a lack of true amiability."[16]

In *Searching for Jane Austen*, Emily Auerbach usefully sleuths some of the reading Austen did from works published in the late eighteenth century—these "conduct books," Auerbach tells us, "iterated the importance of a woman knowing her place and controlling her 'inclinations.'"[17] What they also reveal, though, is the presence of a moral vocabulary that Austen will adopt and transform in her novels. Two brief excerpts of her reading will suffice to make this point, the first from Chase Amos's *The Excellent Female* (1791), and the second from Thomas Gisborne's *An Enquiry into the Duties of the Female Sex* (1797). First, Amos: "Delicacy of manners and purity of speech are so much expected from an amiable, modest female." Then, Gisborne: "Whatever be the influence which the amiable virtues of a wife may obtain over her husband, let not the consciousness of it ever lead her to seek opportunities of displaying it, nor to cherish a wish to intrude into those departments which belong not to her jurisdiction."

We see the virtue of amiability heralded even in Austen's juvenilia, which suggests her early adoption of the idea (likely after reading Amos, Gisborne, and others), but also its gestation in her thinking about "the duties of the female sex" as they relate to social roles. In an early piece, "Jack and Alice," Austen speaks of the character Charles as "an amiable, accomplished, and bewitching young Man."[18] And Charles himself uses the term when rejecting Alice: "Your daughter, sir, is neither sufficiently beautifull, sufficiently amiable, sufficiently witty, nor sufficiently rich for me."[19] In the same story, we hear the two terms arrive in tandem: "she was Religious and amiable, Tho' Elegant and Agreeable, she was Polished and Entertaining."[20]

Later, in *Pride and Prejudice*, Austen's narrator—who rarely makes interventions and comments in the text—takes an occasion to assess Mrs. Bennet's character, and not flatteringly: "I wish I could say [that she became] a sensible, amiable, well-informed woman for the rest of her life," but, as it turned out, she remained "nervous and invariably silly."[21] In the same novel, when he is still in good favor, Wickham is described as "amiable and pleasing"[22]; and we hear of Mrs. Gardiner as "an amiable, intelligent, elegant woman."[23] In *Sense and Sensibility*, Marianne is described as "generous, amiable, interesting."[24] In *Emma*, the eponymous character describes the "amiable, upright, perfect Jane Fairfax."[25] The term "amiable" reaches a crescendo of animated engagement—and oxygenated debate—in that novel when Emma is corrected by Mr. Knightley's virtues-based analysis of Frank Churchill's character:

> "I wish you would try to understand what an amiable young man may be likely to feel . . . ."
>
> "Your amiable young man is a very weak young man. . . . No, Emma, your amiable young man can be amiable only in French, not English. He may be very 'amiable,' have very good manners, and be very agreeable; but he can have no English delicacy towards the feelings of other people: nothing really amiable about him."[26]

Aristotle believed, as MacIntyre puts it, that the "man who practices agreeableness does so from considerations of honor and expediency . . . ; whereas Jane Austen thought it possible and necessary for the professor of that virtue [viz., agreeableness] to have a certain real affection for people as such."[27] And that real affection would be expressed in the higher order virtue of amiability. We can glean this distinction just above when Mr. Knightley contends that Churchill may be "very agreeable," but concomitantly, there is "nothing really amiable about him." Churchill operates at the level of the simulacrum (viz., agreeableness), though, according to Austen's portrait of human ethics, a person is capable of achieving a higher level of fellow feeling, namely via the more esteemed virtue of amiability.

Austen's syncretism does not cease with the difficult task of harmonizing Aristotle and the New Testament. "In fact," MacIntyre eagerly notes, "her views combine elements from Homer as well, since she is concerned with social roles in a way that neither the New Testament nor Aristotle are."[28] For Homer, virtues are anteceded by "well-defined social roles": "It follows that we cannot identify the Homeric virtues until we have first identified the key social roles in Homeric society. [. . .] The concept of *what anyone filling such-and-such a role ought to do* is prior to the concept of a virtue."[29] By contrast in Aristotle, though there are limitations about who can exercise virtues (generally, the wealthy, the male, and the educated are presumed to best exercise them), it is attested that "virtues attach not to men as inhabiting social roles, but to man as such."[30] For Austen, to be sure, "the touchstone of the virtues is a certain kind of marriage,"—a phenomenon very much defined by social roles—and MacIntyre goes further (and has a bit of fun) by adding that such marriage would be achieved with "a certain kind of naval officer (that is a certain kind of *English* naval officer)."[31] MacIntyre is Scottish.

C. S. Lewis writes in "A Note on Jane Austen" about the distinctly Christian nature of her moral vision (and her exemplification of his favored term, "undeception"—a concept with philosophical as well as theological implications, especially in terms of personal redemption), but it is in his *De Descriptione Temporum* (1955) where Austen achieves her apotheosis in the shape of philosophy's long arc: "Roughly speaking we may say that whereas all history was for our ancestors divided into two periods, the pre-Christian and the Christian, and two only, for us it falls into three—the pre-Christian, the Christian, and what may reasonably be called the post-Christian. . . . Between Jane Austen and us . . . comes the birth of the machines."[32]

Another English inheritor, Gilbert Ryle, writes in "Jane Austen and the Moralists" about two dominant—and contrasting—options for "evaluating human character": the Calvinist and the Aristotelian. As John Benson describes the split: "The Calvinist approach appraises people in a stilted, bipolar vocabulary; people are Good or Bad, Virtuous or Vicious, Saints or Sinners." Ryle depicts the other side of this binary: "[T]he Aristotelian pattern of ethical ideas represents people as differing from one another in degree and not in kind, and differing from one another not in respect just of a single generic Sunday attribute, Goodness, say, or else Wickedness, but in respect of a whole spectrum of specific week-day attributes."[33] Using language familiar to Ryle, the Calvinists go in for "sortal" categories (distinguishing, or "sorting," one type from another), while the Aristotelians prefer a "gradal" approach to the same assessments, or as Ryle himself puts it in his characteristically careful philosophical prose: "A is a bit more irritable and ambitious than B, but less indolent and less sentimental. C is meaner and quicker-witted than D, and D is greedier and more athletic than C." John Benson concludes, tying disparate parts together, that "Ryle admires Jane Austen for her Aristotelian approach, derived he suspects from Shaftesbury's adaptation of Aristotle for the needs of the eighteenth century, and manifested in [Austen's] use of 'a copious, specific and plastic vocabulary' in the evaluative description of her characters."[34]

Austen's more nuanced (i.e., gradal) approach to the description of virtues is usefully contrasted with the Calvinists as it is with William Cobbett. "The last man of the old England," as Karl Marx said of him, "and the first man of the new," Cobbett was a radical in the literal sense: he wanted to drive up the roots of society generally and remake it anew.[35] Jane Austen, instead, "tried to discover enclaves for the life of the virtues within" society as she found it.[36] Austen, as MacIntyre writes, "identifies that social sphere within which the practice of the virtues is able to continue," and it is worth dwelling on his sense of this special attribute of her contribution to moral thought:

> It is not of course that she is blind to the economic realities against which Cobbett railed. We learn somewhere in all her novels about where the money of the main characters comes from; we see a great deal of the economic self-seeking, of the *pleonexia* [viz., acquisitiveness] which is central to Cobbett's vision. So much so indeed that David Daiches once described her as a "Marxist before Marx." Her heroines must, if they are to survive, seek for economic security. But this is not just because of the threat of the outside economic world; it is because the *telos* of her heroines is a life within both a particular kind of marriage and a particular kind of household of which that marriage will be the focal point.[37]

MacIntyre's attention to the *telos* (or end, or purpose)—that guides and shapes the lives of the heroines—helpfully points up the Aristotelian quality of her thinking, especially as it distinguishes between outward (or external) demands and inward (or internal) ones. To appreciate Austen's Aristotelian credentials—both how she recovers them by way of Shaftsbury, and also how she transforms them in the expression of her literary imagination—consider her contrast with another of MacIntyre's models of modern virtue ethics: Benjamin Franklin.

Born at the beginning of the eighteenth century, with Austen following him three-quarters of the way in, on the eve of American Independence (viz., 1775), Franklin may—nay, should—be taken as a kind of foil for her approach, especially for thinking about the *telos* of life. "Aristotle," MacIntyre notes, "treats the acquisition and exercise of the virtues as a means to an end, the relationship of means to end is internal and not external." Even though Franklin's depiction of the virtues—most notably and famously in his *Autobiography*—is teleological, the object of his *telos* is not internal, but external, in a word, utilitarian: "The end to which the cultivation of the virtues ministers is happiness, but happiness as understood as success, prosperity in Philadelphia and ultimately in heaven. The virtues are to be useful and Franklin's account continuously stresses utility as a criterion."[38]

Instead of Austen's descriptive, discursive, and decidedly nuanced reading

of the inner nature of human thoughts, feelings, and beliefs, we get in Franklin lists and numbers. A half century later, when we encounter Henry David
Thoreau perched on the shores of Emerson's land at Walden Pond, we have
to wonder if the sinews of Franklin's hand remained intact as Thoreau opens
his book, *Walden*, with its longest chapter, titled "Economy," and therein
sets about to count—to *account* for—all the rice and rye meal, the pork and
pumpkins. It was as if these outward elements were instead signs of inner,
spiritual facts. (Stanley Cavell takes Thoreau's mode of attention as a promising indication of his pursuit of moral perfectionism; Kathryn Schulz, less
charitably, speaks of the "real Thoreau" as "self-obsessed: narcissistic, fanati-
cal about self-control, adamant that he required nothing beyond himself to
understand and thrive in the world."[39]) Needless to say, Franklin's utilitarian
pursuit of happiness—through a similar sort of idiosyncratic tabulation of
personal traits and private behaviors—doesn't square with Austen's Aristotelian sensibilities, especially those that frame the achievement of virtue
within an *internal* (or self-centered) frame of reference. That is, Austen's
preoccupations with the social roles of marriage and the social sphere of
the household do not preclude her commitment to a vision of moral life
that is private, cognitive, and defined by and through the gifts—and
achievements—of reason. Drawing again from a Homeric cast, Austen
regarded society as the site of experiment for the inner life—including *moral*
life—and not its preemption.

With Franklin as foil, and Austen's Aristotelian credentials intact—albeit
with meaningful input from the Homeric and Christian traditions—
MacIntyre helps discern precisely why we should understand "[h]er novels
are a moral criticism of parents and of guardians quite as much as of young
romantics; for the worst parents and guardians—the silly Mrs. Bennet and
the irresponsible Mr. Bennet, for example—are what the romantic young
may become if they do not learn what they ought to learn on the way to
being married." And what they "ought to learn" is not going to be found in
Franklin's utilitarian ledger, but in the development of a supple mind.
Among other traits of her hybridization of traditions of moral virtue, she
"praises practical intelligence [*phronêsis*] in an Aristotelian way and humility
in a Christian way."[40] As MacIntyre concludes, "it is her uniting of Christian
and Aristotelian themes"—Lewis emphasizing the former, Ryle the latter—
"in a determinate social context"—which is a decidedly Homeric
preoccupation—"that makes Jane Austen the last great effective imaginative
voice of the tradition of thought about and practice of, the virtues which I
have tried to identify."[41] She disowns the "competing catalogues of the vir-

tues" so prominent and popular in the eighteenth century (where Franklin stands out as a representative) and "restores a teleological perspective" that is internal and nonutilitarian.[42]

Austen's Novel Approach to the Virtues

MacIntyre is careful to point out that Austen "does not ever merely reproduce the tradition" that we've been engaging—Homer, Aristotle, the New Testament—but "continuously extends it."[43] This must be counted a signal achievement for it is rare among philosophers, and we may say, with a few exceptions, ever rarer among novelists.[44] It is worth, then, articulating explicitly, if briefly, what in Austen's novels stands out as part of that extension.

We have already seen Austen's meaningful refinement (or "extension") of Aristotle in her understanding of agreeableness as a false or counterfeit behavior, especially when contrasted with the genuine virtue of amiability. It's not an overstatement to say that in Austen's time—and for her as a particularly keen observer of human behavior—the threat of fakers was real and potentially dire. Those who would trick others into marriage might gain a fortune, but in the process they might ruin another's life. Discerning genuineness, then, becomes a survival skill—to say nothing of having more than survival, such as experiencing romantic love. Henry Crawford, on MacIntyre's reading, is "the dissimulator *par excellence*. He even boasts of his ability to act parts and in one conversation makes it clear that he takes being a clergyman to consist in *giving the appearance of being a clergyman*. Self is almost, if not quite, dissolved into the presentation of the self. . . ."[45]

What today we may call, perhaps with a bit too much self-congratulation, the "performativity of the self"—theorized famously by Erving Goffman in *The Presentation of the Self in Everyday Life* (1959)—Austen would regard as a "symptom of the vices."[46] Morality, for Austen, is not merely about a series of externally imposed prohibitions one should be obliged to follow but rather, as MacIntyre puts it: "[m]orality is meant to educate the passions."[47] In *Sense and Sensibility*, Marianne Dashwood misses this insight entirely as she allows her reason to become the "servant of the passions." She gets carried away in more than one sense. Marianne's negative example in part helps elucidate another way in which Austen develops the moral tradition she inherits: self-knowledge is a paramount virtue. But her vision of self-knowledge is not Socratic—much less Franklinian—it is Christian, since, as MacIntyre shows us, the knowledge doesn't come through ratiocination

alone but also through repentance. "In four of her six great novels," MacIntyre recounts, "there is a recognition scene in which the person whom the
hero or heroine recognises is him or herself. 'Till this moment I never knew
myself,' says Elizabeth Bennet. 'How to understand the deceptions she had
been thus practising on herself, and living under!' meditates Emma."[48] Austen's depiction of the way characters come to self-knowledge draws together
Homeric social roles, Aristotelian attention to the internal connection
between means and ends, and New Testament bids for absolution and
redemption. Austen's synthetic achievement is formidable, perhaps especially because it appears not as philosophical tractate but, as it did in Dante,
in the guise of ironic comedy. As a Christian, "she sees the *telos* of human
life implicit in its everyday form."[49]

Sussing out the counterfeits and soliciting self-knowledge are comple-
mented by another virtue, the last under consideration here, namely, constancy. Austen sought—or championed figures who sought—"to make of a
human life a unity," what is sometimes referred to as "narrative unity." In
everyday parlance, we may simply say a story, or a life story. For Austen,
narrative unity is not something that precedes the pursuit of a virtuous life,
but something that emerges through the exercise of a virtuous life: "It has to
be continually reaffirmed and its reaffirmation in deed rather than in word is
the virtue Jane Austen calls constancy."[50] Without constancy, MacIntyre
claims, "all the other virtues"—such as authenticity and self-knowledge—
"lose their point."[51] Perhaps we should not be surprised that the characters
who best exemplify constancy are the least charming. For charm is "the
characteristically modern quality which those who lack or simulate virtues
use to get by [. . .] ."[52] Fanny Price, in *Mansfield Park*, for example, is "charm-
less; she has only the virtues, the genuine virtues to protect her, and when
she disobeys her guardian, Sir Thomas Bertram, and refuses marriage to
Henry Crawford it can only be because of what constancy requires."[53] Fanny
Price, like so many of the heroines in Austen's novels, behaves in decidedly
un-Franklinian ways—eschewing utility in order to remain faithful to oneself
(as genuine, as possessed of self-knowledge, and as exercising constancy).
The stakes are indeed high, but as MacIntyre puts it, paraphrasing Matthew,
"she places the danger of losing her soul before the reward of gaining what
for her would be a whole world."[54]

Austen's Descendants

Though our main points of reference have been prominent members of the
established canon of Western thought—Homer, Aristotle, the Gospels, and

others—let's return to an emerging voice, Sparky Sweets, who suggests that "what Austen may be askin' is: how the fuck are people gonna come together in a world of such distances, playa?" *Touché*, Dr. Sweets. Indeed, the question of connection—figured as some form of mutual comprehension, and often the negotiating and achieving of marriage—artfully combines Austen's concern with the nature of individual conduct and the form of institutional culture. While Austen has not once and for all answered this question, she has, according to MacIntyre, proved herself to be an incisive critic of the moral tradition—and perhaps an unanticipated harmonizer of its historically diverse and sometimes puzzlingly contrasting claims.

Lastly, and as a coda to inspire further thought about Austen's place in the grand tradition of moral thinking, we could pause to note that even as MacIntyre heralds Austen as "the last great representative of the classical tradition of the virtues," he also tantalizes us with a suggestive comment drawn from the work of Rudyard Kipling—namely, that Henry James may be the "son"—or perhaps more accurately, grandson—of Austen.[55] Not literally, of course; it would no doubt be a scandal worthy of a novel! But if true in a figurative sense—that is, intellectually, ethically—we have more work to do in our pursuit of virtue in modernity, in modernism, and we must presume, in postmodernism. Kipling would appear to have upset C. S. Lewis's proposed triad (pre-Christian, Christian, and post-Austen), and thus slyly suggest that in James we have a worthy heir to Austen's thinking about courtship, coupling, constancy, and other virtues in some post-classical age, such as our own. These are the enticements of sorting out the history of moral virtue, and so we must continue to debate what it means to think and act "after virtue."

Notes

1. Sparky Sweets, PhD (Greg Edwards), "Thug Notes: *Pride and Prejudice* Summary and Analysis," July 8, 2013, https://youtu.be/5Nm61IoNdHg.

2. "A Phat Spin on Classic Lit," *Entertainment Weekly*, August 21/28, 2015, 105.

3. Alasdair MacIntyre, *After Virtue: A Study in Moral Theory* (Notre Dame: University of Notre Dame Press, 1981), 226.

4. MacIntyre, *After Virtue*, 226.

5. MacIntyre, *After Virtue*, 169.

6. MacIntyre, *After Virtue*, 170.

7. MacIntyre, *After Virtue*, 170, 224.

8. MacIntyre, *After Virtue*, 170.

9. MacIntyre, *After Virtue*, 170.

10. MacIntyre, *After Virtue*, 170.

11. MacIntyre, *After Virtue*, 172.

12. MacIntyre, *After Virtue*, 172.

13. MacIntyre, *After Virtue*, 172.

14. MacIntyre, *After Virtue*, 171.

15. MacIntyre, *After Virtue*, 170–71.

16. MacIntyre, *After Virtue*, 171, 224.

17. Emily Auerbach, *Searching for Jane Austen* (Madison: University of Wisconsin Press, 2006), 45.

18. Jane Austen, *Minor Works*, vol. 6, ed. R. W. Chapman (New York: Oxford University Press, 1954), 13.

19. Austen, *Minor Works*, 26.

20. Austen, *Minor Works*, 13.

21. Jane Austen, *Pride and Prejudice* (New York: Charles Scribner's Sons, 1918), 397.

22. Austen, *Pride and Prejudice*, 157.

23. Austen, *Pride and Prejudice*, 144.

24. Jane Austen, *Sense and Sensibility* (Cambridge: Cambridge University Press, 2006), 7.

25. Jane Austen, *Emma* (London: Richard Bentley & Son, 1886), 207.

26. Austen, *Emma*, 125–26.

27. MacIntyre, *After Virtue*, 171.

28. MacIntyre, *After Virtue*, 172.

29. MacIntyre, *After Virtue*, 171–72 (italics are MacIntyre's).

30. MacIntyre, *After Virtue*, 172.

31. MacIntyre, *After Virtue*, 174.

32. C. S. Lewis, *Selected Literary Essays*, ed. Walter Hopper (Cambridge: University of Cambridge Press, 1969/2013). The passage from *De Descriptione Temporum* is quoted in *The A-Z of C. S. Lewis: An Encyclopaedia of His Life, Thought, and Writings*, ed. Colin Duriez (Oxford: Lion Hudson, 2013), 225; remarks on undeception, 328.

33. Gilbert Ryle, "Jane Austen and the Moralists," *Oxford Review* 1 (1966); reprinted in *Collected Papers* (London: Hutchinson, 1971).

34. John Benson, "Sibley after Sibley," *Aesthetic Concepts: Essays after Sibley*, ed. Emily Brady and Jerrold Levinson (Oxford: Clarendon Press, 2001), 222.

35. MacIntyre, *After Virtue*, 222.

36. MacIntyre, *After Virtue*, 222.

37. MacIntyre, *After Virtue*, 222.

38. MacIntyre, *After Virtue*, 172–73.

39. See Stanley Cavell, *The Senses of Walden* (Chicago: The University of Chicago Press, expanded edition, 1981); and *Emerson's Transcendental Etudes*, ed. David Justin Hodge (Stanford: Stanford University Press, 2003). Kathryn Schulz, "Pond Scum," *The New Yorker* (October 29, 2015), 40.

40. MacIntyre, *After Virtue*, 224.

41. MacIntyre, *After Virtue*, 223.

42. MacIntyre, *After Virtue*, 224.

43. MacIntyre, *After Virtue*, 224.

44. As an indication of an exception, consider Bernard Harrison's argument about Henry Fielding's achievements in *Henry Fielding's Tom Jones: The Novelist as Moral Philosopher* (London: Sussex University Press, 1975).

45. MacIntyre, *After Virtue*, 224 (italics are MacIntyre's).

46. MacIntyre, *After Virtue*, 224.

47. MacIntyre, *After Virtue*, 224.

48. MacIntyre, *After Virtue*, 224.

49. MacIntyre, *After Virtue*, 226.

50. MacIntyre, *After Virtue*, 225.

51. MacIntyre, *After Virtue*, 225.

52. MacIntyre, *After Virtue*, 225.

53. MacIntyre, *After Virtue*, 225.

54. MacIntyre, *After Virtue*, 225.

55. MacIntyre, *After Virtue*, 226.

CHAPTER EIGHT

Jane Austen on Moral Luck

E. M. Dadlez

I will argue that Jane Austen provides a formative account of the phenomenon of moral luck in her novels. The purpose of this project is twofold: first to demonstrate that literature can articulate and clarify a formidable philosophical conundrum and, second, that it can propose solutions to the same. The issue of moral luck, while it is typically said to arise in the philosophical literature with Thomas Nagel's and Bernard Williams's work in the late 1970s and early 1980s,[1] has arguably been of concern in philosophical thinking a lot longer than that. Martha Nussbaum has written on the ancients' concern with the dependence of our well-being and our ability to lead good lives on factors beyond our control,[2] and we can certainly detect the appearance of related discussions in Hume's *Treatise*, when he distinguishes between the possession of a virtue and the practical possibility of exercising it in one set of circumstances or another. However, it was Nagel and Williams who explicitly challenged the well-entrenched view that morality was largely impervious to luck (Nagel via the Kantian conception of acting from a good will) by producing unmistakable cases in which what a subject was appropriately judged *for* was in fact not within the power of the agent to affect. As Nagel puts it, "Where a significant aspect of what someone does depends on factors beyond his control, yet we continue to treat him in that respect as an object of moral judgment, it can be called moral luck."[3] I will show that Jane Austen displays a sophisticated awareness of just this ethical conundrum in both *Mansfield Park* and *Sense and Sensibility*.[4]

There are several ways in which the targets of moral judgment are subject to luck, but only one will be addressed here, since it is most clearly illustrated in the work of Jane Austen: circumstantial luck. Nagel describes it thus:

> The third category to consider is luck in one's circumstances. . . . The things we are called upon to do, the moral tests we face, are importantly determined by factors beyond our control. It may be true of someone that in a dangerous situation he would behave in a cowardly or heroic fashion, but if the situation never arises, he will never have the chance to distinguish or disgrace himself in this way, and his moral record will be different.[5]

Nagel proceeds to offer an example geared to appeal to our moral intuitions. During the Second World War, ordinary German citizens were subjected to a moral dilemma or test to which the citizens of other nations were never subjected. They could choose to oppose the regime at great personal risk or not to oppose it. Most chose not to oppose the Nazis. Even if a similarly high percentage of those who were never put to any such test would also be passively inclined, they cannot be culpable in the same way as the German citizens, since it was not their silence and passivity which enabled the Nazi regime. "We judge people for what they actually do or fail to do, not just for what they would have done if circumstances had been different."[6] This is not unrelated to the well-known claims of researchers like Philip Zimbardo and Stanley Milgram about situational and systemic effects on individual conduct, the upshot of which suggests that certain situations (such as that which obtained in Abu Ghraib) almost invariably affect conduct in ways that are morally disastrous. Naturally, the latter arguments focus more on the prevention of inevitably toxic situations rather than exonerating anyone, but the idea is pretty clearly that there are some moral tests almost everyone will fail and so there are some circumstances that are always unlucky from the moral standpoint. Nagel presents this kind of problem as involving a distinct tension between the intuition that we are not morally responsible for things beyond our control and the fact that those very things may sometimes be at the basis of our moral praise or condemnation.

Nagel, Williams, and others offer detailed examples intended to show us the kinds of judgments we are inclined to make about the cases of circumstantial moral luck under review—indeed, to show us those judgments by prompting us to make them. This kind of philosophical example has sometimes been referred to as an "intuition pump." Intuition pumps, according to Daniel Dennett, are

> wonderful imagination grabbers, jungle gyms for the imagination. They structure the way you think about a problem. These are the real legacy of the history of

philosophy. A lot of philosophers have forgotten that, but I like to make intuition pumps. . . . I coined the term "intuition pump," and its first use was derogatory. I applied it to John Searle's "Chinese room," which I said was not a proper argument but just an intuition pump. I went on to say that intuition pumps are fine if they're used correctly, but they can also be misused. They're not arguments, they're stories. Instead of having a conclusion, they pump an intuition. They get you to say "Aha! Oh, I get it!"[7]

There is a catalog of such examples in Nagel, culled from literature (*Anna Karenina*) as well as history, often featuring the deployment of counterfactuals (conditionals whose antecedents express something contrary to fact) to illustrate how someone happily unaffected by the situation under review *would* have behaved in different circumstances. I will argue that this is precisely the approach taken by Jane Austen in two distinct illustrations of a phenomenon that could only be described as circumstantial moral luck.

Austen employs the same strategy in her two clearest explorations of the phenomenon. In her most explicit illustrations of circumstantial luck, Austen presents us with cases of two very similar characters in radically different circumstances. These are shown to be circumstances to which the characters would respond in similar ways with like conduct, were they to be so placed. One set of circumstances is fortunate in that it would elicit morally appropriate conduct; the other is unfortunate in that it would encourage bad behavior in each character. So it turns out to be largely a matter of luck that one character is respectable while the other is not. Since the respectability in question is in one case sexual respectability, these kinds of literary reflections are doubly surprising, not just for their ethical perspicacity and prescience, but for a (then) controversial attitude toward behavior that would never have been taken to involve things beyond the subject's control.

In *Mansfield Park* the reader is presented with three sisters, two of whom have similar indolent characters that render them largely incapable of exertion, self-sacrifice, or industry. Lady Bertram, the fortunate sister, marries a wealthy, respectable man and happily embarks on a life of leisure. Mrs. Price marries a hard-drinking and relatively impoverished sailor and produces a superfluity of children which their income is not equal to supporting. Lady Bertram is a beacon of respectability while Mrs. Price is a slattern, definitely *not* respectable insofar as her neglect of her children and her care of her family are concerned:

> Of her two sisters, Mrs. Price very much more resembled Lady Bertram than Mrs. Norris. She was a manager by necessity, without any of Mrs. Norris's inclination

for it. . . . Her disposition was naturally easy and indolent, like Lady Bertram's; and a situation of similar affluence and donothingness would have been much more suited to her capacity than the exertions and self denials of the one which her imprudent marriage had placed her in.[8]

The suggestion is unmistakable: Lady Bertram would *not* have been respectable (or, indeed beloved) in Mrs. Price's circumstances, probably making as much of a botch of being the matriarch of a necessitous family as Mrs. Price had done. Conversely, Mrs. Price would have been a pleasant, contented, and respectable woman if she were only to enjoy the wealth and privilege that her sister enjoyed. Respectability is loosely characterized by Austen as an adherence to general rules of morality, politeness, and self-respect. Adherence might encompass such rules as fairness to and care for one's offspring and their moral and intellectual development, having a care for one's own moral and intellectual condition, or not allowing oneself to be treated as a lower form of life by one's husband.

Evidently, Austen brings the same kind of counterfactual moral reasoning to her character dissection as philosophers bring to discussions of circumstantial moral luck. We are led to consider how each character would have conducted herself if her circumstances had been materially altered. Mrs. Price is a bad mother, a sloven, and a doormat. She exhibits a particularly noxious form of favoritism that has an unfortunate effect on her children's moral development, and seems almost incapable of fairness, though much of this may be put down to exhaustion and discouragement and stress. But she would have been none of those things in circumstances of wealth, security, and marital affection. Lady Bertram is a gentle, affectionate, congenial creature entirely content with her lot. But she would have been a complete disaster as the mother of a multitude of clamoring children on a small income. Respectability turns out to be largely a matter of moral luck for Lady Bertram and Mrs. Price.

It is important to note that respectability depends on circumstantial luck only for persons with the particular character deficits that afflict the sisters (a constitutional disposition to inertia) rather than being a matter of circumstantial luck for everyone. Austen does not explore the intriguing question of constitutive moral luck (luck in the kind of character one has, for the formation of which one is not entirely responsible) that philosophers have pursued—at least she doesn't explore it in as recognizably philosophical a way. However, she does present us with a very clear case of circumstantial luck that sheds a new light on disparities in wealth. What is especially inter-

esting here is that Lady Bertram's vaunted virtues are almost entirely negative. She doesn't do anything, and so there is less opportunity for her to
harm others. Servants, indigent relations, tutors, and governesses care for
her children, who are well-fed and well-educated (though, as it turns out,
occasionally morally deficient). The failure of Mrs. Price to exert herself, on
the other hand, has serious consequences for her children's well-being and
for her own self-respect. Thus, being harmless, Lady Bertram is respectable.
Being harmful, Mrs. Price is not. Yet the respectability of one and non-
respectability of the other are both products of the social and economic
circumstances in which they have been placed, and over which they never
had much (if any) control. The subversive suggestion that wealth and privilege may help to disguise vicious traits of character simply by eliminating the
opportunity for their exercise is readily apparent. David Hume suggested that
there can exist "virtue in rags"; that one can possess a virtue despite the fact
that one is never given the opportunity for its exercise:

> Virtue in rags is still virtue; and the love which it procures attends a man into a
> dungeon or desert, where virtue can no longer be exerted in action and is lost to
> all the world.[9]

Similarly, Austen appears to suggest the further prospect of vice in *dishabille*,
the existence of vices that are never manifest because no occasion arises that
would elicit them. It is a surprisingly radical observation for the time period.

Sense and Sensibility offers a very similar comparison of two people of like
character in divergent circumstances. The first of these is an orphan named
Eliza. Colonel Brandon narrates her tragic story—the story of a young
woman whose wealth led his greedy family to force her into an unhappy
marriage with his abusive brother, a circumstance that eventually leads to
complete disaster. The second young woman is Marianne Dashwood, whose
character and personality resemble those of the young Eliza, but who is lucky
enough not to have been forced into an abusive marriage. Brandon compares
Eliza and Marianne:

> If I am not deceived by the uncertainty, the partiality of tender recollection, there
> is a very strong resemblance between them, as well in mind as person. The same
> warmth of heart, the same eagerness of fancy and spirits.[10]

Eliza's initial romantic attachment to Brandon (foiled forever by the forced
marriage) is said by Brandon to be as "fervent as the attachment of . . .

[Marianne] to Mr. Willoughby."[11] Brandon and Marianne are forcibly sepa-rated because of her wealth, just as money and Willoughby's need of it drive him away from Marianne. But Eliza has been forced into a union so intolera-ble that she seeks escape in the arms of a lover and resorts to divorce, eventu-ally becoming dissolute. Brandon discovers Eliza and her illegitimate child only when Eliza is on her deathbed, in a "spunging-house . . . confined for debt," where she finally dies of consumption.[12] Brandon, in comparing Marianne and the unfortunate Eliza, reflects that "their fates, their fortunes, cannot be the same; and had the natural sweet disposition of the one been guarded by a firmer mind or a happier marriage, she might have been all that you will live to see the other be."[13]

As previously, Austen deploys the counterfactual in both directions. We are led to contemplate the fate that would have afflicted Marianne, were she to marry one whom she loathed, and led also to consider the fate of Eliza, were her unfortunate marriage somehow averted. Neither Marianne nor Eliza possess dire character flaws. Rather, they are overemotional and oversensi-tive, unrealistic, and overly idealistic. Such a person is incapable of the kind of stoicism that can withstand cruelty until a remedy is found, and is less likely to seek practical remedies in the first place. That is, such a person is, under adversity, very likely to despair and jettison any effort to ameliorate her condition, and even more likely to be exploited by any apparently pleas-ant individual. And yet such a person flourishes in a loving and supportive environment, one in which affections are nurtured and that allows creative impulses to be followed.

Just as Mrs. Price and Lady Bertram were alike in their indolence, Mari-anne and Eliza share sensitivity, enthusiasm, excitability, impatience, and eagerness—each is ardent, affectionate, and invested in her relationships with others. Each is naive and unrealistic in her expectations. Traits such as these conduce to vulnerability in certain circumstances. Deprived of kind-ness, affection, and support, subjected to cruelty and rejection, such a charac-ter crumbles. And, shockingly, it is not a woman's character but those circumstances that Austen indicates may mark the difference between a respectable woman and a fallen one. Without the circumstance of the forced marriage, Eliza could have been respectable. Without the love and support of her family, Marianne might have wound up in the spunging-house.

Austen is particularly interested in the susceptibility of certain sets of character traits to moral luck. This is understandable enough, given that a novel must narrow the focus of attention to particulars. Nevertheless, she has produced a very clear illustration of the problem of circumstantial moral luck, and has very strongly hinted at a solution to the puzzle well in advance of the solutions that are currently on offer. That solution applies narrowly only to the kinds of circumstantial cases that she canvasses and is never made entirely explicit, but I think that it can be inferred from a number of Austen's observations.

Consider first the kinds of solutions to the problem that are rife in the philosophical literature. Many simply deny that there is such a thing as moral luck, claiming that we can't be held responsible for things beyond our control. Alleged cases of moral luck, the argument might go (and I will focus here only on the question of circumstantial moral luck) involve luck in evading the detection of what one would have done had one been unluckily placed. It is the luck of not being exposed as someone who would have behaved badly in grimmer circumstances. The morally lucky person is actually lucky that her (real) defects escape notice and thereby condemnation. As Nicholas Rescher puts it, "the luck involved is related not to our moral condition but only to our image: it relates not to what we are but to how people (ourselves included) will regard us. The difference at issue is not moral but merely epistemic."[14] Norvin Richards makes a related point by stressing that a "culprit may be lucky or unlucky in how clear his deserts are."[15] Luck doesn't change those deserts, it just affects what observers can infer about them. The epistemic shortfalls afflicting the observer—a dearth of information about what the subject would have done under another circumstance—are what turn out to be fortunate for many subjects. It is not clear how convincing such objections to the idea of moral luck are when we consider the general run of cases, from constitutive luck to causal and resultant luck (to borrow from Nagel). The kind of objection canvassed seems most readily applicable to cases of circumstantial luck construed as Austen has construed them.

If we were to apply the philosophical objections just cited to Austen's examples, here is the kind of result we would get. Lady Bertram is lucky not in her character, but in the wealth that prevents her sloth and inertia from being exposed. Marianne is lucky, not so much in her character (although she is said at one point to have a "firmer mind" than Eliza) as in her avoidance of a situation that would exacerbate her tendency to self-indulgence and her lack of self-control. Yet that doesn't seem quite right. I believe that Austen has made a more nuanced and a more convincing case than this, though it is only applicable to certain situations, in part because she isn't exclusively concerned with the apportionment of blame.

The denial of moral luck, the insistence that we can't be held responsible for what is beyond our control, need not have quite that tenor even if the matter at hand turns out to be epistemic rather than moral. Construed in Austen's terms, an objection of that kind could amount to the recognition of character traits that, while not impervious to change, are sometimes liable to moral assessment independent of circumstances. Considering counterfactual cases isn't useful and informative *only* because it can help us find grounds for blame. It is also useful and important because it can help us discover grounds for mitigating blame or for exoneration. As indicated before, Austen deploys her counterfactuals in both directions. Her interest isn't exclusively in showing us how, for instance, wealth and privilege make it possible to conceal any number of vices because the opportunity to exhibit various vices is so much less likely to arise (she also holds forth about the vices licensed by a surfeit of power, as in the case of Lady Catherine of *Pride and Prejudice*, but that is another story). Her interest also lies in showing how people may sometimes be less to blame if they fall prey to weaknesses and vulnerabilities that are common to the general run of humanity. There may be circumstances that are so grim and vile than no character could emerge from them unscathed. It is difficult to determine the truth of a counterfactual, granted, but considering what someone would do in one set of circumstances or another seems entirely relevant to an assessment of their character.

Notes

1. Bernard Williams, *Moral Luck* (Cambridge: Cambridge University Press, 1981). Thomas Nagel, *Mortal Questions* (ch. 3 on Moral Luck) (Cambridge: Cambridge University Press, 1979).

2. Martha Nussbaum, *The Fragility of Goodness* (Cambridge: Cambridge University Press, 1986).

3. Thomas Nagel, "Moral Luck," in *Moral Luck*, ed. Daniel Statman (Albany: SUNY Press, 1993), 56–72.

4. All examples of Austen's work will be derived from the following editions of her novels: *The Novels of Jane Austen*, 5 volumes, ed. R. W. Chapman, 3rd ed. (Oxford: Oxford University Press, 1988); and to *The Works of Jane Austen*, ed. R. W. Chapman, volume 6, *Minor Works* (Oxford: Oxford University Press, 1988).

5. Nagel, "Moral Luck," 65.

6. Nagel, "Moral Luck," 66.

7. Daniel C. Dennett, "Intuition Pumps," in *Intuition Pumps and Other Tools for Thinking*, excerpted in *Edge*, accessed August 12, 2015, http://www.edge.org/documents/ThirdCulture/r-Ch.10.html.

8. Jane Austen, "Mansfield Park," in *The Novels of Jane Austen*, 5 volumes, ed. R. W. Chapman, 3rd ed. (Oxford: Oxford University Press, 1988), 390.

9. David Hume, *Treatise of Human Nature*, ed. L. A. Selby-Bigge (Oxford: Clarendon Press, 1978), 584.

10. Jane Austen, "Sense and Sensibility," in *The Novels of Jane Austen*, 5 volumes, ed. R. W. Chapman, 3rd ed. (Oxford: Oxford University Press, 1988), 205.

11. Austen, "Sense and Sensibility," 205.

12. Austen, "Sense and Sensibility," 207.

13. Austen, "Sense and Sensibility," 208.

14. Nicholas Rescher, "Moral Luck," in *Moral Luck*, ed. Daniel Statman (Albany: SUNY Press, 1993), 141–66.

15. Norvin Richards, "Luck and Desert," in *Moral Luck*, ed. Daniel Statman (Albany: SUNY Press, 1993), 167–80.

PART III

WEALTH AND CLASS

CHAPTER NINE

Women Owning Property

The Great Lady in Jane Austen

RITA J. DASHWOOD

After commenting on an inheritance received by their wealthy uncle, Mr. Leigh-Perrot, in a letter to Cassandra, in July 1808, Jane Austen writes: "Indeed, I do not know where we are to get our Legacy—but we will keep a sharp look-out."[1] Plainly aware of her and Cassandra's comparatively strained circumstances and of inequality not just within her own family but throughout society, Jane Austen reverses this disparity in her novels. Here, in her narrative economy, propertyless women are given a central position and propertied women become secondary characters. In contrast to the way Georgian genteel women have been represented by scholars of the period, the great ladies in Jane Austen are not portrayed as either creators of spaces, managers of their property, or socially conscientious members of their community. Instead, they share various negative characteristics, with most of them being described as despotic and arrogant. The exception to this is the heroine of *Emma*, in which the future proprietor is central to the narrative. Presented as a potentially tyrannical great lady who does not contribute to the improvement of her community, Emma must reform herself in order to escape this destiny.

While critics including Elsie B. Michie have suggested that through the juxtaposition of wealthy women with the unpropertied heroines Austen invites her readers to value poverty over wealth, Austen depicts wealth and influence as desirable, but as something wasted in the hands of those who do not possess the appropriate education and moral principles prerequisite to their using it wisely. By refuting the idea that during the Georgian period women would not have been expected to manage their property—a position maintained by authors such as Sandie Byrne and Gillian Skinner—Austen does not, as a rule, characterize the great ladies in her novels as property managers, not because this would have been inconceivable but because their education has not prepared them for it.

Indeed, Austen was critical of the faulty female education that made women incapable of undertaking the challenging task of managing property, and she regarded the novel as a means of educating women in ways that will qualify them to do this successfully. In this respect, *Emma* is particularly significant, as the process by which Emma will become a responsible manager—and, after the death of her father—owner of property, is conceivable in this sense as an education that has ethical forms of ownership in view.

The Great Lady

According to Amanda Vickery in *Behind Closed Doors*, during the Georgian period, heiresses and widows were common among the nobility, where as many as a third of all family seats came to women or passed down the female line.[2] In *Women in England* Susie Steinbach supports this and successfully demonstrates the active role these women played in the management of the household and within their communities.[3] Contradicting the stereotype of the languid great lady, this author argues that no aristocratic household would have been left entirely to the staff. Among other managerial tasks, the mistress of the house would have met daily with the housekeeper, kept the household accounts, paid bills, ordered food and other supplies, and overseen the planning of events when the family entertained. Vickery also explores the ways in which women would have contributed to the decoration and shaping of the interior of the house, in spite of the limitations in the law, which denied married women the right to own their own property.

As pointed out by Anne Laurence in *Women in England 1500–1760*, few could have afforded to commission architectural projects at their own expense, since the funds would not have been at their disposal.[4] In spite of this, widowhood, which ended a woman's coverture in common law and restored her full legal personality, would have been, when combined with prosperity, a period of independence and self-expression for women, according to Laurance.[5] This is precisely the situation in which many great ladies in Jane Austen find themselves. However, the connection to a grand domestic space actually works against these women's subjectivity in the novels. Privileged in their social standing and financial situation, these women are only secondary characters, while the unpropertied women are given central positions in the narrative.

In *The One vs. The Many*, Alex Woloch draws attention to the social inequality and the imbalance in Austen's narratives, where privileged women such as Anne de Bourgh, Lady Catherine's daughter, who will inherit "very extensive property" are much "better off than [the] many girls with none."[6] Whereas the heroines are portrayed as possessing moral qualities that would have made them conscientious property managers, the great ladies share strikingly similar characteristics that, taken together, create a negative and unsympathetic portrait of women who inherit substantial property. The injustice of the inequality prevalent in society is thus evidenced by the indications presented throughout the narratives suggesting that the heroines would have made much better use of the property had they been granted the same opportunities and privileges as the propertied women.

Added to the general negative portrayal of the personalities and morals of the great ladies is the fact that Austen does not characterize them as active managers of their property. This is in contrast to the historical cases made by Vickery, Steinbach, and Laurence that demonstrate that such women frequently were active in this role. What are we to make of this generally negative characterization of wealthy and propertied women and its contrast to the positive light in which heroines far less privileged are placed? In *The Vulgar Question of Money*, Michie argues that Austen sees the plots of her novels as a means through which "fiction attempts to counter worldly assumptions by leading readers to value virtue and poverty over wealth."[7] She goes on:

> In the looking-glass logic of Austen's world, to have nothing that would make you desirable on the marriage market, to lack fashionable manners and the rank and possessions that accompany them, is, in fact, to have everything, to possess the value or virtue, the good manners, that will protect you from the corruptions of wealth.[8]

Here Michie suggests that Austen criticizes wealth and exposes its corruptive force in their virtues and manners, while at the same time inviting her readers to value poverty. However, nowhere in her novels does Austen romanticize poverty or present it as an indicator of virtue. In fact, there are several examples in Austen where the morally reprehensible actions of a character are presented as understandable when motivated by poverty or fear of poverty. Mrs. Smith from *Persuasion* would be an example of this, as her desperate situation of poverty and illness leads her to manipulate Anne and encourage a marriage that would be potentially beneficial to her but disastrous to her friend. In *Pride and Prejudice*, Mrs. Bennet's attempts at coercing Elizabeth into marrying Mr. Collins, unlike any manipulation of the sort exerted by the great ladies, is not condemned, as Mrs. Bennet's fear of poverty is the reason behind her objectionable behavior.

While some authors such as Gillian Skinner and Sandie Byrne have argued that women in the Georgian period would not have been expected to manage their own property, other authors have shown that the limits on active management were not so stringent. In fact, we see various examples of women throughout the early modern to the Georgian period who were responsible for commissioning building works in estates either owned by themselves or their husbands. Laurence, for instance, calls attention to the fact that most husbands appointed their wives as executors of their wills and that if a man died intestate his widow was almost always appointed as the administrator of his estate.[9] This disproves the idea that women managing property would have been considered anomalous. In *Women in England, 1760–1914: A Social History*, Susie Steinbach also points out that great ladies would have been expected to undertake important responsibilities as patrons of parish churches and philanthropists.[10]

It is curious to notice, therefore, that having been in the position to portray female agency and philanthropic work, which she is sure to have witnessed, Austen neglected to account for the duties of great ladies in positive and productive terms. As Michie argues, "rich women [in Austen's novels] exhibit engrossment, while rich men demonstrate that it is possible to be both wealthy and virtuous."[11] However, while Michie affirms that the rich woman in Austen represents "the material appeals that threaten to corrupt the moral sentiments," Austen's portrayal of the great ladies is more complex than this.[12] The overall negative portrayal of propertied women in Austen contrasts with the various examples of women who are either capable property managers or have the potential to become so, with household management not being presented as something gendered. In fact, the main reason for the differences between these two sets of characters is illustrated in an excerpt of Fanny Burney's *Cecilia*, familiar to Austen, in which the heroine's household management is described: "The system of her œconomy, like that of her liberality, was formed by rules of reason."[13] The explanation behind the competence of some characters in the administration of the household would be, therefore, the use of reason in the performance of their duties. In Austen, whenever rationality is lacking, it is presented as an indicator of a deficient education that did not prepare the propertied women for their roles.

Education

Mary Wollstonecraft famously argued that traditionally female qualities were not natural but constructed, the result of a limited education. In *Reflections on the Present Condition of the Female Sex; with Suggestions for its Improvement*, Priscilla Wakefield is just as critical of female education when she denounces the faults which prevent women from becoming useful members of society.[14] Arguing that women must be provided with a suitable preparation that allows them to understand their duties and discharge them suitably, these authors defend a revolution in female education that would teach women to become useful members of society. In her novels, Austen contributes to this feminist dialogue on female education by contrasting the consequences of an inadequate upbringing with those of a suitable one. Austen is positive about heroines and other female characters who are well educated, either showing examples of their abilities in household management or indicating that they have the potential to successfully discharge these duties when they marry, such as Anne from *Persuasion* and Elizabeth from *Pride and Prejudice* respectively. These characters are contrasted to those of the great ladies who, through their actions, reveal the consequences of their faulty education: their pride, insolence, and disrespect for those of lower rank and fortune. Wary of wealth and influence being wasted in the hands of women who do not use it in order to improve their communities, but for their own selfish purposes, Austen uses these characters to represent the current system of female education which does not teach women to be rational beings and useful members of society.

Ignorance of their duties and disrespect toward people of lower ranks in society are qualities almost all of Austen's great ladies share. One of the best examples of this is Lady Catherine. This great lady's treatment of her guests when they arrive at Rosings is clearly deliberate and meant as an assertion of her superiority of rank. It is also illustrative of a lack of the good manners and social conscience which should belong to a lady of her position. The episode in which Anne forces Charlotte to stand in the strong wind to speak to her, instead of entering the house, proves her to be her mother's equal in lack of consideration toward people of a lower rank in society. Of a sickly constitution—which may be an excuse for her complete avoidance of responsibility—she does not appear to be educated on how to administer Rosings once it is in her possession. Given her own ignorance of her responsibilities as mistress of a great estate, Lady Catherine is unfit to educate her daughter in these matters. This is evidenced by the description of her discharge of her philanthropic duties, which is extremely ironic:

> Elizabeth soon perceived . . . this great lady . . . was a most active magistrate in her own parish, the minutest concerns of which were carried to her by Mr. Collins; and whenever any of the cottagers were disposed to be quarrelsome, discontented or too poor, she sallied forth into the village to settle their differences, silence their complaints, and scold them into plenty.[15]

As this indicates, in the discharge of her duty, Lady Catherine is neither charitable nor understanding, but only authoritative and condescending, as her approach consists on commanding those less fortunate to be silent and content. There is no indication that this great lady contributes to the improvement of the lives of the poor with either useful advice or financial help, which indicates that these visits are not done out of genuine concern but out of a necessity to display her superiority of rank.

This lack of awareness of their duties is a common characteristic among the great ladies in Austen's novels. Mrs. Ferrars, in *Sense and Sensibility*, is far from being active in her community, as she resides permanently in London and regards her estate merely as a means of income and of manipulating her eldest son into obeying her wishes. In fact, the only episode in which the estate is mentioned by her is during her attempt at persuading Edward to give up his engagement to Lucy Steele and marry Miss Morton, in which it is used as a bribe: "His mother explained to him her liberal designs, in case of his marrying Miss Morton; told him she would settle on him the Norfolk estate."[16] Her administration of her estate and income is never mentioned, except when her daughter describes her reluctance to pay annuities to her former servants: "Her income was not her own, she said, with such perpetual claims on it; and it was the more unkind in my father, because, otherwise, the money would have been entirely at my mother's disposal."[17] Whereas maintaining former servants would have been considered part of the responsibilities of the mistress of the house, Mrs. Ferrars only discharges annuities to the three servants because it was stipulated in her husband's will, making it perfectly clear that had the choice been hers this duty would have been left unperformed. Similarly, in *Sanditon*, the only instances in which Lady

Denham is seen describing her management of the estate are used merely as the means of illustrating that lady's avarice, as she is shown to be concerned about the prospect of a rise in the price of butcher's meat due to the fact that she has "a servants' hall full to feed."[18] The fact that her avarice makes her an unfair mistress is expressed by the declaration of her refusal to accommodate her relatives in her house, since if the servants had more work "they would want higher wages."[19]

Deficient education, both moral and practical, is contrasted, in Austen, with the superior upbringing of other characters. In *Northanger Abbey*, for example, it is indicated that Catherine received lessons on arithmetic from her father, while there is no indication that the propertied women received any such education. The two exceptions to this are Emma and Lady Russell, as the narrative more or less indirectly points toward the fact that they would have been educated in these subjects. Whereas Emma must have a fair knowledge of arithmetic in order to manage the estate by herself, we are informed that Lady Russell, in order to advise Sir Walter on how to best manage his estate, "drew up plans of economy [and] . . . made exact calculations,"[20] revealing her knowledge on the subject. In spite of their other flaws, the portrayal of these two characters is, in contrast to that of other great ladies, a generally positive one, connected in Austen's terms to their superior education. Thus, the propertied woman in Austen is not avaricious and morally reprehensible because she is a woman, but because she received a deficient education that weakened her mind and made her fully unprepared for her role, especially when compared to her male counterparts. For that reason, while most propertied men in Austen—those who have received both a practical and moral education—are both wealthy and well-principled, as Michie affirms, the faults of the women with property are presented as the natural consequences of an inadequate upbringing.

Another common characteristic among the great ladies in Austen is their propensity to tyrannize their dependents or people of lower ranks in society, treating the first as assets in social advancement and the latter as instruments for their amusement, another consequence of their faulty education. When a woman becomes the leader of the family in Austen, it is her responsibility to manage the various economic pressures at its center, her failure in this task becoming another way for Austen to expose the deficiencies of women's education. Mary Wollstonecraft warned against the prejudices that women possessed naturally weaker minds than men, often presented as a justification for their submissive position in the family. According to Wollstonecraft, women's experience of being tyrannized and forced into submission would lead them to, in return, tyrannize those dependent on them.

Originating from a deficient education which weakened their judgment and reason, most of the great ladies in Austen show this willingness to tyrannize, as they attempt to satisfy their insecurities by constantly asserting the power fortune and rank give them. Lady Denham's heir allows her the liberty of selecting a wealthy wife for him, regarding it as the price for the inheritance he expects her to leave him. Lady Catherine also appears to be convinced that she is entitled to manipulate marriages in order to better her daughter's status in society and consequently that of the de Bourgh family. Mrs. Ferrars has the authority to decide when or if her son Edward will inherit and use this power in an attempt to force him to marry whom she pleases and choose his profession, disinheriting him when he opposes these plans. Rather than contributing to the improvement of their community, these women use their position in the family and in society to pursue their own selfish interests. Thus, Austen's characterization of the great ladies does not merely present wealth and rank as something negative or necessarily corruptive, but demonstrates how empty and worthless these privileges are when not accompanied by the moral education and practical preparation that would allow these women to make good use of them.

Emma

Emma is the only Jane Austen novel in which a widowed or unmarried great lady of property does not feature, which means that the position of the two-dimensional character of the great lady appears to be left unfulfilled. However, in contrast with her former novels, in *Emma*, Jane Austen focuses on the figure of the female proprietor and places her at the center of the narrative. Emma, the heroine of the novel, will inherit half of her father's property when he dies, property which, if protected by a trust, would be separate from that of her future husband. In this novel, Austen accompanies Emma's personal development, which may either be satisfactory, turning her into a positive influence in her community, or unsatisfactory, confirming the possibility that she will become the sort of powerful single woman who does not belong to her community, much like the great ladies discussed in the previous sections.

As a literary character, the lack of a positive and moralizing process of personal development in Emma would make her fade from view and join the other less visible female characters of great wealth and little education. As

Woloch affirms, "Power is earned through attention"[21] and, as the main char-acter, Emma is in a position more privileged than any other Austen great lady. According to Frances Ferguson, it is through free indirect speech that Austen brings us much closer to this character than to any other in the novel.[22] By doing so, the reader has access to Emma's thoughts and feelings, her qualities and faults, which altogether make her a complex character and, ultimately, a likable one. As the primary character, Emma undergoes a proc-ess of personal development similar to that of other Austen heroines but unlike anything the other great ladies experience.

Emma loves and actively pursues matchmaking, an inclination which stems out of boredom and lack of occupation, and a sign of the futile lifestyle she will have to abandon in order to become a useful member of her commu-nity. Out of all the great ladies in Austen's novels, Emma is the only one who is involved in the concerns of the parish church of her community and in the philanthropic work which was considered to be part of the responsibil-ities of the mistress of a big house. Episodes in the novel describe Emma as a compassionate and considerate leader in her community, who contributes with money, food, and advice to the well-being of the poor. Nevertheless, and in spite of her potential to become an improver of her community, various factors keep her from realizing it. Indeed, Emma is not just guilty of possessing prejudices toward people of lower social classes, but she also reveals a lack of fortitude in her charity work, avoiding it when possible.

In *A Vindication of the Rights of Woman*, Wollstonecraft asked for "a revolu-tion in female manners" which would restore to women "their lost dignity" and allow them to "labour by reforming themselves to reform the world."[23] Aware of the need for such a reform in women's education, through which women would receive the necessary preparation to successfully help and edu-cate others in return, Austen understands the importance the novelist can have in this process. Seeing the novel as a form of education, Austen denounces the faults of women's current education and places the heroine's process of personal growth and reform at the center of the narrative. Whereas all of Austen's heroines undergo this process, in no other novel is the outcome so uncertain as in *Emma*. In this novel, the faults in the hero-ine's education combined with her extremely privileged social position threaten to turn her into another of Austen's tyrannical great ladies who does not organically belong to her community. By writing stories that edu-cate women in ways that will qualify them to be property owners and manag-ers, Austen does her part in this revolution of female manners. In this context, the representation of philanthropic work becomes essential in

Emma, as the more the heroine understands its indispensable nature, the more prepared she is shown to be for her position as a leader in her community.

Unlike the other great ladies, Emma received a good education from her governess, Miss Taylor, through which she has developed qualities that fit her to become a capable property manager. Mr. Knightley himself, who is not blind to the heroine's faults, recognizes that the values fostered by Miss Taylor are precisely what, combined with a strong mind, make Emma a good person: "Nature gave you understanding:—Miss Taylor gave you principles. You must have done well."[24] Nevertheless, Emma is often neglectful toward those who would benefit from her assistance, particularly Miss and Mrs. Bates, who live in comparative poverty. Emma's refusal to perform demonstrations of solicitude toward the less fortunate families is presented in the novel as something morally wrong and socially irresponsible. Revealing of the faults in her education, this lack of social consciousness must be overcome in order for Emma to adopt an ethical form of ownership and become an improver of her community.

With impeccable morals, values, and consideration for other people, Mr. Knightley leads by example in his own community, which makes him the ideal person to instruct Emma on how to undertake the same responsibilities. Demonstrative of Emma's lack of consideration toward those less privileged at its most extreme, her humiliation of Miss Bates at the Box Hill picnic earns her the reproof of Mr. Knightley. This becomes the most important moment in Emma's process of personal growth. After a second humbling moment in which she regrets the arrogance and conceit that have led her to manipulate Harriet, Emma will be ready to become an active and useful member of her community, embodying an alternative mode to female property management. In *Jane Austen and the War of Ideas*, Butler declares that "At the personal level marriage would mean submitting to continued moral assessment by a mature man, who would fortify the stronger, more rational, objective, and stringent side of Emma's mind."[25] Unlike Butler, however, I do not view Mr. Knightley's mentoring as a patronizing condescension of a man toward a younger woman, but a means for Emma to access and engage with the aspects missing from her education. Throughout the novel, both characters go through a process of personal growth, and at the end of it they admit to their moral failures, with Mr. Knightley not being presented as morally superior to Emma.

The description of Emma's visit to Donwell becomes essential to the understanding of her process of personal development since, in the same way that Elizabeth admires Pemberley in *Pride and Prejudice*, Emma explores Mr. Knightley's estate, approving of everything about it from its tasteful style of decoration to its considerable dimensions, with the estate being presented as the place in which Emma belongs. Mr. Knightley's particular way of managing Donwell is the reason why Emma must develop a social conscience before she can truly belong there. In fact, Donwell is described as an estate in which the source of its prosperity is not hidden, and as a living, growing environment where a relationship of interdependence is established between the owner, Mr. Knightley, and his tenants, whose involvement is solicited and welcomed.

By the end of her process of personal growth, Emma has been saved from the destiny of becoming a tyrannical great lady and has shown that she can organically belong to her community and become involved in managing a large estate. Having freed herself from prejudices and learned to respect people of different ranks in society, she has become the socially conscious mistress that the wife of Mr. Knightley and the mistress of Donwell needs to be. Her happiness secured, we are not meant to doubt that Emma will, after the imminent death of her father, contribute to the maintenance of the respectability and prosperity of Donwell and be a competent manager of her estate and an improver of her community.

At the end of the novel, the danger that Emma may join the morally reprehensible great ladies is no longer a reality. As the central character, Emma goes through a process of personal development which ultimately prepares her for the position of an active member in her community and manager of a large estate. This process, combined with her superior education, saves her from the fate of the other great ladies, who are used as plot devices in order to move the heroine's story further but in whose own story the narrator is not interested. Having gone through a similar process of personal development as those of the other Austen heroines, Emma is allowed, at the end of the narrative, to share the same happy ending, which is intimately connected with the new property in which she has been shown to belong.

In *Emma*, Austen shows that being a woman is no impediment to successful property management, but that the key lies in the appropriate practical and moral education which so many women are denied. The unsatisfactory property management of the other great ladies, therefore, is presented in the novels as a consequence of a deficient education that did not prepare these women for roles of such great responsibility. Austen's portrayal in her novels of the consequences of a faulty system of female education illustrates the influence that contemporary female authors writing about education had on her. Lady Catherine, Mrs. Ferrars, and Lady Denham are portrayed as inactive and ignorant as far as the practical management of property is concerned due to their lack of knowledge of arithmetic and business that authors such as Wakefield, Edgeworth, and West considered essential.[26] By exposing these characters' arrogance and willingness to tyrannize, Austen also demonstrates her accordance with Wollstonecraft's argument that the current system of female education weakens women's minds.

A further important flaw in the management of Lady Catherine, Mrs. Ferrars, and Lady Denham is their lack of a social consciousness, avarice, and reluctance to perform the charitable acts so highly praised by the previously mentioned authors. Due to their lack of an appropriate education and guidance, by the end of the novels these great ladies are just as ignorant of their duties as property owners and managers as they were at the beginning. Whereas Emma avoids doing charitable work whenever it proves inconvenient, she eventually comes to understand the importance of her role as mistress of a large estate and reveals her capacity to improve herself for the benefit of those less fortunate. Her capacity to emancipate her mind and overcome her initial selfishness distinguishes her from the other three great ladies, whose self-centeredness remains unabated. Emma's emancipation is facilitated by the close friendship and trust subsisting between herself and Mr. Knightley who, having enjoyed the benefits of an appropriate education, is willing to communicate it to Emma's advantage. Thus, through her novels, Austen offers a non-prescriptive perspective into what she considers to be the flaws in the education of women, as well as potential alternatives. In doing so, she not only engages with the dialogue on female education, but ultimately offers her own contribution to its reform.

Notes

1. Deirdre Le Faye, ed., *Jane Austen's Letters* (Oxford: Oxford University Press, 2011), 143.

2. Amanda Vickery, *Behind Closed Doors* (New Haven: Yale University Press, 2009), 132.

3. Susie Steinbach, *Women in England, 1760–1914: A Social History* (London: Phoenix, 2005).

4. Anne Laurence, *Women in England, 1500–1760: A Social History* (London: Phoenix Giant, 1996), 153.

5. Laurence, *Women in England*, 220.

6. Alex Woloch, *The One vs. the Many: Minor Characters and the Space of the Protagonist in the Novel* (Princeton: Princeton University Press, 2004), 60.

7. Elsie B. Michie, *The Vulgar Question of Money: Heiresses, Materialism, and the Novel of Manners from Jane Austen to Henry James* (Baltimore: Johns Hopkins University Press, 2001), 57.

8. Michie, *The Vulgar Question of Money*, 39.

9. Laurence, *Women in England*, 235.

10. Susie Steinbach, *Women in England, 1760–1914: A Social History* (London: Phoenix, 2005), 89.

11. Michie, *The Vulgar Question of Money*, 30.

12. Michie, *The Vulgar Question of Money*, 30.

13. Fanny Burney, *Cecilia, or Memoirs of an Heiress* (Oxford: Oxford University Press, 2008), 792.

14. Priscilla Wakefield, *Reflections of the Present Condition of the Female Sex; with Suggestions for Its Improvement* (London: Joseph Johnson, 1798).

15. Jane Austen, *Pride and Prejudice* (Oxford: Oxford University Press, 2008), 143.

16. Jane Austen, *Sense and Sensibility* (Oxford: Oxford University Press, 2008), 200.

17. Austen, *Sense and Sensibility*, 7.

18. Jane Austen, "Sanditon," in *Northanger Abbey, The Watsons and Sanditon* (Oxford: Oxford University Press, 2008), 181.

19. Austen, "Sanditon," 188.

20. Jane Austen, *Persuasion* (Oxford: Oxford University Press, 2004), 13.

21. Jane Austen, *Emma* (Oxford: Oxford University Press, 2008), 60.

22. Frances Ferguson, "Now It's Personal: D. A. Miller and Too-Close Reading." *Critical Inquiry*: 41.3 (Spring 2015): 529.

23. Mary Wollstonecraft, *A Vindication of the Rights of Woman* (London: Penguin, 2004).

24. Austen, *Emma*, 454.

25. Marilyn Butler, *Jane Austen and the War of Ideas* (Oxford: Oxford University Press, 1975), 252.

26. Wakefield, *Reflections of the Present Condition of the Female Sex*; Maria Edgeworth, *Castle Rackrent* (Oxford: Oxford University Press, 2009); Jane West, *Letters to a Young Lady; in Which the Duties and Character of Women Are Considered, Chiefly with a Reference to Prevailing Opinion* (Paternoster-row: Longman, Hurst, Rees, Orme and Brown, 1811).

CHAPTER TEN

Deconstructing Entailment

CHRISTOPHER KETCHAM

A dark cloud hangs over Longbourn, the landed estate of the Bennet family in *Pride and Prejudice* (1813). This dark cloud is called entailment, a legal construct dating back to the thirteenth century in Britain which asserts that an estate in its entirety is inherited (generally) by the eldest male heir. The trouble is that the Bennet's five children are all girls, and the closest male relative is a cousin, William Collins, whom Mr. Bennet dislikes in conjunction with some trouble he had with William's father. Upon the death of Mr. Bennet, Longbourn becomes the property of Mr. Collins, bypassing all of his daughters and his widow, Mrs. Bennet. Mrs. Bennet has her own estate of four thousand pounds, but this is inadequate to support her family without Mr. Bennet's estate.

Jane Austen is a master at creating characters and positioning them in her early nineteenth-century society. Society and its law have great influence upon her characters, the way they act, think, and even how they plan to live out their lives. Sandra McPherson explains the power of property by drawing upon the thought of Alistair Duckworth:

> "The estate as an ordered physical structure is a metonym for other inherited structures—society as a whole, a code of morality, a body of manners, a system of language"—in other words, for the entitlements and conventions of English class structure.[1]

However, Austen is not all that conversant with the intricacies of the law of entailment. Long before Austen wrote *Pride and Prejudice*, the laws of inheritance could be broken by Mr. Bennet through a fairly routine legal process. By the fifteenth century, disgruntled heirs had successfully petitioned courts to produce a remedy that could cure the problem of entailment, effectively favoring other types of estates. Is this glaring mistake a fatal flaw attributable to Austen which serves to sink her story, or, is it emblematic of her contemporary society where laws were not always transparent or understood by lay persons? Peter Appel suggests that the latter may be plausible.[2] He posits that even though Austen herself was familiar with the concept of entailment through the experience of her brother who inherited three estates, it is plausible that both Austen and her early readers did not have a clear understanding of it other than its nasty method of bypassing widows, sisters, and younger brothers for a sole male heir, in this story's case, a distant cousin.[3] Therefore, if Austen had understood the reversibility of entailment, she would have had Mrs. Bennet's brother-in-law who is an attorney (though not a member of the bar) explain to Mr. and Mrs. Bennet the remedies under the law and would have used another legal device to permanently tie up the estate. Even so, the entailment system operates as the story's villain. Yet it was not designed to be villainous, just to solve a very real problem in keeping estates intact and away from money grabbers like the state or wastrel heirs.[4]

Entailment

Estates have been central to the historical culture of Great Britain. Intact, their value as income-producing entities has been well understood. The greater the size of the estate, then the greater prestige a family enjoys by inheriting it. Therefore, for both income and prestige purposes, it has been critical that estates be maintained and kept intact over generations. A legacy passed down through the male heir and namesake in conjunction with any title associated with it is more than an economic boon; it is also a powerfully symbolic achievement in that it operates as a pivotal element of British high society. Historically, estate holders wanted a way of keeping spendthrift heirs in *any* future generation from imperiling the estate by breaking it up. In effect, the idea was to make future heirs custodians of the estate but not really owners because while they had the right to occupy and use the estate, they would not have the right to break it up or dispose of it in other ways. They, of course, could consume the fruits of the estate's labor and industry, but not the real property itself. Entail or, as it is sometimes called, "fee tail" was the instrument passed in 1285 to accomplish this goal.

Entailment has been paired quite often with the idea of primogeniture, which means that the firstborn son (most usually) becomes the sole inheritor of the estate. This combination of fee tail or primogeniture in the form of a legal document is designed to endure into perpetuity, and as such entailments were never subject to the laws that barred perpetuities. With this legal device, the family and its name are maintained in its societal hierarchy by being associated with the property for all time to come. However, this strategy of primogeniture has one fatal flaw: if there is no male heir from the current generation, one must be sought. As we have with the Bennet family, a distant cousin, a Mr. Collins in this case, becomes the rightful entailed heir to the Longbourn estate. While the estate is preserved intact in such a move, and it is possible that the combination of the two estates will produce even a larger estate, the family name Bennet associated with the Longbourn estate no longer will have primacy and will be relegated to the backwaters of the genealogy, buried in the footnotes of the great historical legacy of the estate.

Entailment produces another problem should there be no male child from the current occupant's marriage: what to do with the occupying daughters and widow when the father dies. Entailment is silent on the matter. If there is a male heir, the younger brothers are not entitled to any measure of the estate and are subject to the benevolence of their older brother. While some younger brothers were given modest pensions or other monetary estates, they most often entered into the clergy, accountancy, or law. Through all of these machinations, the corpus of the estate survives by throwing off all who are not essential to its endurance and by preserving the oldest male heir as the only one to retain the prestige of the estate.

Entailment has its purposes and also its problems as we have seen. However, by Austen's time, entailment had been stripped of its absolute power because it could be overturned by the entailed heir through a simple legal procedure to disavow the entailment. Few estates in Austen's time would have been subject to entailment simply because it could be barred.[5] Rather, more estates were subject to a "strict settlement" process which, if set up properly, gave some measure of the estate to the surviving heirs including widows, daughters, and the sons neglected by primogeniture.[6] Strict settlement, however, has the nasty side effect of imperiling the intact estate. Estates produce income. If the family scion gives away too much of the estate in pensions to children or others, the remaining funds may be too small to support the real property of the estate or the lifestyle of its inhabitants. Mr. Bennet regrets that he, himself, has been a spendthrift. Nor was Mrs. Bennet frugal: "Mrs. Bennet had no turn for economy and her husband's love of independence had alone prevented their exceeding their economy."[7]

As the industrial revolution progressed in Britain and around the world, the idea of the estate as a producer of wealth principally through agriculture and some craft making began to decline. However, during this time British society continued to maintain and relish the pomp and circumstance of the wealthy estate holder. Estate holders were expected to live in a manner that would do justice to the name of the estate and, toward this end, maintained lavish lifestyles even when they could not afford to.

So we are left with a conundrum in *Pride and Prejudice*. If entailment could be easily overturned and Mrs. Bennet has a brother-in-law who is an attorney and should have been very familiar with this process, why is the Bennet estate so encumbered? Whether Austen did or did not know that entailed estates could be barred is really not important to her story. What is important is that British society would have such an instrument that guarantees that all but a single individual in sometimes a rather large family (five Bennet girls, for example) can be disinherited with a very real possibility of their being turned out into the cold.

Austen also understands the patriarchal leanings of the society for which male primogeniture is the norm, leaving daughters to fend for themselves, most often in the pursuit of suitable husbands in order to maintain the lifestyle they had grown up in. The dilemma the Bennet daughters wrestle with is whether to marry for money or for love. Mother focuses on the practical economic benefits of marriage. In *Pride and Prejudice* what unfolds is the journey of three daughters into marriage, not all successfully or with large estates.

Austen weaves the two threads of love and money through the choices of men the Bennet sisters eventually marry. Austen doesn't choose between money and love. She shows what can happen when impetuous love is blind through the disastrous marriage between Lydia and Wickham. On the other hand, the cautious Elizabeth chooses a man who has incredible wealth but does so only after carefully considering the ability of Mr. Darcy to love her. Oldest sister Jane falls in love with Mr. Bingley, but it is he who takes his time, influenced by Mr. Darcy, who is against the idea of their marriage. Later in the story, Mr. Bingley and Jane do marry.

While the thread of love is charming, and the thread of entailment hangs over the Bennet family like a sword from a string, a third thread of money operates as an ambivalent dimension. As the middle class grew in the nineteenth century, money became more important than real property because money could be put to diverse use in different investments.

Austen alerts us to the changing nature of society from one of genteel landed gentry into an age where industry and profession are emerging as more powerful economic forces. With entailment, the occupation theory of property reigns supreme. In summary, the occupation theory says that he who first occupies the land or works the material into a product has the rights to do what he wants with the property. After entailment and with the emerging industrial age, an economic theory of property is coming to the fore, meaning that the productivity of the property is more important than its inherited characteristics of ancient ownership.[8] However, Austen shows us a third aspect to private property which is central to how her characters behave in society and that is the concept from Jeremey Waldron, that property is a relationship between people. We cannot have a relationship with property because property cannot reason.[9] As society changes, so do the people and their relationships with one another. Austen dramatizes this change in relationships where property and money operate as central concerns for the Bennet family. The Bennet parents see property as the partner; their daughters see a responsible loving husband as their partner with property just as a tool to provide sustenance to the relationship.

More importantly, as we see with Elizabeth, responsible management of the assets of the estate are as important as the intimate partnership that comes with the marriage union. She will not choose just for money; she will not choose just for love. She needs some assurances that her mate will be responsible to her and their family. The business of marriage, the estate, and money are all intertwined in Austen's tale where property has become not a "being" but a relationship between and among people. Elizabeth is a keen observer. She visits Mr. Darcy's estate. She talks to others who know him, who have worked for him. She sees how he has turned his estate from being a thing to a community. It is his ability to create lasting relationships through his vast wealth that begins to interest Elizabeth in Mr. Darcy.

A Monetized Society

Along with the problem of inheritances in *Pride and Prejudice* there is much talk about money and where it came from in a society where this is simply not a subject for polite conversation.[10] Nor is the story only about lords and ladies who have inherited property from distant ancestors. Included are hard-working merchants and professional persons who earned their estates outright or who put modest inheritances to productive use—or have squandered them. Austen is acknowledging that the conversation of society of old money and its ways is shifting toward entrepreneurship where money is the issue because title and peerage are not available to the nouveau riche. Money has become the topic, the subject of society even though it is supposed to be something one does not speak about. By speaking about it Austen positions the conversation of money, both earned and inherited, at the forefront of the stage. In effect she makes money the mute character who says more by saying nothing, letting the other characters speak for money in the story. It is money that is ascendant in her society, meeting the downward strutting aristocrat halfway up the stairs, declining to give the obeisance that title demands. We see this disdain for the authority of peerage when Elizabeth tacitly rejects Lady Catherine's demands on her not to become involved with the very wealthy Mr. Darcy. Women have their place. Men have their place. Each estate has its place in the hierarchy of society. Lords and ladies have their place, and so do all others in a caste society that is on the verge, as Austen explains it in *Pride and Prejudice*, of rearranging place cards on the society table.

There is a tension in *Pride and Prejudice* between being responsible as in responsible with money, status, and taking the long-term view of inheritance in context of carrying down the male line—and with the idea that a life well lived is with someone you truly love and who is also responsible.

The line of succession of Longbourn continues through the male heir, Mr. Collins. Therefore, after Mr. Bennet's death the estate no longer will be associated directly with the Bennet name. Mrs. Bennet inherited an estate of four thousand pounds. However, Mr. and Mrs. Bennet have been profligate spenders and have not invested her estate well. Mrs. Bennet's meager estate alone is inadequate to support her daughters without Mr. Bennet's contribution, which is one reason why she frantically searches for suitable husbands for her daughters.

Mr. Collins proposes in a letter to Mr. Bennet that he visit Longbourn to consider proposing to one of his daughters. Mr. Collins does visit but does not impress either Mr. Bennet or the two daughters he courts. Mr. Collins cannot not win over the prettier Jane, so he approaches the younger Elizabeth for her hand in marriage, which would have kept at least Elizabeth in Longbourn. She rebuffs the buffoonish Mr. Collins to the consternation of Mrs. Bennet, who says if Elizabeth does not accept Mr. Collins's hand, she will never see her daughter again. Mr. Bennet responds, demonstrating his dislike of Mr. Collins, "An unhappy alternative is before you, Elizabeth.

From this day you must be a stranger to one of your parents—your mother will never see you again if you do not marry Mr. Collins, and I will never see you again if you do."[11]

What we see here is the beginning of the transition from a strictly ordered society based upon tradition and socio-legal structures intended on preserving tradition, toward the emerging awakening of women who begin to take steps to be freed of the traditional, and the first change being a marriage based upon affection and responsibility, not convenience to preserve cultural normativity or please one or more parents. Mr. Bennet with his explanation to Elizabeth that her choosing or not of Mr. Collins will estrange her from one of her parents points to the conundrum of meeting someone's expectations rather than your own. However, Mr. Bennet is also showing her that it is her choosing that is more important than either Mr. or Mrs. Bennet's wishes.

Elizabeth Bennet is no romantic dreamer. After being slighted by Mr. Wickham at the ball in the opening of the story, Elizabeth becomes wary of *all* of her suitors. She turns down Mr. Collins flat. She, at first, turns down the wealthy Mr. Darcy. Not only does she want to experience love, but she is unsure of his capacity to feel it as well as be an adequate provider for her and their future family. It isn't until she visits his estate that she begins to see that Mr. Darcy is a responsible and even kind person, which gives her pause to reconsider her past rejection of him and to become more interested in his entreaties. Elizabeth knows the size of Mr. Darcy's estate; however, Austen helps us understand that Elizabeth is not just estate shopping. Rather than chase after only the money and prestige, Elizabeth desires a responsible partner who not only can be responsible for her and their family's well-being but also responsible to her personally and in her emotional needs as his partner. This is evident through Elizabeth's keen observation of her parents' loveless marriage. From the lesson of her parents, Elizabeth is determined not to make the same loveless mistake. Nor is she likely to become involved with someone whose estate is entailed. She wants the balance of love and security.

A Glimpse into the Future

A hundred years after the publication of *Pride and Prejudice*, the industrial revolution gave birth to a new middle class earning wealth from business and professional activities. Landed estates began to dwindle in number. Revenue from estate-borne agriculture began to decline as many estate holders proved to be poor investors in stock and other schemes.

At the same time of the decline of the English estate, Mary Evans notes through Margaret Kirham that "Jane Austen's heroines are not self-conscious feminists, yet they are all exemplary of the first claim of Enlightenment feminism: that women share the same moral nature as men, ought to share the same moral status, and exercise the same responsibility for their own conduct."[12] Yet men are the providers of income; women run the household.

Austen is conscious of the imperilment of women in her early nineteenth-century society, but her characters are not resigned to their subaltern fate. Elisabeth Bennet is portrayed as being willful, headstrong, quick witted, self-educated, but has a biting tongue that frequently sets her back as the story progresses. Other Bennet daughters handle themselves differently as they confront the law and customs of society. Foremost to Austen is that they are first, people in their own rights, albeit born into a society of titles, estates, gender, and societal hierarchies, whose values are sometimes at odds with what people know instinctively about each other. Austen's characters are just human beings, one as different from the next as to make arbitrary categorization such as male, titled, or entailed difficult to maintain. Austen unravels stereotypes, making both women and men weak or strong. Elizabeth Bennet defies Lady Catherine, which is not only a sign of her independence, but also lack of timidity toward an older woman of a superior class. Austen comments about their first meeting, "Lady Catherine seemed quite astonished at not receiving a direct answer; and Elizabeth suspected herself to be the first creature who had ever dared to trifle with so much dignified impertinence."[13] When Lady Catherine confronts Elizabeth about her intentions toward Mr. Darcy, which she opposes vehemently, Elizabeth produces a vague response to which this short conversation ensues: "Miss Bennet, do you know who I am? I have not been accustomed to such language as this. I am almost the nearest relation he has in the world, and am entitled to know all his dearest concerns." And Elizabeth replies, "But you are not entitled to know mine; nor will such behavior as this, ever induce me to be explicit."[14]

However, title or not, all labor under the same social and legal constraints, of which nothing is more crushing than the weight of entailment. By making her characters believable in all of their human strengths and frailties, Austen gets her message across to her readers without taking a radical feminist position, which would have made it challenging to publish her novels. Given the sensibilities of the time, Austen, herself, did not secure a publisher for her work; her father and brother Henry did.[15] However, her Elizabeth is not one to be pushed around by Lady Catherine, nor is she a slave to money like Mrs. Bennet.

A Certain Tension

Austen uses the legal concept of entailment as a plot device to show the tension in society from the confluence of the estate, money, and the emotional aspect of marriage and family. We know that in Austen's time an entailment could be barred, but we can see how she and others might not have been all that conversant with the law. The tension that the entailment system produces for Mrs. Bennet reveals the genuine urgency of marrying her daughters off as quickly as possible. However, for her daughters Jane and Elizabeth finding the right suitor also involves finding the right provider. Mrs. Bennet seems always to be on the edge of her seat, anticipating the fall of the entail sword upon her and her daughters' heads at any moment. We sense that she and Mr. Bennet married for reasons other than love because their marriage has become somewhat routine.

Her daughters understand the peril of entailment, but it seems they are not overwhelmed by it as is Mrs. Bennet. Mr. Bennet, on the other hand, is disgusted with the prospect of leaving his estate to Mr. Collins, but he is unable do anything about it—as helpless as he feels for any relief from his moribund marriage to Mrs. Bennet. Yet he is also chagrined by his and his wife's lack of frugality during their marriage. As such, the Bennet parents are emblematic of a society whose generations were more interested in spending rather than saving.

From the wreckage of the entailed Longbourn, the next generation emerges. By the end of the story three daughters have married. Yet Austen is not naive; she knows that a loveless marriage and one born in ignorance and impetuosity may both be bad. Lydia's marriage to Mr. Wickham is just such a union. However, what Austen introduces in this story is not only that marriage should be for love, but also that both suitors should look for responsibility in their partners before rushing into marriage. Austen's is a tale as much filled with caution and angst over responsibility as it is with the angst of entailment. By the end of *Pride and Prejudice* the second eldest daughter, Elizabeth, has become the fulcrum between extremes of her mother's frantic anxiety for her daughter's good marriages and the foolish impetuosity of her younger sister, Lydia, who jumps into a disastrous marriage with an irresponsible Wickham. Mr. Bingley serves as the cautionary male suitor, taking his time to know Bennet daughter Jane before marrying her. By waiting, Mr.

Bingley reverses the meaning of the first line of *Pride and Prejudice*, "It is a truth universally acknowledged, that a single man in possession of a good fortune, must be in want of a wife." He has a fine estate of money, not land, but he is not in immediate need of a wife. He takes his time to find the right match so that he can love responsibly. Nor does he immediately purchase a home—he rents. While his estate is not entailed, he appears to understand that it is important to choose the right investment and not just rush into the purchase of property that would give him instant recognition in a society founded upon status that comes from owning real property. It is this recognition that estates are tools and not just image that Austen conveys throughout the book.

Property in *Pride and Prejudice* is much more than the occupation theory that preserves rights forever to the first discoverer or claimant. Property is more than just its economic power to produce productivity. Property serves a function in how people relate to each other, which Austen deftly shows through the Bennet daughters by positioning people in front of other people first, giving property a secondary role as tool. Mother seems to think that the estate confers meaning upon the person and the greater the estate, the more meaningful the person becomes.

We see with Elizabeth that entailment has not clouded her mind or her future. The inheritance system which began the story as the specter of doom and arch villain has been slain, relegated to the backwaters of legality with love and responsibility emerging as the characters to replace it.

Notes

1. Sandra Macpherson, "Rent to Own; or, What's Entailed in Pride and Prejudice," *Representations* 82, no. 1 (2003): 1.

2. Peter A. Appel, "A Funhouse Mirror of Law: The Entailment in Jane Austen's Pride and Prejudice," *The Georgia Journal of International and Comparative Law* 41 (2012): 632.

3. Enid G. Hildebrand, "Jane Austen and the Law," *Persuasions*, no. 4 (1982): 35.

4. J. B. Ruhl, "The Tale of the Fee Tail in Downton Abbey," *Vanderbilt. Law Review En Banc* 68 (2015): 134.

5. Appel explained the use of entail in Austen's time: "Thus, by the time that Austen wrote, the entail still existed, but was used only as a means of preserving distant future interests in land and thus keeping the land within the family as part of a larger settlement" (618).

6. Appel, "A Funhouse Mirror of Law: The Entailment in Jane Austen's Pride and Prejudice," 622.

7. Jane Austen, "Pride and Prejudice," in *Jane Austen, the Complete Collection*, ed. Jane Austen (New York: Bedford Park Books, 1813 original publication). Chapter 8.

8. Morris Raphael Cohen, "Property and Sovereignty," in *Readings in the Philosophy of Law*, ed. John Arthur and William H. Shaw (Boston: Prentice Hall, 2010), 489, 491.

9. Jeremy Waldron, *The Right to Private Property* (Oxford: Clarendon Press, 1988), 27.

10. Mary Evans, *Jane Austen and the State* (New York: Tavistock, 1987), 18.

11. Austen, "Pride and Prejudice." Chapter 20.

12. Evans, *Jane Austen and the State*, 43.

13. Austen, "Pride and Prejudice." Chapter 6.

14. Austen, "Pride and Prejudice." Chapter 14.

15. Hildebrand, "Jane Austen and the Law," 38.

CHAPTER ELEVEN

"Pictures of Perfection Make Me Sick and Wicked"

Privilege and Parody in Emma

NANCY MARCK CANTWELL

Shortly after Jane Austen's death in July 1817, her sister, Cassandra, marked a passage in a poem Jane had dictated in her last days: "When once we are buried, you think we are dead/But behold me immortal!"[1] Cassandra, who had lost the sister she referred to hyperbolically as "the sun of my life," embarked on the process of immortalizing Jane Austen, creating an image of her sister as a paragon, a "gilder of every pleasure," a "dear angel," one of the "pictures of perfection" often ridiculed in her novels.[2] Cassandra, perhaps, cannot be blamed for idealizing the sister who had been her closest friend and companion, but her efforts to erase Jane's less-appealing character traits began the gradual translation of Jane Austen, woman writer, into Jane Austen, paragon and consumer fetish. Now, as Claudia Johnson observes, "it is conspicuously difficult to disentangle the 'real' Austen from the acknowledged or unacknowledged agendas of those discussing her."[3] With distinctly different motives, both scholarly and popular audiences describe Austen and her works in a "language of perfection [that] often turns hyperbolic, habitually exorbitant."[4] In this spirit, Wayne Booth in *The Rhetoric of Fiction* describes Austen as "a perfect human being . . . [whose] character establishes the value for us according to which her character is then found to be perfect."[5]

Emma Woodhouse, however, is far from perfect—although she believes she is a paragon, a model for Harriet Smith to emulate, Emma makes mistakes that show the limitations of her personal ethics. While egoistic perfectionism generally requires that the individual seek the highest degree of self-improvement, it also places personal good alongside the good of others; non-egoistic perfectionism suggests that human beings should be committed to the perfection of others as well as themselves. Through Austen's careful attention to these social implications of perfection, Emma eventually revises her understanding of the ideal self, and once she places it squarely in a social context she is able to strive toward it more effectively.

Austen considers perfectionism in nearly every novel, where questions of moral awareness and the claims of others involve her characters in deep reflection and revision of purpose. However, Austen's presentation of perfection in *Emma* begins on a radically different note—the opening paragraph describes the heroine as a paragon of privilege, endowed with "some of the best blessings of existence," yet, as many critics have observed, sorely lacking in both social and self-knowledge.[6] Rachel Brownstein declares that all Austen's novels interest us "because the positions the novels develop on what constitutes 'right' and 'wrong' conduct and feeling . . . remain elusive"; *Emma* in particular addresses the ethical consequences of behavior motivated by self-interest.[7] Focusing on the development of altruism, Sarah Baxter Emsley views Emma "as primarily responsible for her own moral education" as she learns that truly charitable acts are more than "a matter of style."[8] While Katie Halsey observes that Austen's use of parody creates an alliance between the narrator and the reader that exposes Emma's moral failings, Eugene Goodheart argues that these failings necessarily constitute the moral world of the novel, as without Emma "the imaginist" there would be "no social destiny for the community."[9] "Friendship, ideally an egalitarian relationship, cannot thrive in a hierarchical society," writes Laura Thomason, noting both Emma's unsuitableness as a friend and the loneliness that persists despite the constraints of the small community of Highbury.[10] Emma's moral improvement over the course of her experiences inspires some critics to believe in and some to doubt the lasting effects of the self-awareness she achieves, but most agree that the process necessarily takes place in a social context that informs how much she learns and to what use she is able to put this new knowledge by the closing scene describing her wedding. Andrew H. Miller, in his *Burdens of Perfection*, argues that Emma's development arises from a certain view of perfectionism: "an older, much contested religious meaning of the word [that] emphasizes the role of responsiveness to exemplars. . . . we turn from our ordinary lives, realize an ideal self, and perfect what is distinctly human in us—and that we do so in response to exemplary others."[11] I wish to explore Miller's understanding of the exemplar, the paragon of virtue, extending his discussion to suggest that the novel discloses its skepticism about perfection and perfectibility through parody. With Miller, I view the drive toward moral perfection as socially constructed in Austen's novels, particularly so in *Emma*, where it arises from and in response to the community's understanding of a changing social dynamic. The novel views both moral and economic progress as egalitarian, challenging the existing social structure, which Austen scrutinizes through parody—therefore, Emma's efforts to make Harriet a gentlewoman in her own image follow the very pattern of upward economic mobility that threatens to unseat her own social superiority.

Moral Perfection and Upward Mobility

The novel offers exemplary individuals in a variety of registers—for all her faults, Emma is a dutiful daughter, Mr. Knightley an ideal landowner personally concerned for the welfare of his tenants, Robert Martin a model of sense and industry, Jane Fairfax the consummate accomplished gentlewoman. However, each of these paragons has decided imperfections, as well—Emma's self-absorbed snobbery, Mr. Knightley's brusqueness, Robert Martin's lack of refinement, Jane's reserve—suggesting Austen's view that moral perfection is less often attained than attempted, and that the exemplary individuals in any society are themselves striving for improvement within a social context that alternately resists and supports these efforts. In other words, each person works toward a good that may not be shared by others, and there are limits to how successfully anyone can cultivate perfection in others. We can view Emma's movement toward self-awareness sympathetically by noting how her social circumstances privilege material rather than moral improvement. Although Austen describes *Emma*'s Highbury as "a populous village, almost amounting to a town" situated only sixteen miles from London, it does not appear to engage in the contemporary discourse on moral perfection that informed the nineteenth century's widespread concern with self-improvement and the social good.[12] In many respects, Highbury appears static, characterized by its regard for the hierarchal arrangement of its society, but in fact social relations undergo considerable transformation in the course of the novel's yearlong span. Emma, a paragon of all this society values—birth, beauty, grace, and property—is nonetheless forced to acknowledge important transformations that impact her privileged position in this apparently insulated community.

The expanding social and economic power of the Westons, the Coles, and the Martins exposes the precariousness of the landed class, represented by the Knightleys and Woodhouses. It is interesting that the two oldest families serve as exemplars for those aspiring to higher status, yet movement toward that status involves mimicking and then encroaching on and destabilizing previously well-defined class boundaries. Both Mr. Weston and Mr. Cole are self-made men who have rapidly risen through trade to purchase property; however, Mr. Weston stands as a singular example of the permeability of class boundaries, since he comes of a "respectable family, which for the last two or three generations had been rising into gentility and property."[13] The narrator notes in one breath that Mr. Weston "had made his fortune, bought his house, and obtained his wife," sketching in broad strokes the trajectory by which an industrious tradesman could improve his family's social standing.[14] The wife's role in this arc of ambition is to increase fortune and/or connections, to cultivate gentility, and to provide heirs so that property and status may be transferred to the next generation. Although Miss Taylor is penniless, her "dowry" is her personal refinement and the prospect of higher connections; by marrying her, Mr. Weston gains a stronger affiliation to the Woodhouses, securing his position in the uppermost circle of Highbury society. Later in the novel, Emma affirms this upward move when she considers the future possibility of the infant Anna Weston marrying one of her nephews. And, although Emma would *like* to refuse acquaintance with the Coles, who are "of low origin, in trade, and only moderately genteel," she must reluctantly accept their invitation because they are "in fortune and style of living, second only to the family at Hartfield," a fact further emphasized by the wide variety of guests at their party, which includes Mr. Knightley as well as the Coxes whom Emma thinks vulgar.[15] The Martins offer yet another instance of the meritocratic imitation of gentility, one that Emma at first disparages but eventually conciliates when it serves her own purpose of disposing of Harriet. Mr. Knightley repeatedly applauds Robert Martin's good sense as well as his industriousness—again we are reminded of Miller's observation that the language and intent of moral perfection arose from agricultural and estate improvement—as we chart his rising fortunes through the novel. Returning from her visit at the novel's opening, Harriet reports that the Martins have two parlors, servants, and a summer house to mark their prosperity; Robert Martin later dines with the Coxes after visiting to discuss a matter of legal business, suggesting expanding financial interests, which eventually take him to London, and by the end of the novel, Emma thinks, "it would be a great pleasure to know Robert Martin."[16] Mr. Knightley, despite confessing to Emma that "his rank in society I would alter if I could," actually effects an important change by introducing Mr. Martin into his brother's London household as the bearer of some documents.[17] There he is welcomed and invited to join a family party, affording him the opportunity to renew his proposal to Harriet, while blurring the social boundaries that would once have distinguished tenant farmer from gentleman. Both Knightley brothers respect class boundaries but regard the desire for self-improvement with a tolerant, even approving eye, at least for worthy aspirants like Robert Martin. The drive to perfect himself and his situation as much as he can raises Robert Martin beyond his class and associates him with the meritocracy, already encroaching on Highbury's landed gentry through the social advances of Mr. Weston and the Coles. As a successful barrister making his way in London, Mr. John Knightley also participates in the meritocracy, combining the privilege of the landed class with the active ambition of the professional, even as his brother refuses what he regards as the unnecessary trappings of gentility. Perfectionism complicates previously well-defined class boundaries, and this blurring of formerly clear distinctions also occurs when Emma decides to perfect Harriet Smith by remaking her in her own image.

Emma as Paragon

Because Emma's moral development takes shape within a social context where boundaries are being contested, she is more aware of challenges to her personal superiority. On the surface, Emma seeks out Harriet Smith because she needs a friend and walking companion, though in truth she was trying to replace Miss Taylor, "who had such an affection for her as could never find fault" and thus provided continual affirmation of Emma's superiority.[18] Miss Taylor's marriage and relocation naturally contribute to Emma's growing uncertainty about her perfect state; like her father, she requires the constant reaffirmation of others to maintain a secure sense of self. However, Miss Taylor fails miserably as an exemplar herself, neglecting to inspire Emma to self-improvement or true charity, affirming Emma's mistaken belief that she is already perfect, and lacking the knowledge and mental capacity herself to inspire Emma's more active mind to intellectual attainment. This serves as a reminder that the impulse toward cultivating perfection in others may be unfulfilled, in this case due to Miss Taylor's failure to press Emma to realize an ideal self. Her deficiencies keep the memory of Emma's own mother active for Mr. Knightley, who observes that Emma "inherits her mother's talents"—he speculates that, had Mrs. Woodhouse lived, Emma "must have been under subjection to her" as "the only person able to cope with her."[19] Early in the novel, she establishes Emma's concern to maintain the appearance of perfection for her father, as Emma worries that Mr. Knightley's criticisms will expose "her not being thought perfect by everybody."[20] Mr. Woodhouse *must* find Emma perfect, of course, to sustain his view of himself and his social role—as Goodheart notes, he too is an "imaginist" who struggles to maintain his fantasy, a community secure from change, in which his prominence remains unquestioned.[21] Like Miss Taylor and Mr. Woodhouse, Emma's sister Isabella "could never see a fault in any of them" and "was not a woman of strong understanding or any quickness."[22] Austen makes it plain that those who find Emma perfect are themselves far from reliable judges.

In Jane Fairfax, Emma encounters and heartily rejects the exemplary accomplished young gentlewoman; her better instincts are repeatedly overcome by a gnawing awareness of Jane Fairfax as a rival paragon, one whose superior natural gifts have been improved beyond Emma's by attentive, professional tutelage. Jane's dependence offers Emma the opportunity to cultivate her active familial duty and extend it into the community, thereby widening the perfectionist impulse, but the threat of being supplanted stalls every impulse toward genuine friendship. Emma's worst behavior arises from her need to diminish Jane and raise herself; thus she falls prey to Frank Churchill's misguided gossip about Mr. Dixon and preens when Mr. Weston asks the Box Hill party, "'What two letters of the alphabet are there, that express perfection? . . . M. and A.'"[23]

Emma's belief in her superiority, in her status as a paragon, relies on a steady flow of uncritical adulation that only reiterates her social and economic privilege. Lacking Miss Taylor's daily attentions, Emma selects Harriet, who adds an irresistible deference to a similar lack of understanding. Although Emma decides that Harriet only wants "a little more knowledge and elegance to be quite perfect," she intends not to improve her but to keep her in a permanent orbit of subjection; the determination that follows this initial assessment—"*She* would notice her, she would improve her"— emphasizes Emma's role as the benefactress, whose "kind undertaking" would be "highly becoming her own situation in life, her leisure, and her powers."[24] This is the misplaced form of charity that Emsley describes, noting "the difference between charity as love and charity as image."[25] Emma's unrivaled prominence in Highbury presents a formidable obstacle to self-knowledge.

The only relation she can imagine with less fortunate others is condescension, itself a remnant of feudal social relations predicated on land ownership; it is no mistake that Emma chooses Harriet, the person most remote from landed values, as the object of her charity. Harriet's illegitimacy is not only generally understood and tolerated in Highbury, but the social acceptance she enjoys demonstrates the priority of wealth over morality—she is invited for an extended visit by the respectable Martin family, and Mrs. Goddard, a model of propriety and community improvement (as the educator of future Highbury wives and mothers), introduces her to Emma, who gradually includes her in all social events of significance. The mysterious financial support (as it turns out, a tradesman's profit) that makes Harriet a frequent and welcome customer in the Highbury shops further associates her with goods and commerce, substituting a commercial for a familial identity, financial for moral improvement. Emma's mistakes regarding Harriet take place in a social context where personal good, the goal of perfectionism, is understood chiefly in economic terms.

Harriet's lack of connections particularly suits Emma's plans because, in the absence of fixed class identity, she can imagine Harriet a fit replacement for Miss Taylor, a gentlewoman in appearance and refinement, but lacking dowry and family connections. Shinobu Minma observes that "Emma's assessment of the position of others depends to a great degree on how they satisfy her sense of superiority."[26] This explains why Emma decides Harriet must be a gentleman's daughter, particularly in light of her comment that a successful farmer like Robert Martin is as far above her notice as below it; Emma must raise Harriet imaginatively to mold her in her own image, but not so far as to be above patronage. However, while Emma intends Harriet to endorse her own status as paragon, she makes Harriet into a parody of the gentlewoman, calling further attention to the weakening claims of hierarchy.

Bahktin reminds us that a parody, whether good or bad as a performance, acknowledges the form and style of its canonical original—it is not itself the work but "the *image of a [work]*."[27] Under Emma's tutelage, Harriet attempts to mimic the perfect gentlewoman, but her inadequacies eventually unmask Emma's own flaws, forming the turning point in her self-awareness and moral improvement. Emsley argues that Emma's realization that she is not in love with Frank Churchill is the moral turning point, but while this moment first opens the heroine's ability to consider herself and others analytically, it is Harriet's pretension to marry Mr. Knightley that forcefully alerts Emma to her own moral failings.[28] As a parody of a gentlewoman, Emma's portrait of Harriet raises her visible status in the community by identifying her as a subject worthy of drawing for display in a fine house (i.e., a gentlewoman) and by aligning her socially with the other subjects Emma has attempted, notably Mr. Woodhouse and the John Knightley family. It seems disingenuous on Emma's part to ask Harriet if she has ever had her portrait drawn, but the question refers to a consciousness of commodities at play in the changing social scene; Harriet has means, though she lacks birth, and Emma also regards her beauty as an important asset that, displayed to advantage in the portrait, will help her to marry a gentleman like Mr. Elton or Frank Churchill. The portrait also compares artistic to moral perfection—Emma's artistic skills are limited by her lack of dedication and sensitivity to criticism of flaws in execution, and so are her improvements to Harriet's image, correcting surface flaws as she corrects her manners without any broader social purpose. Perfectionism in this context would require Emma to work earnestly to fulfill her artistic potential and to promote Harriet's self-development toward true gentility; however, the two criticisms of Emma's likeness, deliberate alterations to Harriet's eyes and to her height, point to interior depth and stature—two traits noticeably absent in Harriet's character that are also called out for examination in Emma's. The portrait hollowly conveys the form and style of a gentlewoman, but without Miller's sense of the social purpose of perfectionism, the "fundamental recognition of our susceptibility to influence and our capacities for influencing others" that implicates both awareness of self and of audience for the performance of self.[29] The portrait commands enough importance to be framed in Bond Street, and it returns to a prominent place at Hartfield, "hung over the mantle-piece in the common sitting-room," a location arguably more appropriate for a portrait of Emma herself.[30] If Harriet's image replaces Emma's as the central object on display in the room where the best society of Highbury gathers, it stands to reason that Emma wishes her own work (Harriet's transformation) to be appreciated and commented on, so that it becomes yet another document testifying to her superiority. Emma represents her power to influence perfection in others through the portrait of Harriet, raised above the mantle to the stature of a gentlewoman, one eligible for Mr. Knightley's hand. Although Emma soon learns her own (and Mr. Knightley's) heart, the crisis points to Austen's class analysis, in which clear hierarchal distinctions of the past give way to the rising fortunes of the meritocracy. By remaking Harriet in her own image, Emma threatens to destabilize the inherited basis of social authority, as she realizes while entertaining the possibility of a match between Harriet and Mr. Knightley. Reviewing his past attentions to Harriet at the Crown and at Box Hill, Emma fears his democratic tendencies—his reluctance to order his carriage, his appreciation of Robert Martin and William Larkin, his ability to see beyond class boundaries. Her subsequent reflections show an awareness that the world has changed enough to make such an alliance possible, if not uncontroversial:

> Such an elevation on her side! Such a debasement on his! It was horrible to Emma to think how it must sink him in the general opinion, to foresee the smiles, the sneers, the merriment it would prompt at his expense. . . . And yet it was far, very far from impossible. . . . Was it new for any thing in this world to be unequal, inconsistent, incongruous . . . ?[31]

Emma imagines Mr. Knightley's social humiliation despite Highbury's acceptance of upward mobility and the "unequal, inconsistent, incongruous" society she has unwittingly been promoting through Harriet's ascent. Had Harriet married Frank Churchill and established herself as mistress of Enscombe, it would have been an equally resonant challenge to legitimacy and inheritance, a challenge that Emma does not anticipate when she plans the match. Added to the mortification she experiences after Box Hill, the fear of Mr. Knightley's marriage makes Emma realize that she cares about promoting *his* good, *his* pursuit of perfection, and it consequently forces her to examine his important role in her own moral progress. With the prospect of Harriet supplanting her, Emma's reflections reframe her desire for self-development—she acknowledges the gravity of her arrogance and vanity in the context of Mr. Knightley's moral influence, recalling his "endeavor to improve her" and his "anxiety for her doing right, which no other creature had at all shared."[32] This perfectionist influence is conspicuously missing in the novel's other marriages—Miss Taylor and Mr. Weston, Jane Fairfax and Frank Churchill, Augusta Hawkins and Mr. Elton—but notably present in altered form in Harriet's engagement to Robert Martin, which lies in the "husband as teacher" vein, preserving her from further negative influences while offering her the benefit of her husband's sense.

While Miss Taylor, Jane Fairfax, Augusta Hawkins, and Harriet Smith improve their respective situations through marriage, suggesting the increasing priority of money over birth, the privileged also consolidate power through alliances. Emma may recant the assumption of her own superiority that led her to impose her will on others, but being first with Mr. Knightley also means being first in Highbury society, and "the perfect happiness of the union" can also be imagined in material terms as uniting the two largest estates, at least while Mr. Woodhouse lives.[33] Austen's critique of privilege in *Emma* employs parody to interrogate class constructions; at the very least, Emma's efforts to recast Harriet in her own mold expose her social ignorance and deflate her assumption that class is static and perfection conferred by privilege, without effort. It is certainly possible to imagine future moral challenges for a heroine who glibly declares, "I always deserve the best treatment, because I never put up with any other," and as a crucible dissolving class hierarchy, *Emma* ends by describing the drive for a perfection that could transform social relations as a laborious but worthwhile process.[34]

Notes

1. Jane Austen, "When Winchester Races," in *The Poetry of Jane Austen and the Austen Family*, ed. David Selwyn (Iowa City: University of Iowa Press, 1997), 17.

2. Cassandra Austen, "Letters 95–96, to Fanny Knight, 18 and 19 July 1817," in *Letters of Jane Austen*, ed. Deirdre Le Faye (Oxford: Oxford University Press, 1997), 343–48.

3. Claudia Johnson, "Austen Cults and Cultures," in *The Cambridge Companion to Jane Austen*, ed. Edward Copeland and Juliet McMaster (Cambridge: Cambridge University Press, 1997), 214.

4. James Thompson, "How to Do Things with Jane Austen," *Jane Austen and Co.: Remaking the Past in Contemporary Culture*, ed. Suzanne R. Pucci and James Thompson (Albany: State University of New York Press, 2003), 20.

5. Wayne Booth, *The Rhetoric of Fiction*, 2nd ed. (Chicago: University of Chicago Press, 1983), 265.

6. Jane Austen, *Emma* (Oxford: Oxford University Press, 1995), 3.

7. Rachel Brownstein, *Why Jane Austen?* (New York: Columbia University Press, 2011), 8.

8. Sarah Baxter Emsley, *Jane Austen's Philosophy of the Virtues* (New York: Palgrave, 2005), 129.

9. Katie Halsey, *Jane Austen and her Readers, 1786–1945* (London: Anthem, 2013), 62; and Eugene Goodheart, "*Emma*: Jane Austen's Errant Heroine." *Sewanee Review* 116.4 (Fall 2008): 597.

10. Laura E. Thomason, "The Dilemma of Friendship in Austen's *Emma*," *Eighteenth Century: Theory and Interpretation* 56.2 (Summer 2015): 228.

11. Andrew H. Miller, *Burdens of Perfection: On Ethics and Reading in Nineteenth-Century British Literature* (Ithaca: Cornell University Press, 2008), 3.

12. Austen, *Emma*, 5.

13. Austen, *Emma*, 12.

14. Austen, *Emma*, 13.

15. Austen, *Emma*, 186.

16. Austen, *Emma*, 432.

17. Austen, *Emma*, 429.

18. Austen, *Emma*, 4.

19. Austen, *Emma*, 33.

20. Austen, *Emma*, 9.

21. Goodheart, "Emma," 596.

22. Austen, *Emma*, 84.

23. Austen, *Emma*, 336.

24. Austen, *Emma*, 20.

25. Emsley, *Jane Austen's Philosophy of the Virtues*, 138.

26. Shinobu Minma, "Self-Deception and Superiority Complex: Derangement of Hierarchy in Jane Austen's *Emma*," *Eighteenth-Century Fiction* 14.1 (Oct 2001): 54.

27. M. M. Bahktin, *The Dialogic Imagination: Four Essays*, ed. Michael Holquist, trans. Caryl Emerson and Michael Holquist (Austin: University of Texas Press, 1981), 51.

28. Emsley, *Jane Austen's Philosophy of the Virtues*, 129.

29. Miller, *Burdens of Perfection*, 4.

30. Austen, *Emma*, 62.

31. Austen, *Emma*, 375.

32. Austen, *Emma*, 376.

33. Austen, *Emma*, 440.

34. Austen, *Emma*, 430.

CHAPTER TWELVE

"The Middle Classes at Play"

Austen and Marx Go to Hollywood

CHARLES BANE

As the title of this series indicates, Jane Austen (1775–1817) is a great author. She is not only great in the sense that she was a best-selling writer in her own time, but also great in the sense that she has remained a best-selling writer ever since. Though this can be said of many great authors including Nathaniel Hawthorne, Ernest Hemingway, and Edith Wharton, these other writers remain current mainly through their inclusion in academic settings in that they continue to be taught and written about. Austen, on the other hand, often finds her way into the hands of general readers. And we don't just read her books; we are interested in Austen herself as writer, her readers, and her place in popular culture. For proof, consider such films as *Becoming Jane* (2007) based on the 2003 book *Becoming Jane Austen* by Jon Hunter Spence, *The Jane Austen Book Club* (2007) based on the 2004 novel by Karen Joy Fowler, and the upcoming *Pride and Prejudice and Zombies* (2016), based on the 2009 novel by Seth Grahame-Smith (and Jane Austen). But perhaps the best indicator of her continued popularity is not these spin-offs or the numerous editions of her novels published each year, but the fact that each generation produces new film adaptations of those novels. These adaptations range from attempts to capture the authentic time and place of Austen and her characters, *Sense and Sensibility* (1995), to complete reappropriations of her works to modern times, *Clueless* (1995), based on Austen's 1815 novel *Emma*.

Though these adaptations could simply be attempts to cash in on Austen's continued popularity, they often speak to how we read Austen and understand her relevance in our own times. It is for this reason that adaptations of her novels are so often successful and praised by both critics and audiences as "faithful" representations of Austen's works—not because they are big budget productions of our favorite love stories, but because they show the depth and continued relevance of Austen. This essay will focus on one of the most enduring adaptations of Austen's 1813 novel *Pride and Prejudice*: the 1940 version directed by Robert Z. Leonard with Greer Garson and Laurence Olivier as Elizabeth Bennet and Mr. Darcy. But first, a brief overview of adaptation criticism is in order.

George Bluestone and Fidelity Criticism

As its name suggests, "fidelity" criticism focuses on the faithfulness of an adaptation to its source material. Critics who adhere to this principle judge a film and measure its value against the novel on which it is based in hopes of determining the degree of "faithfulness" to the source text and, therefore, the success of the film in question. Brian McFarlane provides the most complete definition to date:

> Fidelity criticism depends on a notion of the text as having and rendering up to the (intelligent) reader a single, correct "meaning" which the filmmaker has either adhered to or in some sense violated or tampered with. There will often be a distinction between being faithful to the "letter," an approach which the more sophisticated writer may suggest is no way to ensure a "successful" adaptation, and to the "spirit" or "essence" of the work. The latter is of course very much more difficult to determine.[1]

In short, a film adaption is considered successful if it adheres to the source texts as closely as possible (the "letter") without making any major alterations to the story ("the spirit").

One of the first and most influential adaptation scholars is film critic and author George Bluestone, whose *Novels into Film* (1957) is widely accepted as the seminal text in the canon of film adaptation criticism. Bluestone's book is both theoretical and practical—divided into two sections, one covers "The Limits of the Novel and the Limits of the Film," while the other analyzes six adaptations, including Leonard's *Pride and Prejudice* (1940). In his introductory essay, Bluestone argues that there are so many crucial formal differences between the two media that a perfect correlation between novels and their adaptations is simply not possible. In fact, he claims that only in the script phase—a medium of words—do films resemble novels. Since a perfect correlation is not possible, film adaptations can only hope to provide a "kind of paraphrase" in which characters and incidents have "somehow detached themselves from language and, like the heroes of folk legends, have achieved a mythic life of their own."[2] As a result, the filmmaker does not translate the novel for the screen; rather, he or she becomes the author of a new work. Because of statements like these, Bluestone has become the champion of those who want to move completely away from fidelity criticism.

Throughout his study, Bluestone questions fidelity critics, claiming that they are inconsistent in their criticism. In general, he argues that fidelity critics only complain if they do not like the film in question. If a film is well received and "succeeds on its own merits," then the "question of 'faithfulness' is given hardly any thought" and the film "ceases to be problematic."[3] Audiences, according to Bluestone, will likewise accept films that deviate from their source as long as the film is enjoyable. So, if a film is successful—either financially, critically, or both—questions of fidelity disappear on "the assumption that [the filmmakers] have mysteriously captured the 'spirit' of the book."[4] Bluestone criticizes the equating of "faithful" and "unfaithful" with "successful" and "unsuccessful" by calling it a "stubbornly casual, persistently uncritical approach" to the study of film adaptation.[5] But even Bluestone, who argued for the autonomy of novels and films and claimed that any comparison is "fruitless" since in "the last analysis each . . . is characterized by unique and specific properties," was not immune to questions of fidelity.[6] Bluestone, too, slips into issues of fidelity throughout his "reading" of *Pride and Prejudice* (1940).

Pride and Prejudice According to Bluestone

Bluestone attributes the success of Leonard's *Pride and Prejudice* (1940) to the fact that Austen's novel "possesses the essential ingredients of a movie script" by meeting the requirements of "Hollywood's stock conventions."[7] The novel follows the "shopworn formula of boy meets girl; boy loses girl; boy gets girl."[8] In addition, it provides an "individual solution to general problems" and, above all, "the story has a happy ending."[9] Furthermore, as detailed as Austen is in developing the "psychological timbre of her characters," the "absence of minute physical detail" in her style allowed Leonard to make his own decisions regarding the physical appearance of the characters and setting.[10] In fact, Bluestone further attributes Leonard's ability to bring *Pride and Prejudice* to the screen to Austen's "lack of particularity, absence of metaphorical language, omniscient point of view, [and] dependency of dialogue to reveal character."[11] In Austen's defense, her novels are not as shallow as the above descriptions would make them appear. Her great talent lies in the theme of irony that pervades all of her works, and Bluestone makes this fact clear, describing Austen's ability "to range one set of principles against another . . . the polarities . . . the interpenetration of opposites . . . the poles attracting each other toward a more or less agreeable center."[12] The very titles of Austen's novels bear this statement out: *Persuasion*, *Sense and Sensibility*, and, of course, *Pride and Prejudice*. *Pride and Prejudice* is successful *as a film* because it plays out this theme on screen. Bluestone describes the plot of the novel in terms of a great dance:

> The lovers proceed through a series of misunderstandings and revelations which culminate in the two central climaxes of the book—Elizabeth's rejection of Darcy, completing the initial movement of the lovers away from each other; and Elizabeth's acceptance of Darcy, completing the final movement of the lovers toward each other. . . . To anyone thinking of the book in cinematic terms, the word "movement" is inevitably arresting [and] corresponds exactly to the movements and rhythms of a dance, movements and rhythms which, I suggest, have been caught by the film.[13]

To prove his point, Bluestone focuses on the film's dance sequence at the Assembly Ball in which "all the dramatic relationships are enunciated in terms of dance relationships."[14] I will not go into Bluestone's detailed shot-by-shot analysis of the sequence, but I agree that the sequence does capture the "movements and rhythms" of the characters throughout the novel as the dancers move "toward and away from each other, exchanging partners . . . in a kind of party prattle [none] takes very seriously."[15] This sequence is an example of what films can do that novels cannot: provide simultaneous action. Novelists must alternate dialogue with narrative description, but film can dispense with narrative description since the images being described in the book are visually realized. Furthermore, since the sequence stands for the book as a whole, dialogue and incidents can be moved from various parts of the novel and incorporated into a single scene in order to establish continuity. As Bluestone points out, the film's Assembly Ball scene draws on material from chapters 3, 10, 15, and 16 of the novel. The effect of "combining snippets" from four of the first sixteen chapters creates "unity of place" and "compresses the chief plot points" so that the viewer becomes an "omni-scient observer . . . roving from couple to couple, seeing them now from one point of view, now from another."[16] In the end, all of the "dramatic and psychological relationship[s] . . . in the novel's opening events" are realized in the dance sequence in which "choreography becomes an exact analogue of the social game."[17]

The film does have a few additions to the novel, but Bluestone defends these additions by arguing that they are not "mere appendages" but "credible . . . probabilities of Jane Austen's world."[18] He points to the film's opening Meryton sequence to prove his point. Though this long sequence does not appear in the book, it is "a transposition of incidents" from various places in the novel.[19] In fact, much of the dialogue in the opening sequence is lifted from dialogue that appears throughout Austen's novel. The carriage race that ends the opening sequence has, for Bluestone, "more than a merely capri-cious function . . . [since] the visual competition becomes the exact forecast of what is to come."[20] The carriage race is a visual metaphor for the social contest between the Bennets and the Lucases. When Charlotte marries Col-lins, it appears that the Lucases have the upper hand; when Jane and Eliza-beth agree to marry Bingley and Darcy, the Bennets emerge as the social victors.[21] Bluestone argues that this scene, as well as the other additions, deletions, transpositions, and alterations of the filmmakers are minor and only help to advance the primary story line of the novel by allowing the audience "to 'see' what is not [in the novel]" and that, in the final analysis, the film's changes have "a rightness which seems wholly appropriate to Jane Austen's intentions."[22]

Perhaps it is this ability to "see" what is not in the novel while still attempting to adhere to Austen's intentions that has made *Pride and Prejudice* one of the most popular films among fidelity critics. In fact, this adaptation is turned to again and again as an example of a successful, faithful adaptation. In his analysis of *Pride and Prejudice*, Bluestone argues that in "rendering the quality of Jane Austen's intentions, in finding cinematic equivalents for what Jane Austen, by choice, merely implied, the film-makers successfully rethink the material in terms of their own medium. The screen writers, reading closely . . . divine the meaning of Jane Austen's aristocratic dance."[23] So, Bluestone is both defending the right of filmmakers to alter details as long as those details are "equivalent" to the original author's "intentions." In short, he is arguing that films can still practice fidelity to the source text even if they aren't completely faithful. One issue with this approach is that some alterations are not simple "cinematic equivalents" but actually change the

"intention" of Austen's novel as seen in the Meryton Ball sequence in Leonard's 1940 adaptation.

Pride and Prejudice According to Marx

Bluestone points out that although Leonard's adaptation is faithful, there are
"several significant changes" that even the most "casual reader of Jane Austen's novel will observe."[24] But again, Bluestone defends these changes
because they do not "alter any of the essential meanings in the original."
Altered or additional dialogue in the film "bears an unusual ring of probability . . . [and] represents the kind of thing which Jane Austen *might* have
said."[25] This is an interesting stance to take considering that one of the
altered lines carried a powerful political punch in an important time in film
history.

In the novel, the Bennet sisters meet Bingley and Darcy at the Meryton
Ball. When Darcy, "the proudest, most disagreeable man in the world,"
refuses to dance with any of the young ladies, Bingley attempts to persuade
him to dance with Elizabeth.[26] Darcy replies that though she is "tolerable,"
she is not "handsome enough" to tempt him, and furthermore he is "in no
humour at present to give consequence to *young ladies* who are slighted by
other men."[27] In the film, this scene remains intact except that Darcy's line
as delivered by Laurence Olivier is "Yes, she looks tolerable enough, but I am
in no humor tonight to give consequence to *the middle classes* at play."[28]
This alteration is anything but slight. Although Bluestone acknowledges this
alteration, he states that this line, along with others, has been altered "to
make [it] more pertinent."[29] More pertinent to what? There is a great chance
that more was going on in this alteration than Bluestone is willing to admit
and that the line is not simply a "reasonable equivalent."[30] The term "middle
class" had a different connotation in 1940 than it would have had for Austen.
Though the term dates back to at least the mid-1700s, during Austen's time
it generally referred to the intermediate bourgeois class between the nobility
and the peasantry.[31] While the nobility were the landowners and the peasantry made their living working the land for the nobles, the middle-class
bourgeois were those who made their living from the manufacture and sale
of merchandise, sometimes amassing enough wealth to rival the nobility. In
the world of the novel, the Bennets and the Lucases actually belong to the
lower gentry, a lower aristocratic class that owns its own land. Though they
hold no titles of nobility, the land ownership provides them with enough
annual income to eliminate the need to work for a living. Upper levels of

the clergy are also considered gentry, which is why Mr. Collins, as both a clergyman and heir to his estate, is a "suitable" marriage for the Bennets' and Lucases' daughters.

However, in a post-Marx world, the term "middle class" more often refers to the working class, not major industrialists or those who have inherited wealth. This concept puts the middle class of 1940 more in line with the peasantry of Austen's day. The Darcy of the novel sees Elizabeth simply as a young lady who has been slighted by another man, but the Darcy of the film sees her as part of the middle class who is *playing* at being upper class. This reference to separate classes, along with the suggestion that the lower of the classes is attempting to rise up, hints at class struggle, a touchy subject in early mid-twentieth century America when the fear of Communist infiltration and socialism was beginning to take hold.

The 1940 film adaptation of *Pride and Prejudice* was released just seven years before the House Un-American Activities Committee (HUAC) blacklisted more than three hundred Hollywood professionals. Though a committee to investigate subversive acts had been established in 1919 just after World War I, in 1938 Congress formed HUAC to investigate U.S. citizens with ties to Germany's Nazi party. By 1945, HUAC had changed the focus of its investigation to individuals and organizations suspected of having ties to communism, a political ideology many believed threatened American democracy. This period, from the mid-1940s to the late 1950s, is often termed "McCarthyism" because of its association with Senator Joseph McCarthy. As a senator, McCarthy had no direct involvement with HUAC but was chair of the Senate's Permanent Subcommittee on Investigations. He was such a powerful presence during the Red Scare, he is often mistakenly believed to have been in charge of the HUAC hearings. In 1947, a series of hearings was held to consider allegations of communist propaganda and influence in Hollywood. These hearings led to the conviction of the "Hollywood Ten," screenwriters and directors who refused to "name names" of alleged communists within the movie community. Eventually, film studios blacklisted more than three hundred suspected subversives. Were the creators of *Pride and Prejudice* some of the "subversives" that Senator McCarthy and HUAC were trying to silence? Unfortunately, we cannot look at the list because the majority of the records of the proceedings were ordered sealed until 2026. Bluestone makes no direct reference to the blacklist, but he does question the reputation of the film by pointing out that though the film's stars went on to have successful careers, the talent behind the script and the camera were not so fortunate. Bluestone states that director Robert Z. Leonard did "little serious work" after *Pride and Prejudice*.[32] In Leonard's defense, the fifty-one-year-old filmmaker had directed an astonishing 135 films when he began work on *Pride and Prejudice*. As for screenwriter Jane Murfin, it is true that she was "rarely heard from" again.[33] Whether or not she was on the Hollywood blacklist is uncertain, but she did begin to write screenplays under a pseudonym, a common practice for writers who had been black-listed.[34] In 2001, the ruling that the records be sealed was overturned, and the public was allowed access to the documents, but access is governed by Rule 7 of the House of Representatives, which establishes the eligibility criteria for viewing noncurrent, permanent records of the House.[35] This rule creates a Kafkaesque nightmare of bureaucracy seemingly intended to deter anyone in the public from actually accessing the records. As such, we will have to wait until 2026 to see if Murfin was on the list.

Regardless of what is revealed about the screenwriter when the documents are opened, the 1940 film version of Austen's novel is not the simple "boy meets girl story" that Bluestone claims the novel is. The film is a story of haves and have nots, of distinct social classes who—depending on their class—try either to raise themselves to a higher class or to keep the lower classes out. Darcy, whom Austen describes as being "proud" and "above his company" and having "a most forbidding, disagreeable countenance," could very well represent the bourgeoisie.[36] After all, he does make "ten thousand a year."[37] By the same token, the competition between the Bennets and Lucases to be the first to marry off their daughters could represent the attempts of the proletariat to achieve political power, an attempt that, according to Marx, "is continually being upset again by the competition between the workers themselves."[38] Though the Bennets and Lucases are not "workers" in the sense that Marx intended, they do represent class struggle, or at least they do in the film version. Audiences in 1940, or now for that matter, may not understand the differences between the aristocracy, gentry, and peasantry, but they knew what "middle class" meant to them. The line change informs and, in fact, influences how the audience views the film.

Whether or not a Marxist reading of Austen is what Leonard and Murfin intended in their adaptation is irrelevant. What is relevant is that the film-makers have done something with the text that allows the viewer to raise questions about the text and to read it outside of the constraints of Austen's time and place. As stated earlier, "fidelity" criticism focuses on the faithful-ness of a film adaptation to its original source. For George Bluestone, this means finding "cinematic equivalents" for an author's implied intentions. For Bluestone, the screenwriters of the 1940 film version of *Pride and Preju-*

dice have by "reading closely . . . divine[d] the meaning of Jane Austen's aristocratic dance." But 1940 America is not 1813 England. Leonard and Murfin have not simply come up with cinematic equivalents that lead to a single *intended* reading that Bluestone seems to think is there, but a *possible* reading that opens the text up to other, broader interpretations. Regardless of what the filmmakers meant by the alteration, the line does suggest a Marxist view of class and conveys a snobbery that extends beyond the novel's comment about "young ladies." If Austen wrote simple "boy meets girl" love stories, her novels may not have endured in the way that they have. But if we see Austen as a writer of ironic novels that push the socially constructed boundaries of her time, whether those boundaries are dictated by class, gender, or race, we see her novels not only as texts but also as cultural constructs that have a life outside of the bound pages of literary history. The 1940 film adaptation allows us to do this with the altering of one line. And, as Bluestone suggests, the line "bears an unusual ring of probability . . . [and] represents the kind of thing which Jane Austen *might* have said." By not constricting Austen's text, and by allowing changes through adaptation, the text can speak to other times and places. That Austen's texts can both withstand and support alteration suggests she is not simply a popular author of nineteenth-century love stories, but a great author for all times.

Notes

1. Brian McFarlane, *Novel to Film: An Introduction to the Theory of Adaptation* (Oxford: Clarendon, 1996), 8.

2. George Bluestone, *Novels into Film: The Metamorphosis of Fiction into Cinema* (Berkeley: University of California Press, 1957), 62.

3. Bluestone, *Novels into Film*, 114.

4. Bluestone, *Novels into Film*, 114.

5. Bluestone, *Novels into Film*, 114.

6. Bluestone, *Novels into Film*, 6.

7. Bluestone, *Novels into Film*, 117.

8. Bluestone, *Novels into Film*, 144.

9. Bluestone, *Novels into Film*, 144.

10. Bluestone, *Novels into Film*, 118.

11. Bluestone, *Novels into Film*, 118.

12. Bluestone, *Novels into Film*, 117.

13. Bluestone, *Novels into Film*, 124, 126.

14. Bluestone, *Novels into Film*, 127.

15. Bluestone, *Novels into Film*, 127.

16. Bluestone, *Novels into Film*, 131.

17. Bluestone, *Novels into Film*, 132.

18. Bluestone, *Novels into Film*, 137.

19. Bluestone, *Novels into Film*, 137.

20. Bluestone, *Novels into Film*, 137.

21. Interestingly, Joe Wright's 2005 film version, based on Deborah Moggach's (and an uncredited Emma Thompson's) screenplay, completely ignores the "social contest" between the Lucases and the Bennets. In fact, Mr. Collins, as played by Tom Hollander, is used for comic relief, while Charlotte Lucas, as played by Claudie Blakley, is a minor character.

22. Bluestone, *Novels into Film*, 138–39.

23. Bluestone, *Novels into Film*, 136.

24. Bluestone, *Novels into Film*, 130.

25. Bluestone, *Novels into Film*, 130.

26. Jane Austen, *Pride and Prejudice* (New York: Penguin, 2002), 58.

27. Austen, *Pride and Prejudice*, 59.

28. *Pride and Prejudice*, directed by Robert Z. Leonard (1940; United States: MGM), DVD.

29. Bluestone, *Novels into Film*, 130.

30. Bluestone, *Novels into Film*, 131.

31. According to the *Oxford English Dictionary*, the first known recorded use of the term "middle class" is in a 1745 pamphlet by James Bradshaw titled *Scheme to Prevent Running Irish Wools to France*.

32. Bluestone, *Novels into Film*, 145.

33. Bluestone, *Novels into Film*, 145.

34. It is also possible that Murfin wrote under a pseudonym because of the fact that it was often difficult for female screenwriters to see their work to production. The fact that she chose a male pseudonym, "Alan Langdon Martin," lends credence to this argument, but we do not know for certain.

35. "Office of the Clerk," pdf, House of Representatives Committee on Rules, https://rules.house.gov/resources.

36. Austen, *Pride and Prejudice*, 58.

37. Austen, *Pride and Prejudice*, 58.

38. Karl Marx and Friedrich Engels, *The Communist Manifesto* (New York: Monthly Review, 1964).

PART IV

CONCEPTS AND CLARIFICATIONS

CHAPTER THIRTEEN

Do You Want to Know a Secret?

The Immorality and Morality of Secrets and the Subversive Jane Austen

ELIZABETH OLSON AND CHARLES TALIAFERRO

Jane Austen knows well the power of a secret. Although it is not difficult to observe that plot in general depends on secrets—the reader knows something the characters don't, one character knows something other characters don't, neither reader nor characters know a secret that is eventually revealed by the author, and so on—Jane Austen is remarkable for the variety of ways she represents secrets in her work and in the ways secrets not only propel plot, but represent a moral hazard . . . or a virtue.

What Are Secrets and Why Do We Find Them Fascinating?

Before we are able to examine the moral role played by secrets, though, Austen has to establish their importance and has to make them interesting for us. Here, Austen shows herself to be an astute judge of human character, depicting how people are drawn to the excitement of the unknown, drawn to having *and* discovering secrets. When in *Sense and Sensibility* Mrs. Jennings says, "Come, come, we shall have no secrets between friends," she is not only admonishing against the keeping of secrets; she is expressing the near-universal wish to be *in on* the secret. To some extent, then, shared secrets can be a way of establishing bonds and securing friendships in an exclusive fashion. Arguably, part of the nature of good friendships is that we give our friends access to truths about us that we might be reluctant to make public. Austen knows this and skillfully weaves secrets into her narratives so that we as reader are hooked and, in a sense, brought into a kind of friendship with the author.

What counts as a secret? Consider what we think is a promising but incomplete analysis from Sissela Bok in her important book *Secrets: On the Ethics of Concealment and Revelation*:

> Anything can be a secret so long as it is intentionally kept hidden. It may be shared with no one, or confided on condition that it go no further. . . . To keep a secret from someone is to block information about it or evidence of it from reaching that person, and to do so intentionally; to prevent him from learning it, and thus from possessing it, making use of it, or revealing it.[1]

We will not quibble about the possibility of someone coming to have a secret unintentionally or accidentally; for while we believe that this can occur, these would not reflect clear, central cases of what is a secret. Our worry instead is that there seems to be an important difference between having a secret and being modest or decorous or bashful. Someone may not disclose the fact that she dislikes zombie films or has a phobia about bats or is romantically excited by a flight attendant, yet while she may seek to block this information or evidence of these facts, they are not so much secrets as they are facts about persons that others have no right or expectation to know. Consider an analogy with wearing clothes. Perhaps in a nudist colony, someone's wearing clothes might be considered a peculiar covering up of one's body, but ordinarily clothing is not a matter of keeping one's naked body a kind of concealed secret. We propose, then, an amendment to Bok's definition to make explicit that secrets involve the concealing or blocking of evidence of some fact that would otherwise (in the normal conventions and practices at issue) be public. Consider, then:

> Some fact (e.g. one's engagement to be married or one's intent to elope with someone and use this to extract money) is a secret when, in the conventions and practices of the time, it would normally be publicly known or conventionally discoverable (e.g. by asking whether someone is engaged or asking someone about their real intentions), and yet a person or people conceal public awareness of this fact, intentionally blocking information about it or engaging in deception to prevent its discovery or revelation.

With this definition in place, and noting how secrets can be used as one aspect of forging friendships, we should also note the ways in which secrets can cover up what might otherwise be dangerous vices or be used for good. These will be unpacked in Austen's novels. But let us take note here of Thomas Hardy's observation about how the lack of concealment of our true feelings might present us with a ghastly world.

> If all hearts were open and all desires known—as they would be if people showed their souls—how many gapings, sighings, clenched fists, knotted brows, broad grins, and red eyes would we see in the market place![2]

We add, only, that these vices are only secrets insofar as they are the kinds of traits and dispositions that it is conventional or expected that we disclose. An interesting borderline case that addresses Hardy's rather grim portrait of the marketplace would be if you asked the butcher, "What do you think of the lord of the manor?" and he answered, "Oh, he is a fine gentleman" when in reality the butcher loathes the lord and would butcher him if he could get away with it. In this case, we might naturally say that the butcher is keeping his loathing a secret because we might not expect full disclosure, but still we would not expect such a total, radical disassemble or disingenuous response.

We believe that the case for our definition of a secret is supported by a very interesting, potentially borderline case of where we think Emma is guilty of impropriety and the vice of humiliation and self-promotion whereas some readers might think of it as a case in which Emma has a secret she should have concealed. Consider, then, the incident in which Emma divulges her lack of respect for Miss Bates. Is this a case in which Emma has a legitimate attitude toward Miss Bates but should have kept it a secret, perhaps sharing it only with Mr. Knightley? We do not think so; we suggest, instead, that the incident reveals Emma being doubly wrong: she is wrong on the level of her feelings (whether disclosed or not) and she is wrong in terms of breaking the conventions and expectations of her society in which persons who are privileged do not speak haughtily of those less privileged.

In the dialogue that follows, what becomes clear is that it is Emma's attitude as well as its disclosure that are the problems. Here, through Mr. Knightley, Austen is commenting on the ways the powerful or aristocratic are wrong (and cruel) in their condescension toward the poor. It is the poor, the dispossessed, and those who are not privileged who should be not just protected from humiliating disapproval, but who merit the compassion of those better off economically and socially. Emma is here criticized for her lack of feelings, not just her inappropriate disclosure.

> "How could you be so unfeeling to Miss Bates? How could you be so insolent in your wit to a woman of her character, age, and situation?"
>
> "Oh!," cried Emma, "I know there is not a better creature in the world, but you must allow, that what is good and what is ridiculous are most unfortunately blended in her."
>
> "They are blended," said he. "I acknowledge, and, were she prosperous, I could allow much for the occasional prevalence of the ridiculous over the good. Were she a woman of fortune, I would leave every harmless absurdity to take its chance, I would not quarrel with you for any liberties of manner. Were she your equal in situation—but Emma, consider how far this is from being the case. She is poor, she has sunk from the comforts she was born to . . . her situation should secure your compassion! It was badly done, indeed! You, whom she had known from an infant, whom she had seen grow up from a period when her notice was an honour, to have you now, in thoughtless spirits, and the pride of the moment, laugh at her, humble her—and before her niece, too—and before others, many of whom (certainly some,) would be entirely guided by your treatment of her.—This is not pleasant to you, Emma—and it is very far from pleasant to me; but I must, I will,—I will tell you truths while I can."[3]

We find this rebuke not a rebuke that Emma should keep her contempt a secret; rather, it is a rebuke that she should not have such contempt. More importantly, though, in support of our definition, if Emma had kept her contempt to herself and her peers, this still would not have been a secret because it was not part of the customs and conventions of her society that Emma would make such a disclosure.

With these preliminary observations in place, let us explore the secrets in Jane Austen's work.

The Craft and Ethics of Secrets

Northanger Abbey, the book Austen wrote first but which was only published posthumously, has a markedly different tone than her later work, as she in essence satirizes the popular gothic novels of her time. The use of secrets in *Northanger Abbey* is less subtle than in her later work, but even here, Austen establishes the secret as something we must figure out. We meet Catherine, who has an almost breathless sense of the excitement of a secret. Catherine fantasizes that the abbey will contain great secrets. It does not, but the description of the potential secret is witty, drawing on conventional expectations of the genre and playing against type at the same time:

> "What! Not when Dorothy has given you to understand that there is a secret subterraneous communication between your apartment and the chapel of St. Anthony, scarcely two miles off? Could you shrink from so simple an adventure? No, no, you will proceed into this small vaulted room, and through this into several others, without perceiving anything very remarkable in either. In one perhaps there may be a dagger, in another a few drops of blood, and in a third the remains of some instrument of torture; but there being nothing in all this out of the common way, and your lamp being nearly exhausted, you will return towards your own apartment. In repassing through the small vaulted room, however, your eyes will be attracted towards a large, old-fashioned cabinet of ebony and gold, which, though narrowly examining the furniture before, you had passed unnoticed. Impelled by an irresistible presentiment, you will eagerly advance to it, unlock its folding doors, and search into every drawer—but for some time without discovering anything of importance—perhaps nothing but a considerable hoard of diamonds. At last, however, by touching a secret spring, an inner compartment will open—a roll of paper appears—you seize it—it contains many sheets of manuscript—you hasten with the precious treasure into your own chamber, but scarcely have you been able to decipher 'Oh! Thou—whomsoever thou mayst be, into whose hands these memoirs of the wretched Matilda may fall'—when your lamp suddenly expires in the socket, and leaves you in total darkness."[4]

In Austen's other novels, we continue to see the liberal use of secrets, and Austen is masterful at drawing us in and making us realize their importance. The frequent secret engagements are obvious in their importance (e.g., Jane and Frank in *Emma*, Fanny and Edward in *Sense and Sensibility*, etc.), but the use of secrets to highlight morality or character flaws and virtues is more subtle and usually more interesting than the secret engagement.

Austen knows that when people are told not to do something, it becomes almost a compulsion to do that very thing. So we are told, and shown, not to keep secrets. This seems a straightforward piece of advice; Austen is simply stating obvious morality for the "good" person. Secrets (e.g., secret engagements, deceptive characters, and illegitimate children) disrupt the social order, thwart happiness, and cause real harm. Secrets introduce a very real element of danger and chaos, and they are a corrosive influence in the lives of Austen's characters. We review these dangers and then consider the ways in which some secrets may be honorable, though in the work of Austen these are mostly cases of when some base secret is either exposed or some wrong is rectified. How can we tell the difference? We suggest that assessing the value (that is, the merit or demerit) of secrets takes place from the standpoint of the reliable narrator. Secrets are permissible from the standpoint of an impartial judge who knows all the relevant facts and who has an affective appreciation of the points of view of all involved parties. We would be entitled to keep a secret from you if it would be deemed acceptable from the standpoint of an authoritative, affective narrator. As it turns out, this is precisely the point of view that Austen offers us in her novels, putting her readers in a position to judge the value of the secrets of the different characters. In what follows, we illustrate this from different angles.[5]

One stark illustration of the danger and chaos caused by secrets is Wickham and Lydia's secret elopement in *Pride and Prejudice*. We can easily read it as the thoughtless act of a silly girl and a dissolute man. In reality, though, such a rash action represents the potential to destroy the Bennet family's economic and social standing and leaves the other four Bennet girls with severely reduced prospects for marriage and, well, food and shelter—their very survival. With marriage as the overwhelmingly primary avenue to economic stability for women, "reduced prospects" were not merely theoretical. No suitor of any economic substance would make an attachment to such a family with one sister so morally compromised. The secret Lydia and Wickham share has the power to irreparably damage the futures of the Bennet family. As readers, we rightly see this concealment to be cruel and wrong.

Similarly, Colonel Brandon's secrecy in *Sense and Sensibility* regarding Willoughby's immoral behavior provides another example of the harm caused by secrets. Marianne is devastated after being jilted by Willoughby, whom she had adored and idolized as her soulmate. Had she known that he impregnated and then abandoned a woman and infant, she would surely not have come so close to ridicule and serious damage to herself. In Austen's work, keeping secrets—and living in such a way that secrets must be kept—is shown to be wrong and should be avoided.

While keeping secrets often has destructive consequences, it is Austen's genius to subvert this societal norm and show us why secrets can sometimes actually be the vehicle for a moral good. Even as she writes at length about the evils of keeping secrets, Austen clearly illustrates how secrets create and cement bonds between friends and lovers, how they provide a way to do good without being self-aggrandizing, and how keeping secrets can maintain order in society and protect the feelings of others. It is our contention that by showing her readers the way secrets function in these different ways, Austen provides us with the tools to differentiate between good and bad secrets.

Secrets in Austen, as in most domestic novels, are a major way of establishing a bond between people, whether relatives, friends, lovers, or even adversaries. (They are also a significant plot device, and Austen uses them liberally to move her stories along, but that is a topic for a different essay.) Lucy Steele, for example, forges a bond with a somewhat reluctant Elinor Dashwood in *Sense and Sensibility* when she confesses her secret engagement to Edward Ferrars. Elinor feels honor-bound to keep the secret, and it creates an instant relationship between the two women, closer than Elinor would have chosen otherwise. We thus learn of Elinor's integrity and Lucy's duplicitous nature.

It is clear that the relationship between Elinor and Marianne in the novel would have been stronger, but very different, had Elinor shared her secrets with Marianne. She would not have been *giving up* having a secret, but it would have been a shared secret, one that indicated trust of her sister and esteem of Marianne's judgment. A mutual knowledge of Elinor's hopes regarding Edward—and an observation of Elinor's continued forbearance and calm—could well have guided Marianne's behavior, and would perhaps have helped her avoid further humiliation at the hands of Willoughby in London:

"How long has [Edward's engagement] been known to you, Elinor? Has he written to you?"

"I have known it these four months. When Lucy first came to Barton Park last November, she told me in confidence of her engagement."

At these words, Marianne's eyes expressed the astonishment which her lips could not utter. After a pause of wonder, she exclaimed "Four months! Have you known of this four months? . . . while attending to me in all my misery [since being abandoned by Willoughby], has this been in your heart . . . So calm! So cheerful!—how have you been supported?"

"Yes. But I did not love only him—and while the comfort of others was dear to me, I was glad to spare them from knowing how much I felt . . . I acquit Edward of all essential misconduct. I wish him very happy; and I am so sure of his always doing his duty, that though now he may harbor some regret, in the end, he must become so . . . time and habit will teach him to forget that he ever thought another superior to [Lucy]."

"If such is your way of thinking," said Marianne, "if the loss of what is most valued is so easily to be made up by something else, your resolution, your self-command, are, perhaps a little less to be wondered at."

"I understand you. You do not suppose that I have ever felt much . . . If I had not been bound to silence, perhaps nothing could have kept me entirely—not even what I owed to my dearest friends—from openly shewing that I was very unhappy . . . I have had [Lucy's] hopes and exultation to listen to again and again.—I have known myself to be divided from Edward for ever. . . ."

Marianne was quite subdued. "Oh, Elinor," she cried, "You have made me hate myself forever. How barbarous have I been to you!"[6]

In this dialogue one can observe the painful way in which one can look back at secrets and judge, from a distance, whether or not they were justified.

Austen offers the affective, impartial reader a vantage point for seeing when secrets can also play a role in redemption and setting things right without drawing attention to oneself. This desire for modesty and humility are admirable qualities in Austen's characters. Darcy in *Pride and Prejudice* is perhaps the most famous example of how secrecy can be a morally good thing in this way. When he pays to ensure that Wickham and Lydia have married and will be set up with a commission in the army, Darcy does so secretly, avoiding self-aggrandizement and saving Lydia's—and Elizabeth's—reputation. He is able to rectify what he believes to be a wrong on his part, namely his previous secrecy regarding Wickham's venal nature which was the cause of the whole disastrous elopement.

Secrets in Austen are more complicated than we are initially led to believe. Austen first masterfully gets us to care about her characters' secrets, then takes the societal and seemingly sensible position against keeping secrets, illustrating their potential to harm and corrode morality and social order. One reason Austen remains fresh to us now, though, is her intelligence in showing the nuances of the secret and the potential good that can come from keeping things to oneself. Through the actions of her characters, we see that keeping secrets is more complex than just concluding secrets are "bad." Secrets can, in fact, be useful and important as a vehicle for moral good in Austen's world, and it is our delight to discover this. Reading her novels can itself be an instructive moral exercise in developing the skills at recognizing when secrets may be good or bad, merciful or cruel. We also believe that in pointing out that the case of Emma and Miss Bates is not a matter of Emma making the mistake of not keeping secret something she should have, we can appreciate when Austen is condemning the haughtiness of the upper class. She is not, in that case, cautioning her character and readers that they should keep their contempt quiet; she is rather exposing how such contempt is simply wrong and reprehensible.[7]

Notes

1. Sissela Bok, *Secrets: On the Ethics of Concealment and Revelation* (New York: Pantheon, 1982), 5.

2. Thomas Hardy, *The Later Years of Thomas Hardy*, ed. F. E. Hardy (Cambridge: Cambridge University Press, 2011), 133.

3. Jane Austen, *Emma* (London: Richard Bentley & Son, 1886), 323.

4. Jane Austen, *Northanger Abbey* (London: Little, Brown, & Company, 1907), 191–92.

5. This is a version of what is called the ideal observer theory, according to which the ideal conditions for moral judgments consist of those that would be made by an observer who is all-knowing of the relevant facts, impartial, and affectively aware of the points of view of all involved parties. Taliaferro has defended this account in various places, most recently in *Environmental Ethics: Contemporary Prospectives* (New York: Linus Pulications, 2016).

6. Jane Austen, *Sense and Sensibility* (London: Cassell, 1908), 210–13.

7. Our thanks to Fiona Macauley and to Alexander Quanbeck, as well as to fellow contributors to this book, for assistance on this chapter.

~

CHAPTER FOURTEEN

Persuasion, Influence, and Overpersuasion

KEITH DROMM AND HEATHER SALTER

Changeability in one's tastes, enjoyments, or affections—commonly called fickleness—is widely regarded as a character fault. We probably condemn it because it makes predictions about the fickle person's behavior so difficult. For instance, it complicates making plans with them. You arrange a party and bake a chocolate cake because last week the guest of honor posted on Facebook that she adores surprise birthday parties and chocolate is her favorite dessert ingredient. When you serve her a slice, she says she would have preferred strawberry and the surprise has interfered with her plans. You throw up your hands in exasperation. However, since the harm it causes is only annoyance, fickleness probably does not rise to the level of a vice. Fickleness differs from changeability in *beliefs*, which concerns how we think the world is, not only what we like or dislike about it. The latter, our tastes, are a reflection of our subjective states, which change according to the vagaries of our minds; beliefs can be acquired through a more deliberate process. Beliefs can be evaluated, and then affirmed, rejected, or held in suspension. Since beliefs are more under our control, objections to a person's changing his or her beliefs, like those made by Captain Wentworth in Jane Austen's *Persuasion*, seem more reasonable than objections to another's fickleness. Wentworth considers changeability in belief a vice and has no respect for those who exhibit it. Clearly, his own experience of being a victim to another's change of beliefs has caused his strong dislike of this trait. This victimization occurred when his fiancé, Anne Elliot, broke their engagement because, as he sees it, she had allowed herself to be persuaded by Lady Russell to adopt a negative view of the planned union. However, Wentworth is wrong both about Anne's reasons for breaking the engagement and his objections to anyone changing their beliefs.

What Is Persuasion?

Persuasion is one of the mechanisms by which our beliefs about a matter can change. This change in belief may result in a change in actions, and persuasion is often attempted in order to change what someone does, not merely what he or she believes. Still, persuasion acts first on an agent's beliefs, in ways that we will elaborate upon here. To begin, persuasion *changes* our belief about some matter; it does not fill in our ignorance about it. When Sir Elliot or Miss Elliot looked into the ledger for Kellynch Hall for the first time—or more likely, were informed of its contents by Mr. Shepherd, for whom, as they likely thought, such an activity would be more appropriate—and learned the exact amount that they were in arrears, the resulting belief of theirs in the amount of their debt was not the result of persuasion. This was a number they had hitherto not known, although its size might have surprised them. Persuasion implies the overcoming of resistance posed by an already held but conflicting belief, not merely the learning of a new fact. Persuasion is needed to convince Sir Elliot and Miss Elliot to cut their expenses, and to an extent that goes well beyond Miss Elliot's suggestions to stop donations to "unnecessary charities"[1] and presents for Anne. Mr. Shepherd demurs from this task, so it is entrusted to Lady Russell and her "excellent judgment"[2] to come up with some plan and present it to the Elliots. Since they believe they can continue to live at Kellynch Hall with little change to their lifestyle, Lady Russell must somehow dislodge this belief and replace it with the belief that staying on at Kellynch Hall would require a drastic reduction in expenses. If she succeeds, this would be a case of persuasion, because it would involve replacing a strongly held conflicting belief. Alas, she does not convince them to revise their lifestyle at their current home, but her efforts still achieve their ultimate aim, which is getting the Elliots to cut their expenses. They decide to leave Kellynch Hall rather than live there in greatly reduced style, which, once rented out to its new tenants, will set the stage for Captain Wentworth's return and thus the novel's central drama.

The example of Lady Russell's efforts with the Elliots highlight some other aspects of persuasion. First, there must be some agent doing the persuading. This will be a person, and the object of their persuasive efforts will be a person as well. But there are many ways a person can change another's belief. Only some of these ways are examples of persuasion. For example, in order to get the Elliots to believe that they should leave Kellynch Hall, Lady Russell and Anne could have perpetrated the ruse that it was haunted. They rattle chains at night, dress-up in sheets and stalk the halls, and so on. This might convince the Elliots that they should change residences, yet it is not a case of persuading them that they should leave Kellynch Hall. It is not the deception involved that disqualifies it from being persuasion. To see this, consider another technique they might have employed: they physically torture the Elliots until they agree to leave. Such a change in belief could only ironically—say, by a gangster in a film—be described as a case of persuasion. As in the haunting case, they are similarly presented some facts—the pains they endure from the torture—and then reason that it would be best to leave Kellynch Hall. The reasoning is done entirely by the targets of the belief-changing methods. If Lady Russell and Anne were not merely to present facts to the Elliots, but present them in a way that clearly showed that their best course of action would be to quit Kellynch Hall, then they would be attempting to persuade. That is, if they showed them an *argument* whose conclusion was the Elliots should move, they would be performing the reasoning that, if successful, would guide them to the conclusion that they should move (and since their efforts would replace a belief that staying is financially innocuous with the belief that it is financially deleterious, it meets the first condition of persuasion that we identified). The Elliots would not need to perform the reasoning themselves. This is what distinguishes this case from the haunting and torture; in those cases the Elliots needed to construct their own arguments—based on the facts they were given—as to why it would be best to leave.

Other examples of persuasion from the novel include Mrs. Clay's efforts to persuade Sir Elliot to rent Kellynch Hall to Admiral Croft. She begins by attesting to her knowledge of those in his profession. They are "'so neat and careful in all their ways,'" she exclaims. So, Sir Elliot can be confident that his valuable paintings would "be perfectly safe" and his "gardens and shrubberies" will be maintained to the same standards. In an additional reason directed toward Miss Elliot, she says she need not fear her "own sweet flower-garden's being neglected."[3] Mr. Shepherd continues these efforts and notes "the circumstances . . . indisputably in their favor," such as their "age, and number, and fortune; the high idea they had formed of Kellynch-hall, and extreme solicitude for the advantage of renting it."[4] Both Mrs. Clay and Mr. Shepherd have selected the facts they present to the Elliots—these include ones that they know will be effective with them, particularly those that appeal to their vanity—and they have presented them in a way that is intended to support the idea that it would be to their advantage to have the Crofts as tenants. Since they are doing all the reasoning for the Elliots, they are attempting to persuade them.

So, persuasion involves at least two persons, one to do the persuading and the other to be the target of these efforts.[5] The act of persuading involves sharing with the target the reasoning that supports the belief the agent wants him to accept. Given these conditions, persuasion is always *rational*. It operates directly on the reasons a person has for holding a belief by presenting an argument in support of a change of belief. But to say that persuasion is rational does not mean that the arguments must be good ones. For example, one can be persuaded by false reasons. Lady Russell could have exaggerated the debt of the Elliots in order to convince them to reduce their expenses. If successful, this would still be a case of persuasion even though the reasons are false. The reasons might be true but not very good ones for the belief they are intended to support. For example, that the Crofts are grateful to reside at Kellynch Hall is not a good reason for thinking they would be good tenants, yet it manages to persuade Sir Elliot. On the other hand, good reasons may have no success at persuading. If Anne had tried to persuade her father and sister of anything, even something they were otherwise inclined to believe, she would most likely fail.

There is a nonrational way of changing another's belief that is often referred to in *Persuasion*. This is influence, and the word "influence" is used almost as often as "persuasion" in the novel.[6] Influence is the power another person has to change another's belief simply by virtue of who they are. In an article on persuasion, the philosopher J. N. Garver says that with persuasion, it is ultimately "something which the person says or does"[7] that persuades; that would be to offer an argument, as we have explained. With influence, the "person *per se*,"[8] as Garver explains, is responsible for changing the belief, rather than any argument they may present.[9] Mr. Shepherd enlists Lady Russell's help in convincing the Elliots to reduce their expenses not because she is "rational and consistent;"[10] these qualities only ensure that she agrees with him on what is required for the Elliots to overcome their financial difficulties. Rather, it is her influence over the Elliots that makes her the better person to present these requirements to them. Anne, despite her "elegance of mind," has no such influence; she "was nobody with either father or sister: her word had no weight."[11] Anne also recognizes it in Lady Russell: "She rated Lady Russell's influence highly."[12] The Elliots are more likely to listen to her advice than that of anyone else.

Influence is a nonrational change in belief because the arguments presented by the person, if any, are not responsible for the change. Rather, it is the person's charisma, authority, attractiveness, social status, or other facts, all irrelevant to the truth of any belief, that are responsible for changing the belief. Wentworth uses some of these qualities to get the Musgroves' wayward son to write his parents while serving under him at sea.[13]

Persuasion and influence can work together to change beliefs. Mr. Shepherd knows that the reasons presented to the Elliots will be good ones, but given his lack of influence over them, they would likely not be accepted as such. Lady Russell, even though she would be presenting the very same reasons, would be more effective at persuading them. Another character remarks about her: "I have always heard of Lady Russell as a woman of the greatest influence with every body! I always look upon her as able to persuade a person to anything."[14] Despite its lack in relation to her father and oldest sister, Anne was "[k]nown to have some influence with [Mary]."[15] Mary's husband, Charles, and her in-laws frequently ask her to exert it. Charles says to Anne: "I wish you could persuade Mary not to be always fancying herself to be ill."[16] The reasons expressed by a person with influence can seem more persuasive than someone without influence, even though they might be the very same reasons. As a corollary of this, someone without influence can try to persuade with very good reasons but be unsuccessful.

It can be difficult to resist the influence of some people on our beliefs. These people can be friends or family members; they can also be important social or political figures. Political campaigns and celebrity endorsements exploit the fact that we are all susceptible to influence to some degree. However, we should always oppose the effect that influence can have on our beliefs. When we believe on the basis of influence, we have not assessed the belief's truth. In contrast to persuasion, we are not believing because we're convinced by the reasons or evidence that support the belief; rather, we believe only because of our faith in the person influencing us. As young children, before our reasoning abilities have fully developed, we are not capable of assessing these reasons. Therefore, we need to submit to influence in order to acquire the beliefs that will form the basis of all our subsequent learning. But as adults, with fully-formed reasoning abilities, as well as the knowledge or the means to obtain it in order to make informed judgments, there is no longer a need for us to submit to influence.

Since influence should be avoided, its effects on persuasion should be eliminated. However, should we also avoid persuasion, as Captain Wentworth seems to believe?

Is Persuadability a Vice or a Virtue?

Captain Wentworth believes that persuadability is a vice. His own experience as a victim—as he sees it—of another's persuadability seems to have strengthened him in this belief, although it could very well have been the origin of it. He believes that because of the combined influence and persuasion of Lady Russell, Anne unilaterally ended their engagement. In doing so, besides having "deserted and disappointed him," she revealed herself to be of a "persuadable temper"[17] and thus guilty of "feebleness of character," as well as "weakness and timidity."[18] He declares that his next engagement will be with a woman of "strong mind";[19] that is, someone who possesses "the character of decision and firmness."[20] He repeats his views about persuadability on several occasions, conveniently in the hearing of Anne. Louisa Musgrove, who appears to be auditioning for the role of Wentworth's next fiancée, expresses her agreement: "I have no idea of being easily persuaded. When I have made up my mind, I have made it."[21] Instead of persuadability, Wentworth values *firmness of mind*. Louisa, as we will discuss, eventually suffers from a weakness of mind, both literally and figuratively.

One does not need to be a spurned fiancé to regard persuadability as a vice. Others hold this view; for example, some voters disdain changeability in belief in their political candidates and have used the sobriquet "flip-floppers" to label those who change their positions. It seems that one does not need to be frequently guilty of this in order to deserve this title; just one change in position will warrant its application. For so-called flip-floppers, it is rarely clear whether they have changed their beliefs as a result of persuasion, influence, or simply political expedience (in which case their beliefs do not change, but only what they claim their beliefs to be). However, when we give the flip-flopper, or someone in Anne's position, the benefit of the doubt and assume that she has been persuaded to change her beliefs, such a change is not obviously a fault.

It is clear that Wentworth has a grievance against someone whom he believes was persuadable, but he is not very forthcoming on why he believes persuadability is a vice. He says of minds that are not very firm, "You are never sure of a good impression being durable."[22] But this seems to be the same complaint made against fickle people; it concerns not any serious harm they do to us, but simply the unreliability of our beliefs about them. Nevertheless, he insists, "[L]et those who would be happy be firm" and then analogizes someone with a firm mind to a hazelnut, one of which he has plucked from a tree he is standing under to illustrate. Since it had remained attached to the tree (analogous to someone sticking with their beliefs), it is unblemished, "a beautiful glossy nut . . . still in possession of all the happiness that a hazel-nut can be supposed capable of."[23] He is still only talking about appearances. That might be the only happiness a hazelnut can be capable of, but the happiness of humans certainly depends on more than how they might appear to others. Wentworth's complaint against the persuadable person seems almost aesthetic, so it can vary according to different tastes. Anne expresses an alternative preference for "those who sometimes looked or said a careless or a hasty thing, than of those whose presence of mind never varied, whose tongue never slipped."[24] Certainly, a reason to oppose a politician who has a mind that varies is that with such politicians it is difficult to know for whom one is voting. A candidate who is inconsistent in what he says or does does not present a stable enough impression from which a voter can acquire this knowledge. However, when Anne states her preference for carelessness, she is criticizing Mr. Elliot, the presumptive heir of Sir Elliot; she believes that she can "depend upon the sincerity"[25] of those who change their beliefs more than on one who is always consistent in what he says or does. To be constantly perfect in the impression one gives requires practice; it is more often a matter of rehearsal than a firmness of mind. So, we should suspect such persons of insincerity, rather than trusting that they hold the beliefs they espouse.

Unlike the perfect politician, or the committed dogmatist, most people will undisguisedly change their minds on some matters. Captain Wentworth should be more forgiving of alternations in belief. Also, he should be willing to accept that some changes in belief are innocuous, if not beneficial. It would be more reasonable for Wentworth to oppose persuadability with respect to beliefs about certain matters, such as those the politician takes public positions on, or about the suitability of a prospective spouse for oneself. We will borrow a term from the novel and say of those who change their beliefs on such matters that they are guilty of "overpersuasion."[26] They are willing to change their beliefs about important matters, including ones they have already deliberated over and have made decisions about. Yet, the reasons to oppose overpersuadability are as lacking as those against persuadability on less important matters. We will argue that not only is persuadability of any sort not a vice, it is actually a virtue. We should be open to being persuaded to change all of our beliefs that we could possibly change. This does not mean that we should *easily* change our beliefs. Persuasion, as we have explained, is a rational process. For it to succeed, the target must understand and accept the reasoning presented to him for an alternative belief. This is not a simple process. But it is a process that should be continually engaged in, because the happier person is the persuadable person, even if this person is overly persuadable.

Our argument for persuadability being a virtue, and not a vice, is adapted from an argument for a different, but related, conclusion found in John Stuart Mill's (1806–1873) classic book in political philosophy, *On Liberty*. Mill argues that people should enjoy a wide range of rights that protect their liberty from interference from both governments and others.[27] He does not argue that we possess such rights innately or that we have been endowed with them by a benevolent creator. Instead, he gives purely utilitarian arguments for these rights; he argues that societies that respect these rights will have happier citizens than those which do not. Among these rights are those of "thought and discussion."[28] Mill holds that a society that affords its citizens the greatest possible freedom of expression would flourish more than one that withholds it. He identifies two reasons for this: first, such a society would have the opportunity of exchanging its false beliefs for true ones; and, second, for its beliefs that are true, this society would possess a "clearer perception"[29] of their truth.

These reasons work also on the individual level. In fact, they must in order for the arguments for the societal level to work. If we replace *freedom of expression* in his argument with *persuadability*, we can see that the reasons that support the former also support the latter. A person who is persuadable will be, all else being the same, happier than a person who possesses Wentworth's preferred firmness of mind. As Anne proposes, "a persuadable temper might sometimes be as much in favour of happiness as a very resolute character," contrary to Wentworth's "opinion as to the universal felicity and advantage of firmness of character."[30] A persuadable person will listen to arguments whose conclusions conflict with her already held beliefs. Unlike the censor working at the level of society, she will not try to silence them, but listen to, and even encourage, them. In doing so, she will enjoy the same benefits of an open society. First, she will have the "the opportunity of exchanging error for truth."[31] An assumption behind both dogmatism and persuadability is that true beliefs are useful. As Mill puts it, "The truth of an opinion is part of its utility."[32] True beliefs help us make it through the world safely and successfully. Someone who is by principle unpersuadable will stubbornly hold onto his false beliefs. He will never have the occasion to replace those beliefs with ones that are true. He will inevitably suffer because of his false beliefs. Just imagine the consequences for the Elliots if they allowed themselves to persist in their false belief that their finances needed no radical improvement. To afford oneself the opportunity to replace false beliefs, it is essential, as Mill describes it, that one "has sought for objections and difficulties, instead of avoiding them, and has shut out no light which can be thrown upon the subject from any quarter."[33] While it was almost forcibly shined upon them, the Elliots finally permitted the light that exposed the difficulty of their finances.

Seeking "objections and difficulties" is also the only way to be assured that one's beliefs are true. The second benefit enjoyed by the persuadable person is the confidence he can have in his beliefs. Even if all his beliefs are true, he cannot know this unless he is willing to measure the reasons for his beliefs against those for opposing ones. To do so sincerely and thoroughly is to leave open the possibility of being persuaded to change to an opposing belief. Even if persuasion does not occur, he will acquire more confidence in the truth of his already held beliefs. As Mill explains, such confidence is only allowed to the person who "has kept his mind open to criticism of his opinions and conduct."[34] As with the Elliots, some of us need to be forced into this openness. Mill shows us why we should willingly subject our beliefs to criticism.

The novel contains an ingenious metaphor for the dangers of firmness of mind in the character of Louisa Musgrove, who had declared to Captain Wentworth that once she's made up her mind, she never changes it. It is such stubbornness that leads to her fall from a seawall, from which she insisted on jumping despite the warning of Captain Wentworth. "I am determined I will,"[35] she exclaims. She lands on the lower pavement and receives a severe, although undiagnosed, injury to her head. She eventually recovers, but her firmness of mind is gone. Her pursuit of Wentworth is over, and she instead marries the bookish Captain Benwick. The same happiness is in store for Anne, but she must first convince Captain Wentworth that her character and affections have not altered since they were engaged. To get him to change his mind about her she will use persuasion and not an injury to his head.

Duty and Belief

It turns out that Anne was being neither fickle nor persuadable when she ended her engagement with Wentworth. She was also not being influenced in the sense we defined earlier. She was none of these things because she never changed her beliefs about Wentworth and their prospective marriage, and she certainly never lost her affections for him. In the novel's penultimate chapter, she explains to him that when she broke off their engagement, it was to fulfill a duty she believed she owed Lady Russell: "When I yielded, I thought it was to duty." Lady Russell had been like a mother to her. If she had not followed her advice, she says, "I should have suffered in my conscience." She does not believe the advice given by Lady Russell was correct, but she believes she was "perfectly right in being guided by it" and she "was right in submitting" to it.[36]

In acting out of "a strong sense of duty,"[37] Anne acted in a way that did not reflect her true beliefs about Captain Wentworth and their prospective marriage. Her particular reason for doing so probably seems alien to many in a contemporary audience, where we find more people who believe that marriage should be exclusively a matter of individual choice. Yet, the idea of acting in ways that do not conform to our beliefs is familiar to us in other ways. For example, it is a requirement for participation in democratic institutions. Let's imagine that the majority in our Jane Austen book club votes to read *Mansfield Park* next and not, as we would prefer, *Persuasion* (and not only because we just read it, but because we think it is the better novel). We will not show up at the next meeting with our copies of *Persuasion* and talk about it throughout the meeting. Even though it would be inconsistent with our belief that *Persuasion* is the novel we should be discussing, we will do what the majority wishes. We should, of course, recognize limits to conforming our actions to majority decisions. If the book club voted—to adapt an example used earlier—to torture Phyllis if she forgets to bring the pinot grigio again, we are not obligated to follow their wishes in these circumstances and should probably actively oppose their implementation. Identifying the occasions when our duty requires us to act contrary to our beliefs, as well as the limits of such duty, can be difficult, but it would require the kind of "elegance of mind"[38] that Anne possesses and not the stolid, rigid sort of mind esteemed by Wentworth.

Wentworth's ideal mind will have further problems. As we have argued, someone who resists persuasion can never have the assurance that his beliefs, which his resistance so adamantly protects, are even true; he also denies himself the opportunity of exchanging his false beliefs for true ones. For these reasons persuadability is a virtue and not the vice that Wentworth had considered it. It is not clear whether Wentworth ever changes his view, but it is only his relenting to Anne's persuasion that allows them to be reunited in the end.

Notes

1. Jane Austen, *Persuasion*, ed. John Davie (New York: Oxford University Press, 1990), 15.

2. Austen, *Persuasion*, 16.

3. Austen, *Persuasion*, 23.

4. Austen, *Persuasion*, 28.

5. While some cases might be described as persuasion *by the facts*, we regard these cases as ones of *self*-persuasion in which an agent fits the facts into an argument, such as in chapter 7 of *Persuasion* when Charles Musgrove persuades himself that it would be okay to attend the dinner at his parents' house even though his son has just suffered a terrible injury, given the facts that the apothecary assures him that his son's condition will not worsen and (the spurious fact) that caring for children was the job of women. In cases of self-persuasion, there is still a person doing the persuading, and the object of that persuasion is a person; they just happen to be the same person.

6. Some philosophers talk about *nonrational persuasion*. We believe the cases they discuss are better captured by the word "influence," as we define it in this chapter, or words like "entice," "manipulate," or even "seduce." We also believe that our definition of "persuasion" fits its use in the novel.

7. J. N. Garver, "On the Rationality of Persuading." *Mind* 69 (1960): 167.

8. Garver, "On the Rationality of Persuading," 170.

9. Garver actually uses the term "irrational persuasion," rather than "influence." So, he is one of the philosophers we refer to in the earlier note. But it is clear that he is referring to what we, and the novel, call "influence."

10. Austen, *Persuasion*, 17.

11. Austen, *Persuasion*, 11–12.

12. Austen, *Persuasion*, 18.

13. Austen, *Persuasion*, 67.

14. Austen, *Persuasion*, 100–101.

15. Austen, *Persuasion*, 46.

16. Austen, *Persuasion*, 46.

17. Austen, *Persuasion*, 113.

18. Austen, *Persuasion*, 62.

19. Austen, *Persuasion*, 62.

20. Austen, *Persuasion*, 86.

21. Austen, *Persuasion*, 85.

22. Austen, *Persuasion*, 86.

23. Austen, *Persuasion*, 86.

24. Austen, *Persuasion*, 153.

25. Austen, *Persuasion*, 153.

26. Austen, *Persuasion*, 62.

27. He coins the famous phrase "tyranny of the majority" in the book.

28. John Stuart Mill, *On Liberty and the Subjection of Women*, ed. Alan Ryan (New York: Penguin, 2006), 22.

29. Mill, *On Liberty*, 23.

30. Austen, *Persuasion*, 113.

31. Mill, *On Liberty*, 23.

32. Mill, *On Liberty*, 29.

33. Mill, *On Liberty*, 27.

34. Mill, *On Liberty*, 27.

35. Austen, *Persuasion*, 106.

36. Austen, *Persuasion*, 232.

37. Austen, *Persuasion*, 232.

38. Austen, *Persuasion*, 11.

CHAPTER FIFTEEN

The Language Games of Persuasion

RICHARD GILMORE

Secrets are wise persuasion's keys unto love's sanctities.

—Pindar

The same word used in different contexts can have different meanings. It is persuasion that convinces Anne to break off her engagement with Captain Wentworth, but, of course, it is persuasion that brings them back together again at the end of the novel. It is not just that different evidence is adduced in the two dramatic shifts in the novel. The very meaning of the word, the phenomenology of the experience of persuasion, is different. The same word will mean different things in different contexts, just as the same person will mean different things using the same word in different contexts. There is, then, a parallel between the changes in the meaning of "persuasion" and the changes in the people persuading and in the people persuaded.

Jane Austen can be a very funny writer. When she opens *Persuasion* with a description of Sir Walter Elliot, of Kellynch Hall, perusing the *Baronetage* to read about himself, which he seems to have often done, it is amusing. We are amused by a person of such social eminence who is so silly about it, but it does not seem to be a particularly nefarious failing. The author concludes this amusing description with this summary judgment: "Vanity was the beginning and the end of Sir Walter Elliot's character; vanity of person and of situation,"[1] and then goes on to describe his infatuation with his own beauty. But two chapters later, when she recounts Sir Walter's direct response to the praise by Mrs. Clay and her father, the lawyer Mr. Shepherd, of men of the navy, a different response is elicited. Sir Walter says, "The profession has its utility, but I should be sorry to see any friend of mine belonging to it" and then gives his two objections to men of the navy, "First, as being the means of bringing persons of obscure birth into undo distinction . . . and secondly, as it cuts up a man's youth and vigour most horribly"[2] our amusement is pushed up into incredulity and laughter. We now see that vanity really is the beginning and the end of Sir Walter Elliot's character in a kind of horrifying way, and our sympathy goes out to Anne to have such a father.

Austen's real strength, however, is in her use of irony. The form of irony most prominent in her writing, especially in *Persuasion*, is what is known as the litotes, the irony of understatement (usually, but not always in the form of a negative for a positive). "Not bad" does not mean "not bad." It means "Good!" More is meant by means of saying less. As with all irony, it is not always obvious or even easy to detect. In this way it is like Anne herself, mostly unseen by those who surround her and yet always meaning much more than is ever understood by most.

Juliet McMaster, in her essay "Young Jane Austen: Author," draws our attention to the wild ebullience of Austen's early explorations in writing. Some adjectives that she suggests might apply to that writing are "irreverent, rollicking, spontaneous, hyperbolic, violent, indecent, indecorous, outrageous."[3] She goes on to suggest that this wild ebullience never really leaves her writing although it gets considerably subdued in her mature novels. "Listen, and you can often hear that zestful teenage voice in the work of the seasoned novelist."[4] Let me just remark on two litotic understatements that generate giant swerves of meaning, quiet ironies that suggest the real dramas of the novel *Persuasion*.

The first has to do with her relationship to Lady Russell. To set up the point, Fiona Stafford in her essay on *Persuasion*, referring especially to the description of Mrs. Musgrove's "large fat sighings" over the death of her son, bravely suggests that the descriptions by the author Austen may be meant to largely overlap with the inner experiences of Anne the character. As Stafford says about the "large fat sighings": "Although these details have often been attributed to the narrator by those unwilling to associate such unkindness to Anne, the distinction between narrator and heroine is not always clearly defined."[5] Another case of such an overlap occurs, I want to argue, in one of the very earliest descriptions of Lady Russell. The first description of Lady Russell is as "a sensible, deserving woman."[6] A slightly later description of her, however, is: "She was a woman rather of sound than of quick abilities. . . ."[7] The question is raised, litotically, just how not quick Lady Russell actually is. This question is raised again later in that same paragraph when she is described as having "a cultivated mind, and was generally speaking, rational and consistent—but she had prejudices on the side of ancestry. . . ."[8] The ironic swerve of these passages is in the "rather sound than quick abilities" and in the "—but. . . ."

It is as though the narrator wants to fully praise Lady Russell, but the truth constrains her. The desire on the part of the narrator to think well of Lady Russell's character notwithstanding, the truth seems to be that her abilities may not be that far beyond Sir Walter's. Certainly her limitations have nothing to do with vanity, but that "sound rather than quick" and "but" are pretty damning, and they cannot be the narrator's perceptions alone. If that is the way it is, then Anne must see it that way as well. This should color our thinking about Anne's being persuaded by Lady Russell about who it is appropriate to marry. There is some sense to saying she should have known better than to trust Lady Russell's advice, and she seems to regret her decision to be persuaded by Lady Russell almost immediately after the fact: "A few months had seen the beginning and the end of their [Anne's and Wentworth's] acquaintance; but, not with a few months ended Anne's share of suffering from it. Her attachment and regrets had, for a long time, clouded every enjoyment of youth; and an early loss of bloom and spirits had been their lasting effect."[9]

The second bit of ironic understatement I want to consider is the whole treatment of Anne's and Captain Wentworth's first romance. So much seems to be predicated on that romance. The significance of their reunion, hence the significance of the novel as a whole, seems to depend on the depth of that first love and the pain of its dissolution. Yet here is the description of that important time in its near entirety:

> He [Wentworth] was, at that time, a remarkably fine young man, with a great deal of intelligence, spirit and brilliancy; and Anne an extremely pretty girl, with gentleness, modesty, taste, and feeling.—Half the sum of attraction, on either side, might have been enough, for he had nothing to do, and she had hardly any body to love; but the encounter of such lavish recommendations could not. They were gradually acquainted, and when acquainted, rapidly and deeply in love. It would be difficult to say which had seen the highest perfection in the other, or which had been the happiest; she, in receiving his declarations and proposals, or he in having them accepted. A short period of exquisite felicity followed, and but a short one.—Trouble soon arose.[10]

This is a pretty breezy account of what becomes such a fraught and weighty period. She is influenced by her father's disapproval, minutely, and by Lady Russell's, preponderantly, and meets with Captain Wentworth to break off the engagement. The account of his response is equally brief: "—a final parting; and every consolation was required, for she had to encounter all the additional pain of opinions, on his side, totally unconvinced and unbending, and of his feeling himself ill-used by so forced a relinquishment.—He left the country in consequence."[11]

These accounts of their romance and its dissolution hardly seem to prepare us for the intensity of feeling Anne will feel having a child lifted from her back by Captain Wentworth or his at hearing in the tone of Anne's voice some promise of her continuing affection for him. There is, no doubt, understatement and irony at work here, but what does it mean?

There are three interrelated points and three interrelated arguments that I want to make in this essay. First, Austen's novel *Persuasion* is also a philosophical rumination on the phenomenon of persuasion. Second, Austen's thoughts on persuasion reflect Plato's analysis of persuasion taking two very different forms, which I will call Persuasion I and Persuasion II. In relation to Plato's ideas about persuasion I will also adduce Wittgenstein's analysis of language in his later philosophy, where he sees the meaning of a word as something not fixed and universally determined, but as something that emerges from a specific context. "Persuasion" will mean something quite different in different contexts of use. Finally, I will consider the trajectory of the plot of *Persuasion* in light of Stanley Cavell's analysis of what he calls "the comedy of remarriage."[12] *Persuasion* is not exactly a comedy, except in the Aristotelian sense of being a narrative that begins in a worse place and ends in a better. But I take Cavell's analysis to be generalizable beyond the genre of Hollywood romantic comedies.

The power and meaning of persuasion is a philosophical topic that goes back to Plato's *Gorgias*. Plato has Socrates arguing with some professional orators about what constitutes authentic persuasion. This invokes the most basic philosophical distinction, the appearance versus reality distinction. There is, Socrates argues, a kind of apparent power of persuasion that seems to persuade, seems to change people's minds but does not; and there is another form of persuasion that is an authentic power and really persuades, and can really change a person's mind: Persuasion I and Persuasion II. The distinction that Socrates makes to clarify these two forms of persuasion is between persuasion without knowledge, which does not really change anyone's mind, and persuasion with knowledge (philosophy), which really does change people's minds. As Socrates says, "Would you like us then to posit two types of persuasion, one providing conviction without knowledge, the other providing knowledge?"[13] Gorgias assents to this distinction, to his own eventual undoing.

Just to be clear, apparent persuasion (Persuasion I), persuasion that does not really change people's minds, may very well influence a person's behavior. To say that it does not really change people's minds means that one's basic schema of value, a schema of value based on appearances, does not change. Authentic persuasion (Persuasion II), persuasion with knowledge, changes the very schema of values from which one operates. The first schema of value, based on appearances, is about short-term pleasures, desires unrelated to virtue, and social conformity; the second schema of value is about the authentic good, genuine virtue, and the way to real happiness. This is the basic philosophical desideratum, to move from valuing appearances to valuing reality.

Related to this distinction is a philosophical perspective on how language functions. In his early philosophy Wittgenstein argued that in order for language to be possible, that is, in order for us to be able to say something true about the world, there must be some direct connection between language and the world. If that were true, then words would connect with reality in a pretty direct and inflexible way. A word would mean what it means and not any other thing. There would be only certain things that could be said, and for the rest, "Whereof one cannot speak, thereof one must remain silent."[14]

In his later philosophy Wittgenstein abandoned this view of language and shifted to a notion of meaning that did not depend on some direct connection between language and the world, but rather was the function of use. As Wittgenstein says in *Philosophical Investigations*, "the meaning of a word is its use in the language."[15] The name he gave for a general context of use was a "language game."[16] Words get their meaning from the roles they play in language games. Language games are determined by what Wittgenstein calls "a form of life." What we must look to to understand how a word is being used, which will determine its meaning, is to a language game that is being played as a part of a form of life. "What has to be accepted, the given, is—so one could say—forms of life."[17] A consequence of this understanding of language is that the same word (or words) can have different meanings in different language games. "Persuasion" can mean very different things in different language games.

A beautiful example of how the same words can mean different things in different language games is illustrated in Stuart Tave's chapter on *Persuasion* in his *Some Words of Jane Austen*. He begins that chapter by observing, "The first sentence that introduces Anne Elliot's name tells us that with either her father or her sister 'her word had no weight . . . she was only Anne.'"[18] Throughout the course of the chapter Tave argues for Anne's quiet, but-there-for-those-with-the-eyes-to-see-them, integrity, strength, and power of mind and emotion. He ends the chapter saying, "Her feelings and her exertions have maintained an active and balanced integrity and neither can be explained away as woman's nature or as man's nature. Only Anne." Now, "only Anne" takes on an entirely different meaning from the use at the beginning of Austen's novel. A different language game is being played, and the identical words, referring to the same person (character), mean completely different things. This, I want to say, is what Austen does with "persuasion" in *Persuasion*.

We clearly see Austen distinguishing between uses of "persuasion" within just a few pages in the chapter recounting Anne's earlier attachment to Captain Wentworth. The first version is the description of the influence of Lady Russell's persuasion on her: "She was persuaded to believe the engagement a wrong thing—indiscreet, improper, hardly capable of success, and not deserving of it." Just a few pages later, however, and referring to a time some eight years later, we get another description of "persuasion" that seems to be very different in kind: "She was persuaded that under every disadvantage of disapprobation at home, and every anxiety attending his profession, all their probable fears, delays and disappointments, she should yet have been a happier woman in maintaining the engagement, than she had been in the sacrifice of it; and this, she fully believed. . . ." How and why are these two forms of persuasion so different? The criteria upon which the first version of persuasion is based are entirely social and conventional. It is a form of persuasion based entirely on appearances, which, pretty clearly, she does not "fully believe." The language game being played is the language game of prudence, not, perhaps, the best language game for adjudicating questions of love and marriage. The second use of "persuaded" is in the language game of sincere reflection upon what is really valuable in this life. It is a reflection upon the real sources of happiness, counter-appearances notwithstanding. It is the language game of philosophy.

A final yet related point and argument that I want to make is to read *Persuasion* as a version of what Stanley Cavell calls the "genre of remarriage."[19] The genre or narrative of remarriage is about the problem of legitimizing a marriage. As Cavell says, "its subject is the legitimizing of marriage, as if the pair's adventures are trials of their suitability for that condition."[20]

The idea is that marriages, in their initial stages, are necessarily illegitimate and that some process has to be undergone to legitimate them. Marriages are initially illegitimate because what legitimates a marriage is a certain kind of knowledge, specifically, a knowledge of oneself and of the other person in the relationship. This knowledge is usually not available to newlyweds for two reasons. The first is because they will not have spent enough time with each other in the right capacity of intimate marriage to be able to fully know the other. The second is because, lacking such knowledge, each must act on what amounts to a projected understanding of the other, the other becoming more or less a projection of what each wants and hopes and expects the other to be. What has to happen, what will happen, is, eventually, there will be an encounter with the other as fully other. This will be somewhat horrifying, but certainly disappointing, to learn that the other is not the projected ideal that one wanted and hoped and expected them to be. This will instigate a "divorce." What each must discover in their turn is that the other that each lost, but is once again learning to know, is even more attractive ultimately than the other that they had been projecting. It is the other precisely in their otherness that each desires. This will become the grounds of a remarriage. In working out the terms of the remarriage the marriage itself is legitimated.

All of this is meant very symbolically. An actual legal marriage need not have occurred nor any kind of official divorce. What has to happen is only some shared experience of intimacy, some period, however brief, of "exquisite felicity," and then a more or less sudden loss of that felicity, the divorce, and then a realization of what really has been lost, and the willingness to try to recover that lost thing, but now in full (more or less) knowledge of who the other is, and with full compassion and appreciation for their differences.

This is pretty much a literal description of what happens in *Persuasion*. I will just point out a unity of themes among my three points and arguments. If we take the first "marriage" as Marriage I and the second remarriage as Marriage II then we can say that "I love you" would mean something very different in Marriage I than it does in Marriage II. The difference in those meanings can be accounted for, in part, by a certain lack of knowledge in Marriage I and the painful acquisition of knowledge in Marriage II. In fact, the knowledge acquired and necessary for Marriage II is necessarily acquired only through pain. It is the kind of knowledge that ancient Greeks referred to as *pathei mathos*, the knowledge that is gained through suffering. There is something that persuades the couple to unite, and there is something that persuades the couple to separate and, finally, there is something that persuades the couple to unite again, after much suffering, and not just in spite of, but because of the suffering. More or less inevitably, the first two forms of persuasion will be forms of Persuasion I. The form of persuasion that persuades to remarry will finally be Persuasion II, which must be considered an achievement, in fact, a philosophical achievement. It is the achievement of finally seeing the real through the veil of appearances.

The legitimating of a marriage, then, really depends, first of all, on the legitimating of each person's individual self. The reason that Austen treats the original attachment of Anne and Captain Wentworth, and its subsequent dissolution, so breezily, I take it, is because they were not really fully formed as selves and so could not really be in a position to legitimize a marriage. Anne was too easily persuaded by persuasion, persuasion based on appearances and without knowledge. Captain Wentworth was too quick to judge Anne's susceptibility to persuasion as a sign of an inconstant character. He too is persuaded by a version of Persuasion I, persuaded by appearances rather than what he should have known better, the goodness of Anne's character, in spite of appearances.

It is only after they have each suffered from their earlier seduction by appearances that each can achieve, through reflection and self-knowledge, a real knowledge of the other. Only then can each see the other for who the other really is, in their goodness, integrity, and exceptional and unique suitability as a complement to one another's particular characters. There is a sense, I think, in which if Anne had remained unpersuaded by Lady Russell in the first case, and had married Captain Wentworth, the union of Anne and Captain Wentworth would have been less. The relationship between Anne and Lady Russell would certainly have been damaged, perhaps irreparably, and that would have been a hard thing to bring into the marriage. More importantly, however, Anne's knowledge of Captain Wentworth, and Wentworth's of Anne would have been relatively shallow and unformed. It is not that they could not have deepened their knowledge of each other over time, but that it may not have ever gotten to the depths of understanding that is achieved after the eight years of separation. Most specifically, what Anne comes to know is how deeply she appreciates the fact that Captain Wentworth has a mind that can appreciate her mind, and vice versa for Captain Wentworth with respect to Anne's mind. They each now know what they could only know because of their separation, how thin the world is without the other.

It is a rich irony that what precipitates the reunion of Anne and Wentworth is an argument over "constancy." It begins somewhat obliquely with

Anne overhearing a conversation between Wentworth and Louisa. In that conversation Wentworth is applauding Louisa's firmness of mind and affirming the value of such a mind in general, "let one who would be happy be firm."[21] He follows this with the praise of the firmness of a nut he finds on a bush. It is an amusing swerve that is hard to read. In a sense, he has not been firm of mind himself, swerving from the serious to the amusing and then back again. It could be that in his greater maturity, after eight years, his commitment to one kind of firmness may be softening. In any event, whether he knows she is there or not, it is as if he were speaking to Anne herself.

In the culminating scene in the novel, a scene that mirrors the earlier scene of Wentworth and Louisa conversing while Anne overhears, Wentworth now overhears a conversation between Captain Harville and Anne. The conversation begins with Captain Harville wondering about the apparent inconstancy of Benwick, who seems to be more or less done with his mourning for his dead Fanny, and has turned his attentions to a future with Louisa. Anne responds by, as it were, agreeing with Captain Harville by affirming the greater constancy of women to that of men. To that, "Captain Harville smiled, as much as to say, 'Do you claim that for your sex?'" To which Anne replies, to the asked but unspoken question, "Yes. We certainly do not forget you, so soon as you forget us. . . ." Captain Harville affirms the superiority of men's constancy as a thing of nature: "I believe in a true analogy between our bodily frames and our mental; and that as our bodies are the strongest, so are our feelings. . . ." To which Anne replies, "the spirit of analogy will authorize me to assert that ours are the most tender. Man is more robust than woman, but he is not longer-lived; which exactly explains my view of the nature of their attachments."[22]

Captain Harville then gives an impassioned description of the pain a man feels when he leaves his wife and children to go again to sea. To which Anne gives an equally impassioned response, at once acknowledging Captain Harville's claim to strong feelings, yet simultaneously insisting on the peculiar intensity of feeling that a woman might experience: "'All the privilege I claim for my own sex . . . is that of loving longest, when the existence or when hope is gone.'"[23] Anne speaks as if she were speaking directly to Wentworth.

It is hearing Anne's defense of the constancy of woman that persuades Wentworth that she still feels passion for him. The irony of this, as it were, ongoing argument between Anne and Wentworth on what constitutes constancy is that neither has been, putatively speaking, very constant with respect to the other. Is there a Constancy I and a Constancy II distinction that can capture the ways in which, even as each has failed the other with respect to constancy, each also rivals the other in his own, truer form of constancy? Austen's answer is clearly yes. The two forms of constancy are nicely given in the thoughts of Anne after witnessing the disastrous form of Louisa's firmness of mind, which leads to her uncaught fall on the Cobb in Lyme. Anne wonders if it might give Wentworth some pause. "She thought it could scarcely escape him to feel, that a persuadable temper might sometimes be as much in favour of happiness, as a very resolute character."[24] Which is to say, there is a form of constancy that is about being unchanging, and there is a form of constancy that is about being always willing to change when one sees a real reason for one to change. Anne and Wentworth both demonstrate their constancy that takes the form of a willingness to change when change is warranted.

At the end of the novel, when Anne and Captain Wentworth have been reunited in their love, Anne explains to Captain Wentworth the change in her thinking about persuasion from the time when she was persuaded to reject his marriage offer. She is responding to a comment made by Captain Wentworth explaining his slowness to respond to Anne the second time around, and his fear that her attentions might turn to Mr. Elliot. He has seen her with Lady Russell and, "the knowledge of her influence, the indelible, immovable impression of what persuasion had once done—was it not all against me?" To which Anne replies: "You should have distinguished. . . . You should not have suspected me now; the case is so different, and my age so different. If I was wrong in yielding to persuasion once, remember that it was to persuasion exerted on the side of safety, not of risk. When I yielded, I thought it was to duty; but no duty could be called in aid here. In marrying a man indifferent to me, all risk would have been incurred and all duty violated."[25] It is not that the concern for duty has been abandoned, but the very concept of what duty is and what it entails has changed. Duty was originally in the service of a false prudence. Now, duty is determined by the requirements of love; all other values are measured against that one. This is a different language game of persuasion.

Both Anne and Captain Wentworth had their secrets, then, at the time of their separation, and, again, at the moment of their reuniting. Anne's secret, then, was that she was doing it for him. As Austen writes, giving us insight into the thinking of Anne, "Had she not imagined herself consulting his good, even more than her own, she could hardly have given him up."[26] Wentworth's secret, then, was that he was hurt by *her*. In both cases, their secrets were secrets of what the existentialists call "bad faith." Anne's secret was bad faith because it is not true. It is hypocrisy to formulate her rejection of him as *for* him. It is to hide from herself her own capitulation to a false prudence, and an insincere sense of duty. Wentworth's secret is that, as is clear from his simultaneous wooing of, or, at least openness to the charms of, either of the two Musgrove sisters, that Captain Wentworth thinks that it does not really matter whom he marries. His outrage is not that *Anne* refused him, but that *he* was refused. He is not honest with himself about his own anger and that is his bad faith, his hypocrisy.

They each hold a new secret at the moment of their reunion. Anne's new secret is that she recognizes fully, unequivocally, and passionately that it is to Captain Wentworth alone in the world whose intimate disclosure she most wants to allow and to whom she most wants to disclose her most intimate self. Captain Wentworth's secret is that he has come to see that it does matter whom he marries, that not anyone will quite do. What he recognizes is that it is only Anne who can fully appreciate who he is, what he has done, and what he can do. It is only Anne he really wants to understand. It is only Anne he wants to understand him. These secrets are wise persuasion's keys to loves sanctities.

Notes

1. Jane Austen, *Persuasion* (London: Penguin, 1985), 36.

2. Austen, *Persuasion*, 49.

3. Juliet McMaster, "Young Jane Austen: Author" in *A Companion to Jane Austen*, ed. Claudia L. Johnson and Clara Tuite (Malden, MA: Blackwell, 2012), 81.

4. McMaster, "Young Jane Austen: Author," 82.

5. Fiona Stafford, "*Persuasion*: The Gradual Dawning" in *A Companion to Jane Austen*, 148.

6. Austen, *Persuasion*, 36.

7. Austen, *Persuasion*, 42.

8. Austen, *Persuasion*, 42.

9. Austen, *Persuasion*, 56–57.

10. Austen, *Persuasion*, 55.

11. Austen, *Persuasion*, 56.

12. Stanley Cavell, "North by Northwest," in *Themes Out of School: Effects and Causes* (San Francisco: North Point Press, 1984), 153. See also his *Pursuits of Happiness: The Hollywood Comedy of Remarriage* (Cambridge: Harvard, 1981).

13. Plato, *Gorgias*, trans. Donald J. Zeyl (Indianapolis: Hackett, 1987), 12 (454e).

14. Ludwig Wittgenstein, *Tractatus Logico-Philosophicus*, trans. Frank Ramsey and C. K. Ogden, ed. Marc A. Joseph (Peterborough, Ontario: Broadview Editions, 2014), §7.

15. Ludwig Wittgenstein, *Philosophical Investigations*, ed. G E. M. Anscombe and R. Rhees, trans. G. E. M. Anscombe (New York: Macmillan, 1953), §43.

16. Wittgenstein, *Investigations*, §7.

17. Wittgenstein, *Investigations*, 226e.

18. Stuart Tave, *Some Words of Jane Austen* (Chicago: The University of Chicago Press, 1973), 256.

19. Cavell, *Pursuits of Happiness*, 1.

20. Cavell, "North by Northwest," 154.

21. Austen, *Persuasion*, 110.

22. Austen, Persuasion, 236.

23. Austen, *Persuasion*, 238.

24. Austen, *Persuasion*, 136.

25. Austen, *Persuasion*, 246.

26. Austen, *Persuasion*, 56.

PART V

MONSTERS AND ZOMBIES

CHAPTER SIXTEEN

Dead and Alive

Austen's Role in Mashup Literature

AMANDA RITER

Jane Austen's *Pride and Prejudice* was first published in 1813 and has since been considered a masterpiece of English literature. *Pride and Prejudice and Zombies* was published by Seth Grahame-Smith in 2009 and depending upon the reader has been either lauded as a brilliant parody or derided as an abhorrent insult to Austen. However, no matter the perception, *Zombies* has undeniably brought literature mashups into popular culture, spawning a sequel, a prequel, a film adaption, and dozens of imitators, all of which embrace the idea that no work or author is so esteemed as to be safe from mashing. Despite this disregard for the traditional sanctity of the written word, mashups still require that their readers have some sense of the unadulterated source in order to function. By simultaneously requiring familiarity with *Pride and Prejudice* and disregarding the prestige typically associated with it, *Zombies* creates a unique relationship with Austen, where she both cannot and must influence the mashup for it to succeed.

The first step to unpacking the complicated relationship these mashups have with Austen is understanding the hybrid structure that makes a novel a mashup. *Zombies* uses this structure to critique Austen's source, accentuating the aspects of *Pride and Prejudice* that Grahame-Smith finds flawed by putting zombies alongside them. The next step is acknowledging that for these mashups to exist at all, Austen must be both literally dead and metaphorically "dead." But at the same time, the mashups must engage with a living Austen to achieve their purpose. There is a distinction between the "dead" Austen that enables the mashups to exist, and the "living" Jane that *Zombies* seeks to undercut. It is this hybrid form of Jane Austen that *Pride and Prejudice and Zombies* engages with, reacting against the living Jane and believing it to be the dead Austen.

Although mashups have been staples in mediums like music and film for several years, *Pride and Prejudice and Zombies* marks the first time that the concept of mashups has been applied to literature. Mashups in any genre are a contemporary product because modern technology has created a world where texts largely exist digitally, making it easy for amateurs to edit and distribute them in a way that would have almost been unthinkable in the era of vinyl and film. For mashup literature, these technological advancements mean that rather than purchasing a hard copy of the novel and retyping it, a source with an expired copyright can simply be copied and pasted into a document where the secondary author can begin editing. While music and film mashups typically involve merging two complete, preexisting sources into one, literature mashups instead take a single source novel and add newly written material. Different mashups vary in the amount of material added, ranging anywhere from 5 percent new material in *Mansfield Park: The Wild and Wanton Edition* to 40 percent new material in *Sense and Sensibility and Sea Monsters*, but the presence of this new material among the source is what makes the novel a mashup.

Because of the popularity of *Pride and Prejudice and Zombies*, people often assume that the additions to a mashup must come from a genre oppositional to the source in order to qualify. The juxtaposition between the source's genre and the mashup's additions serves to comment on the source material. As Eckart Voigts-Virchow explains in one of the few—but comprehensive—definitions for mashup literature, a mashup novel contains "two antithetical, distinctly marked, generically crystallized genres . . . best represented by the 'vs.' frequently used with audio remixes: the Austen canon vs. zombie canon."[1] While the conflict between Austen and zombies is an accurate definition of *Pride and Prejudice and Zombies*, it fails to take into account those mashups where the additions are not supernatural.

At this point, there are two subgroups of literary mashups: the more well-known supernatural, and romance. Contrary to the antagonism that Voigts-Virchow sees in *Zombies* and select other supernatural mashups, the romance mashups embrace the Regency world that Austen presents but alter the source's restrained courtship by adding anything from flirtatious conversations to clandestine sexual encounters. While the behavior of the characters in these romance mashups might seem out of place in Austen's source, it lacks the genre conflict that characterizes *Zombies*. The correlation between these two groups of literary mashups lies not in the kind of material that they are adding to the source, but in a structure that has them add material at all. Although each individual mashup seeks to achieve different things with their additions and pulls on a different canon of material from which to draw those additions, each mashup novel consists of a complete source work with added material that is designed to function in conjunction with the source.

In the case of *Zombies*, the additions are designed to not only alter the narrative by adding zombies and ninjas, but also to use those additions to comment on the source.[2] Specifically, Seth Grahame-Smith uses the presence of zombies to accentuate the aspects of *Pride and Prejudice* that he considers flawed. Grahame-Smith has been clear about his dislike for Austen's work, explaining in an interview that at the time he wrote *Zombies*, "I hadn't read [*Pride and Prejudice*] since I was 14, and when I read it at 14 I found it sort of slow and unenjoyable."[3] That dislike carries over into Grahame-Smith's reinterpretation of the novel. *Zombies* treats Austen's classic as a deeply flawed text. Though the male, teenage dislike of Austen has become almost culturally axiomatic—whether that presumption is based on fact or not—for Grahame-Smith that dislike endures into his reinterpretation of the novel. By adding zombies to *Pride and Prejudice* Grahame-Smith not only creates humor from juxtaposing the grotesque additions and the elegant source, but he also accentuates those elements of *Pride and Prejudice* that he deems worthy of ridicule.

Specifically, Grahame-Smith has said that he believes "the characters in Jane Austen's original books are rather like zombies because they live in this bubble of immense wealth and privilege and no matter what's going on around them they have a singular purpose to maintain their rank and to impress others."[4] Out of all the potential issues with the text that a mashup might introduce material to critique, Grahame-Smith narrows his focus to the novel's presentation of class, reacting against *Pride and Prejudice* as though it really is such a one-dimensional portrait. The mashup maintains the characters as they are portrayed in the source but juxtaposes their as-written actions against a zombie plague that logically ought to change their behavior. When the characters keep going to balls and worrying over marriage, their concerns appear ludicrous in comparison to the problems the mashup has introduced. The zombification of the characters' world is meant to exaggerate the absurdity that Grahame-Smith sees in the behavior in such a way that readers can't miss it.

By placing the source and its parody together in the same work and forcing the reader to consume them simultaneously, the mashup is meant to show the reader not only the obvious distinction between the works, but also the lack of distinction. The ridiculous, supposedly out-of-place behavior that comes from interacting with zombies is interwoven with the supposedly mercenary world of Austen's original in such a way that the reader cannot tell what outlandish behavior can be attributed to Grahame-Smith, and what to Austen.

As an example of this, Grahame-Smith is fond of accentuating Mrs. Bennet's dramatics to the point where even the Reader's Discussion Guide questions ask, "Does Mrs. Bennet have a single redeeming quality?"[5] The most casual of readers still ought to be able to determine from among the dramatic "tears and lamentations of regret, invectives against the villainous conduct of Wickham, and half a bucket's worth of vomit" which actions are explained by the kind of language that would have been used in Regency England and thus are mashup additions.[6] However, this dramatic overreaction to the situation is in alignment with Mrs. Bennet's behavior in the source. It is so much in alignment that when Mrs. Bennet's "joy burst forth" and she is "in an irritation from delight, as she had ever been fidgety from alarm and vexation" about Lydia's impending marriage, her actions feel as though the passage ought to be one of Grahame-Smith's additions, but instead, it is actually untouched Austen.[7]

The entire mashup attempts to call into question what the reader thinks he knows about the prestige of Austen's story, though whether Elizabeth's contemplations of murder or Mr. Darcy's violent ridicule actually parallels their characters well enough to make commentary on them is up for discussion. Either way, in these moments the reader is meant to have trouble drawing a line between which dramatics are additions and which are part of Austen's original. With Austen's elevated literary status, the reader assumes that anything ridiculous will come from Grahame-Smith. However, when the line between the two is blurred, all of the reader's assumptions about the height of Austen's work are subverted. Whether the ridiculous material is one of Grahame-Smith's additions or not, when the reader cannot tell the difference, the mashup achieves its purpose.

Although Grahame-Smith is explicitly clear in his interviews about using the mashup to target the perceived ridiculousness of Austen's characters, he himself doesn't seem certain about what kind of behavior constitutes ridiculous. In various comments, he points to the characters' focus on maintaining their social standing as the chief behavior to be ridiculed, and his mocking treatment of Mrs. Bennet for her obsession with seeing her daughters married and denying her own culpability in Lydia's behavior parallels that statement. However, for all Grahame-Smith's arguments that *Zombies* is designed to critique the class-centric behavior in *Pride and Prejudice*, he fails to carry that critique through to arguably the novel's bastion of class-conscious behavior: Lady Catherine de Bourgh. Despite her class-centric focus, Lady Catherine is presented as the "greatest of all zombie slayers"[8] in a society that Grahame-Smith has fashioned to value a person's ability to fight off zombies. Whatever value characters like Mrs. Bennet might still place on marriage, Darcy's definition of a truly accomplished woman requires that she be "not only a master of the female arts, but the deadly as well"[9] and it is Lady Catherine who is "so great a slayer" that "there had been no reports of zombies in Hunsford for years" because "the stricken [zombies] dared not venture too close to her home."[10] Despite being the pillar of everything Grahame-Smith claims is ridiculous and deserving of critique in Austen's novels, Lady Catherine is the paragon of what the characters in his zombie-riddled society are meant to value. The disparate ways that Grahame-Smith deals with the commentary about these characters suggest that despite his statements to the contrary, Grahame-Smith chooses to critique characters, not for their focus on maintaining wealth and privilege, but because of his own personal dislike for them.

The very existence of mashup literature and the notion that Grahame-Smith has the authority to rewrite Austen's work in accordance with his own, personal views of her characters is rooted in the idea that no work and no author are too hallowed to be beyond ridicule. It is one thing to analyze Austen's works from the perspective of a scholar and find them deficient, but it is something else to rewrite Austen's works with the intent to point out all the things that the secondary author as an individual finds deficient. Though in our modern era of adaptation and remixing, the acceptability of mashing a novel might seem obvious, it is actually a fairly recent concept in the history of literature.

In 1967 literary critic Roland Barthes published "The Death of the Author," an essay in which he asserts that to properly study texts they need to be freed from "constraints of fidelity to an origin, a unified meaning, an identity, or any other pregiven exterior or interior reality," including that of their author.[11] More simply put, Barthes rejected a critical tradition that regarded the author of a text as godlike, limiting the interpretation of the work to one "correct" reading that the author always intended to be the true meaning. However, by disregarding assumptions about what the author intended a text to mean, the reader is repositioned as the primary means of understanding a work.

Barthes explains that to "give a text an Author" as a source of ultimate authority over interpretations of the work "is to impose a limit on that text, to furnish it with a final signified, to close the writing."[12] This closing of the text removes any opportunity a reader might have to interpret the work in a way contrary to what the author might have originally intended. However, by removing the godlike author the text is reopened to a multitude of different interpretations that venture beyond anything that the author may have originally imagined for her work. Opening the work to varied interpretations has allowed Austen's texts to be examined through the lens of everything from feminism to history, from economics to colonialism, from sequels to variations, and now for mashup literature to not only reinterpret Austen's work but to go so far as to rewrite it. By removing Austen's authority the text ceases to be "a line of words releasing a single 'theological' meaning (the 'message' of the Author-God) but [instead becomes] a multi-dimensional space in which a variety of writings, none of them original, blend and clash."[13] The different interpretations of readers and scholars alike can be applied to the text rather than solely the intentions of the author, a concept that stretches so far as to include mashups that rewrite the very novels themselves, pointing out the elements that a singular reader deems flawed.

While the Barthesian death of Austen enables the existence of mashup literature, it also directs how Grahame-Smith interacts with the source text. Austen's literal death allows him to mash up Austen's works without violating copyright, but her Barthesian death allows him to reinterpret her work. Out of all Grahame-Smith's interviews, it is in one with *Time* magazine that he offers his most complete rationale for the critique in *Zombies*. He reiterates his belief that Austen's characters act like zombies themselves, then explains:

> They're so preoccupied with the little trivial nothings of their lives—who's dating who, who's throwing this ball, or having this dinner party. As long as there's enough lamb for the dinner table, they could care less what's falling apart around them. So in this book, in this version, it literally is falling apart around them, and they sort of carry on writing letters to each other about hurt feelings and loves and passions and all these things. It's ridiculous![14]

As we have discussed, the line that Grahame-Smith claims to draw about what makes a character's behavior ridiculous enough to critique is not so clear-cut as he suggests, but his explanation for the critique does indicate what he believes *Pride and Prejudice* to be, and it is that interpretation of the work that his mashup is designed to react against.

Grahame-Smith sees *Pride and Prejudice* as class-centered and obsessed with petty concerns at the expense of being engaged with the real world, and it is this version of *Pride and Prejudice* that he reacts against. Grahame-Smith is not alone in this presumption about the focus of Austen's works. So long as there has been an analysis of Austen's texts, there have been readers who consider them just like Grahame-Smith does. Even Austen's first professional biographer reported in 1890 that, "There is not hidden meaning in Austen; no philosophy beneath the surface for profound scrutiny to bring to light; nothing calling in any way for elaborate interpretation."[15] He considered any further commentary unnecessary because Austen's works were one-dimensional enough to not require deeper analysis. While Grahame-Smith considered that supposed simplicity part of the novels' charm, he deems it an insurmountable flaw that mashing is necessary to point out.

The disconnect between the *Pride and Prejudice* that so many consider worthy of reading and the *Pride and Prejudice* that Grahame-Smith critiques as inferior is at the core of many negative *Zombies* reviews. One of the most thorough of these came from Cynthia Kartman, a contributor to AustenBlog. In her review, she wrote from the point of view of Jane Austen looking down on *Zombies* from heaven and expressing her opinion on the mashup. She pointed out that the readers of *Zombies* seem to be divided into four major categories, those who like both Austen and zombies, those who like Austen enough not to mind the zombies, those who like Austen and are upset about the zombies, and those who hate Austen but like zombies. While the first three groups she understands, "[t]he fourth category, in turn, divides into two subcategories: those who are looking forward to a medium that finally makes P&P palatable; and those who are looking for [Grahame-Smith's] work to vindicate their long-held belief that P&P is the most overrated book in the English language."[16] The reaction of this particular subset of readers—who are arguably the main audience that Grahame-Smith wrote for—rebel not against the actual novel, but against the tradition that has established it as a classic deserving of attention. Grahame-Smith embraces the idea that Austen's work is simple and beneath any real notice, targeting a Regency society devoted to class and appearances, and one so incapable of confronting the harsh realities of the world that they mostly ignore the presence of zombies in their midst. While class was obviously important in Regency England, the presumption that Grahame-Smith has about the immaculateness of the rest of Austen's world is inaccurate. Kartman explains from the point of view of Austen, changing those assumptions about Austen's actual Regency life

> would have interfered with [Grahame-Smith's] main goal: ridiculing the reaction of stodgy upper-class 19th century Britons to a life filled with gore and bloodshed. In one interview, in fact, you stated that it was the people on whom my characters are based who behaved like zombies. But you err when you suppose that the society these people lived in was not already a gory and bloody one. I had two sisters-in-law who died in childbirth. One of my dearest friends was killed when she was thrown from her horse. Two of my brothers served gallantly in His Majesty's Navy, where they undoubtedly witnessed scenes of horror during battle and while stationed in foreign lands. In short, there was plenty of vice and violence in the real world of my time without resorting to the undead.[17]

Kartman's review of *Zombies* taps into the disconnect that readers familiar with Austen see in Grahame-Smith's writing. That disconnect is one where he critiques a version of *Pride and Prejudice* that they don't know as readers.

While Kartman's review assumes a factually historical stance in order to take Grahame-Smith to task for misunderstanding Austen's novel, it also has the presumption to assume Austen's viewpoint and speak on her behalf. Though there is nothing wrong with this particular method of argument, it is symptomatic of the relationship that the reading public possesses with Austen. While Jane Austen, the actual person, is both literally and figuratively deceased, devoted fans have created a version of her that is still functionally alive, constantly being re-created in films, sequels, variations, and even mashups of her works. This manufactured Austen is the one Grahame-Smith engages with, critiquing what society *thinks* her works say rather than what Kartman and other Austen devotees would argue they actually do. Although the literal and Barthesian death of Austen is what allows mashups to exist, *Zombies* is not actually dealing with the works of a "dead" Austen, but the personage of a still very much "alive" *Jane*.

The living version of Austen bears the same name and is regarded as indistinguishable from the actual author, but rather than founding this identity on historical fact, she is based on an edited version of Jane. While there is almost always a distinction between the author as an actual person and the literary concept of author, in the case of Austen the divide between those two people is enormous. Beginning with her brother Henry's Biographical Notice soon after her death, Austen was presented to the public as "[f]aultless herself, as nearly human nature can be" and claimed that she "never uttered either a hasty, a silly, or a severe expression."[18] At the same time, he emphasized her piety and humility, beginning the still-standing tradition of Austen as the infallible Divine Jane. Though this tradition of divinity peaked with the Victorians, our contemporary presentation of Austen embraces this image that has "sweetened her image, weakened her words, and softened her bite."[19]

Almost all well-known authors go through a separation between the actual person who is doing the writing and the person they are perceived to be. But for authors like Austen who have been in near-constant circulation for decades, the false creation of the author supplants the foundation in fact. Authors like Austen become a creation on par with their works that can be consumed alongside the text itself. The death of the author that allows the creation of mashup literature also allows for the real personage of the author to be buried underneath the version of the author who has been constructed by culture. This effect is particularly potent for Austen because of her incredible popularity and the industry that has been built up around her name. Eckart Voigts-Virchow, in his own discussion of *Zombies*, likens Austen's works unto furniture because "her texts become objects not just to read, but to reckon with, to be moved around, to delight and wallow in," while at the same time Austen herself has "long been the bone of contention in illicit readership debates. . . . Academic readers, working-class readers, female readers, American readers, non-English readers, chick-lit readers may be seen as battling over 'ownership' via reading, very much as one may debate ownership of furniture."[20] Both Austen and her texts are regarded as public property, a *thing* that different subgroupings of readers seek to lay claim to and regard as their own rather than an actual person who is no one's by her own. As Claire Harman points out in *Jane's Fame: How Jane Austen Conquered the World*, Austen's contemporary popularity has grown to such an extent that "Austen's name bears such a weight of signification as to mean almost nothing at all."[21] For all but the most diligent of readers, the idea of Austen has supplanted the facts. Her Barthesian death has stretched to the point that not only does Austen no longer have a say in the interpretation of her works, but also in the version of her self that is being presented to the public. Just as with her novels, Austen has ceased to be a person and instead has become a character to be rewritten in whatever manner suits the reader.

This representation of Austen is what Grahame-Smith reacts against rather than the actual author. He attempts to use his mashup to point out the defects in this one-dimensional portrait of *Pride and Prejudice*. However, the image that he possesses of Austen as a saintly woman writing works obsessed with class and courtship is not the actual author or the actual focus of her text. Although the courtships within *Pride and Prejudice* have allowed the work to be written off as just another romance, and Austen considered a woman capable of writing only such a genre, a deeper analysis allows readers to see the texts as far more complicated. Austen's supposed sweetness is counteracted by the biting sarcasm with which she treats Lady Catherine de Bourgh—a character which Grahame-Smith sets up among the best in his zombie-riddled world—while her propriety is juxtaposed against Lydia's scandalous behavior—for which Lydia is arguably not at all punished—and Austen's romantic focus by the emphasis that the narrative actually places on the relationship between Elizabeth and Jane. All of the complexity that dwells within Austen's text is disregarded by the mashup because it doesn't fall into alignment with the caricature of Austen that Grahame-Smith regards as the truth. The historical Austen with all her human frailties and complex works is not what Grahame-Smith attempts to critique with his mashup. Instead, he reacts to the image of a living Jane who is constantly being re-created and diluted by popular culture.

For Grahame-Smith's parody to function, it is not the "dead" Austen the reader must have a familiarity with, but the "living" Jane of popular culture. Even if his audience has never read the source before—and thus is unaware of the complexity that Austen actually brings—they still need to be aware of the prudishness, romance, and other stereotypes that Jane is typically considered to represent. Austen's physical death allows the mashup to exist legally while her Barthesian death allows it to exist psychologically, both of which create the opportunity for the mashup to react against the literary tradition that has elevated both her and her works. But at the same time, Jane must still be living, constantly portrayed as the saintly, marketable, spinster whose textbook romances are what the mashup is actually critiquing. This juxtaposition of needs places the mashup's source author in the strange position where she must both be Jane, exerting her influence over the mashup's view of her work, and be Austen, who is so safely buried that the mashup can exist at all. While it is not the true Jane Austen whose stature and skill the mashup rails against, it is still her work that is deemed so flawed that a horde of zombies can make it better.

Notes

1. Eckart Voigts-Virchow, "Pride and Promiscuity and Zombies, or: Miss Austen Mashed Up in the Affinity Spaces of Participatory Culture," in *Adaptation and Cultural Appropriation*, ed. Pascal Nicklas and Oliver Lindner (Berlin: de Gruyter, 2012), 48.

2. Although there are now numerous literary mashups for Austen's major novels, I will constrain the bulk of my discussion to *Pride and Prejudice and Zombies* because of the wealth of conversation that has been had about that particular novel, and the familiarity readers are more likely to have with it as compared to mashups generally.

3. Seth Grahame-Smith, interview by Lev Grossman, "Pride and Prejudice, Now with Zombies!," *Time.com*, April 2, 2009, http://content.time.com/time/arts/article/0,8599,1889075,00.html.

4. Seth Grahame-Smith, interview by Tim Masters, "It's . . . Darcy of the Dead," *BBC News*, April 8, 2009.

5. Seth Grahame-Smith and Jane Austen, *Pride and Prejudice and Zombies* (Philadelphia: Quirk Books, 2009), 319.

6. Grahame-Smith, *Zombies*, 229.

7. Grahame-Smith, *Zombies*, 256.

8. Grahame-Smith, *Zombies*, 121.

9. Grahame-Smith, *Zombies*, 34.

10. Grahame-Smith, *Zombies*, 119.

11. Roland Barthes, "The Death of the Author," in *The North Anthology of Theory and Criticism*, 2nd ed., ed. Vincent B. Leitch, trans. Stephen Heath (New York: W. W. Norton, 2010), 1318.

12. Barthes, "Death of the Author," 1325.

13. Barthes, "Death of the Author," 1324.

14. Grahame-Smith, interview by Lev Grossman, "Pride and Prejudice, Now with Zombies!"

15. *Jane Austen: The Critical Heritage, Volume 2, 1870–1940*, ed. B. C. Southam (New York: Routledge, 2002), 190.

16. Cynthia Kartman, "Reader Review: Pride and Prejudice and Zombies by Seth Grahame-Smith," AustenBlog. August 6, 2009. http://austenblog.com/2009/08/06/reader-review-pride-and-prejudice-and-zombies-by-seth-grahame-smith-and-jane-austen/.

17. Kartman, "Reader Review."

18. Henry Austen, "Biographical Notice of The Author." *Austen*.com. http://www.austen.com/persuade/preface.htm.

19. Emily Auerbach, *Searching for Jane Austen* (Madison: University of Wisconsin Press, 2004), 3.

20. Voigts-Virchow, "Pride and Promiscuity and Zombies," 39–40.

21. Claire Harman, *Jane's Fame: How Jane Austen Conquered the World* (New York: Henry Holt, 2009), xvii.

CHAPTER SEVENTEEN

Pride and Prejudice and Zombies

Regency, Repression, and Roundhouse Kicks

ANDREA ZANIN

It is a truth universally acknowledged that a zombie in possession of brains must be in want of more brains.

—*Pride and Prejudice and Zombies*

Zombies in corsets—your brain will resist, but *Pride and Prejudice and Zombies* doesn't give a shit; it'll take you *there*, against your better judgment. In Seth Grahame-Smith's zombie adaptation you'll find relief in the familiar pomp and ceremony that characterize Jane Austen's original nineteenth-century novel *Pride and Prejudice*—it's all there, but the reprieve is short-lived, as most everything else "familiar" has been semi-obliterated by a mysterious plague that kills and then causes the dead to return to "life." Once-dead men, women, and children—*zombies*—blunder through the English countryside (towns and cities, too) without aim or purpose, devoid of consciousness, but with a partiality for human meat—kicking, scratching, and mauling to get their fill. Grahame-Smith thrusts Austen's characters into a savage world where survival is not (only) dependent on being born into wealth or marrying well; survival is conditioned upon the decimation of the zombie threat. In Austen's pre-apocalypse society, a quick wit and sharp tongue were what it took for heroine Elizabeth Bennet to find love and fend off a life of mediocrity, but in zombie-land, it's a very literal *kill* or *be killed*. And so Grahame-Smith embellishes Elizabeth's intellectual fighting arsenal with a blade, to complement her gall and guts—and boy, does she use it with relish!

Pride and Prejudice and Zombies conceptualizes a violent and deeply cathartic alternative to the polite impertinence suggested by the prescribed values of the Regency society explored by Austen in *Pride and Prejudice*. Drawing on Austen's penchant for parody, Grahame-Smith uses the language of horror (in all its glorious excess) to accentuate the discernible criticism of the highly prescriptive social constructs that contextualize her novels. Rewritten against the backdrop of a zombie apocalypse, "polite society" is transformed into the home of horror's most manky metaphor—rotting corpses, once human but supernaturally resurrected, without soul or essence.

The notion of the "living dead" accentuates Austen's ideas on the effects of conformism, suggesting that the repression of thoughts, desires, and passions for the sake of "proper behavior" has a degenerative effect (like a plague of the mind that if manifest in the flesh would cause the skin to rot and the brain to putrefy) leading to the ultimate disintegration of the self into something *unmentionable*, as the zombies are so named in the adaptation. With mindlessness a mere bite away, Grahame-Smith uses the concept of the "philosophical zombie" to imply a scenario in which thought is contrived and action is manipulated—and "zombification" is liberal in its infestation, inflicting both plebeian and patrician with vigor alike.

The zombie apocalypse reorders civilized society; no longer do "us" and "them" refer to "rich" and "poor," "married" or "unmarried," "gentlemanly" or "un-gentlemanly," but rather "alive" or "dead," in the most visceral of terms. The words (and concepts) traditionally used by Regency denizens to locate themselves (hierarchically) within the society of which they are a part have been rephrased. That which is "Other"—*unmentionable*—in the context of a zombie apocalypse, the thing that exists in opposition to the self (that which heroine Elizabeth Bennet parallels her identity against), is a soggy ex-human that fancies brains for dinner. In defiance of all things contextually appropriate, Elizabeth Bennet's ability to extricate the enemy adds a new dimension to her sense of self. Under the weight of Grahame-Smith's pen, not only is she something of an antidote to the trappings of social propriety, as Austen intended, but a zombie assassin with skills far superior to the men and women in her company. Perhaps only Lady Catherine de Bourgh and delicious Fitzwilliam Darcy can rival Elizabeth's fighting prowess; de Bourgh ends up almost dead and Darcy married—"owned" by lethal Lizzy.

In a world where mornings are spent sharpening daggers and polishing muskets, and minds are engaged in "the deadly arts" rather than "clouded with dreams of marriage and fortune,"[1] Elizabeth Bennet is afforded a fortuitous outlet for the frustration nurtured by impulses forcibly submerged and stifled in a society governed by gender stereotype, class structures, and behavioral dictates. *Pride and Prejudice and Zombies* is a metaphorical conjecture into the mind of Elizabeth Bennet; hypothesizing the nature of her subconscious—what she would *really* wish to do to those who fall under the gaze of her contempt. As it turns out, a well-executed roundhouse kick goes a long way to assuaging repressed emotion.

Her Hand Met the Dagger Concealed Beneath Her Dress

Regency society couldn't have been better at constraining humankind's natural impulses if it had tried. Austen's world was governed by enigmatic social intercourse with no scope for direct conversation or emotion; meanings were frustratingly implicit. If you *really* liked someone, forget "hey, wanna go on a date"; rather, you'd *dare* to ask them for a second dance, as Bingley does the lovely Jane Bennet at the Meryton Ball; and if you were incensed because some guy had totally dissed your sister (by leading her on, dancing with her *more* than twice and then rolling out of town without so much as a personal "goodbye"—*ehem* . . . Mr. Bingley), the extent of your fury would manifest in "speaking ill" of said guy—to no one *but your sister*. Harsh?—*Not*. The hyper-euphemistic manner of the expression that characterized Regency society cannot have been healthy; all that submerged emotional surplus had to go somewhere.

Sigmund Freud (1856–1939), the father of psychoanalysis, had a lot to say about repression, the affirmation of which is essential to a comprehensive understanding of the unconscious mind as well as the doctor-cum-philosopher's psychoanalytic theory, the goal of which was (and still is) to make the unconscious *conscious*, in an effort to treat mental illness and rectify inappropriate behavior. Psychoanalysis is based on the existence of unconscious mental processes that comprise thought and inform our interactions with the world. Freud theorized two primary instincts: aggression, which represents the death instinct; and sex (libido), representing the life instinct. Freud said that these two instincts are opposing drives and are thus in constant conflict. He believed that the aggression instinct needs to be controlled; if it is not controlled, psychosis will result. So when Darcy insults Elizabeth at the Meryton Ball by saying to Bingley (within earshot of our fabulous heroine), "*You* are dancing with the only handsome girl in the room" also calling her "tolerable, but not handsome enough to tempt" him, in Austen's version, Elizabeth reacts with "no very cordial feelings" toward Darcy and retells the story with "great spirit" among her friends.[2] Elizabeth takes the proverbial high road in spite of the fact that she is hurt and angry—as suggested by the Georgian euphemism "not very cordial." In *Pride and Prejudice*, Jane Austen alludes to a society vastly diverse in the enactment of its public and private self, which is emphasized when Elizabeth represses her annoyance for the sake of social decorum (aggression buried—*check*; psychosis avoided—*check*), and she has her superego to thank.

The *superego* was an integral part of Freud's personality theory, which introduces the model of the id, ego, and superego. The id is our pleasure impulse; the superego is our internal voice of authority and morality; and the ego, which is governed by the reality principle, mediates between these two opposing forces. So not only are the sex and aggression drives battling for domination within the id, but the id is battling for domination against the superego (no wonder life is hard!). Elizabeth's reaction to Darcy's insult was expertly mediated by her ego, which responded to the superego's need to conform to the social propriety demanded by the context. Elizabeth is pissed, but she balls her fists, stiffens her backbone, and stares Darcy down, rather than dishing him a fat slap in the face. But what if Lizzy had lost control, her id slam-dunking superego through the hoop, with hang time to boot? Well, chaos—basically; *Lord of the Flies* on steroids. An exaggeration, perhaps, but you get the point, right? Regency would freak out. Freud chalks up much of mankind's elemental craziness to a base aggressive instinct that is not adequately controlled—too much control results in passivity, too little control results in murder and other types of psychopathological behavior. According to Freud we require the perfect balance of control. *No pressure.*

Freud claimed that we control aggression by repressing it, but it needs an outlet; otherwise it builds up and explodes with devastating effect—Incredible Hulk, *anyone?* This is where the subconscious joins the conversation. The subconscious is the part of our mind that is not currently in focal awareness—it's where we send the stuff that consciousness does not want to or cannot deal with, like emotions that are red-lighted as "inappropriate." Psychoanalysis says that the aggressive impulses that have been exiled from conscious thought into the subconscious are relieved through fantastical imaginings that often manifest in dreams (and daydreams). Freud called it *catharsis*, which comes from the Greek word *catharsis*, meaning to "purge" or "purify."

In Aristotle's (384–322 BC) *Poetics*, a study on poetry, the philosopher uses the term *catharsis* to explain the release of emotions (like pity and fear) built up during a dramatic performance. Although the context is disparate, the principle translates in psychoanalytic terms—the need for the mind to disgorge pent-up emotional angst. In the zombie apocalypse, instead of euphemizing Darcy's insult with her supposed good nature, Elizabeth turns immediately to the violent-type fantasies that characterize Grahame-Smith's adaptation. As she hears Darcy defame her appearance, our heroine's blood turns cold, having never in her life been so insulted. Elizabeth reaches down to her ankle for a dagger concealed beneath her dress; "She meant to follow this proud Mr. Darcy outside and open his throat."[3] The zombie apocalypse offers the perfect opportunity for what Freud called "sublimation," which is all about satisfying an instinct (like aggression) with a substitute object, in a socially acceptable way. So although it would not have been socially acceptable to slit Darcy's throat over an insult, it would be socially acceptable to disembowel a hoard of threatening zombies—the "substitute object." It is through this violent extremity and the metaphoric language of horror that Grahame-Smith contemplates a society that has a superego operating in overdrive, exerting too much control over its members.

Sloppy Seconds

Elizabeth Bennet is commanded by a world organized *by* men *for* men and not just any men: *wealthy* men—who were lucrative property in Regency society. Marriage (not love!) was what it took for a woman to be recognized as a person of value (as much as a woman could be at this time) and was thus top of the priority list for most Georgian ladies. Marrying a man of wealth gave a woman prominence in society and was critical for what Austen terms "preservative from want."[4] A woman's identity was summated by her marital status. Charlotte Lucas, Elizabeth Bennet's dear, desperate friend, sums up marriage as what is, essentially, a surrender of self: "Without thinking highly either of men or of matrimony, marriage had always been her object; it was the only honorable provision for well-educated young women of small fortune, and however uncertain of giving happiness, must be their pleasantest preservative from want."[5]

Charlotte's reflection is a response to her acceptance of Mr. Collins's marriage proposal—*sloppy seconds* after Elizabeth rejects life with a man she finds "neither sensible nor agreeable"; a man who is irksome, conceited, pompous, narrow-minded, and silly.[6] Or in the words of Elizabeth Bennet, zombie slayer: "[Does] this fat little priest mean to take [me] as a wife?" She was horrified at the thought of marrying a man "whose only skill with a blade was cutting slivers of gorgonzola"[7]—*how useless*. But Charlotte *does* marry Collins because at the age of twenty-seven (ancient, right!?) she has no alternative. It's totally sigh-worthy; the ultimate non-fairy tale—a horrendous anticlimax.

In Grahame-Smith's adaptation, Charlotte's marriage to Mr. Collins is almost a direct result of her being stricken by the dreaded plague *because, of course, that's the only reason one would marry such a douche bag*. She longs for a "proper Christian beheading and burial,"[8] and a husband alone can offer her dignity in death. The comment is poignant; it is only through marriage that Charlotte's life is granted worth, but it comes at great cost—a death of soul, which is symbolized by her physical decay. After a few short months of marriage, Charlotte's "skin was quite gray and marked with sores, and her speech appallingly labored"; she hovers over her plate "using a spoon to shovel goose meat and gravy in the general direction of her mouth, with limited success. As she did, one of the sores beneath her eye burst, sending a trickle of bloody puss down her cheek and into her mouth. Apparently, she found the flavor agreeable. . . ." Best yet is that Collins has no idea that his wife is three-quarters dead, not even when she "dropped to the ground and began stuffing handfuls of crisp autumn leaves into her mouth" and on another occasion, proceeded to gnaw on her own hand.[9] Charlotte's descent into zombieness and her husband's lack of consideration is an allegorical rendition of Austen's contempt for Regency society and its attitude toward women, who were forced into relationships of convenience in an ultimate repression of self and loss of authenticity—any desire for happiness quashed by the need to be "seen." Ironically, Charlotte's plague-ridden death is anything but dignified, making her marriage to Collins utterly redundant. Another slam dunk of a point.

It thus comes as no surprise that the girls go wild (with asphyxiated smiles and slight gestures of hand) when Bingley and Darcy roll into town. Rich, eligible men, *omg!* Who cares if they've got crappy personalities; a girl's got to get herself hitched unless your name is Elizabeth Bennet and you're the subject of Jane Austen's utopian romance, in terms of which you get to have your cake and eat it too. Of course, from Lizzy's perspective (not Austen's), she's a woman in control of her destiny—she wants a partnership and will have both love and security if it kills her.

"Your Balls, Mr. Darcy?"

Lizzy gets the guy—against all the odds and in the severest contravention of reality. Darcy is out of her league, not because he's better looking or more intelligent (or a more efficient zombie slayer) *because he's not*, but because he is of noble birth, as noted by Lady Catherine, to whose daughter Darcy is betrothed:

> My daughter and my nephew are formed for each other. They are descended on the maternal side, from the same noble line; and on the father's, from respectable, honorable, and ancient though untitled families. Their fortune on both sides is splendid. They are destined for each other by the voice of every member of their respective houses; and what is to divide them? The upstart pretensions of a young woman without family, connections or fortune. Is this to be endured! But it must not, shall not be.[10]

By all rights, Lizzy should have married Collins but ends up with Darcy; a love match—a happy ending . . . *a myth.* Not only do Elizabeth and Darcy overcome the edict of their social context, but they are able to transcend the limitations of their respective characters—both pride *and* prejudice. It's nothing less than heroic. Not even the violent fantasies lived out in cathartic expulsion are enough to keep Elizabeth and Darcy apart—ego somehow manages to do its job (yet again) in the face of some pretty gruesome stuff. Sure, Lizzy attacks Darcy when he declares his love for her (the first time), with one of her kicks sending the man careening "into the mantelpiece with such force as to shatter its edge,"[11] but she manages not to murder him with the fire poker in her grasp nor rip his heart from his chest and hold it, still beating, in her hand as she swore to do "before her time in Kent was concluded."[12]

The violence and aggression that sends Elizabeth into "a kind of darkness; a kind of absence as if her soul had taken leave, so that compassion and warmth could not interfere"[13] is a form of self preservation, literally (zombie apocalypse and all), but figuratively too, as Lizzy fights to protect her heart. And yet "the darkness" is mediated by an equally strong life instinct (libido) that punctuates the death and decapitation with some life-affirming innuendo. The repressed sexual tension between Elizabeth and Darcy is immutable, even early on, as illustrated by an innocent discussion about the upcoming soirée at Netherfield, which turns into something hilariously bawdy:

> "I should like balls infinitely better" [Miss Bingley] replied, "if they were carried on in a different manner."
>
> "You should like balls infinitely better," said Darcy, "if you knew the first thing about them."

> Elizabeth blushed and suppressed a smile—slightly shocked by his flirtation with impropriety, and slightly impressed that he should endeavor to flirt with it at all.[14]

When it comes to "balls," Darcy just can't help himself. The "sex-text" pops up again when Elizabeth remembers the lead ammunition in her pocket and offers it to dear Darcy: "'Your balls, Mr. Darcy?' He reached out and closed her hand around them, and offered, 'They belong to you, Miss Bennet.' Upon this, their color changed, and they were forced to look away from one another, lest they laugh."[15] And no, the "bawd" has not yet left the building! Lady Catherine's passive-aggressive assault against Elizabeth is countered by Darcy at his smart-ass best: "'Miss Bennet would make a fine showing of Leopard's Claw if she practiced more, and could have the advantage of a Japanese master. She has a very good notion of fingering,'" to which Darcy replies, "'That she does' . . . in a manner such as to make Elizabeth's face quite red."[16] Elizabeth and Darcy can't have sex (until they are married, at least), but they can sure as heck think about it, and in the zombie apocalypse, they can *even* allude to it.

The (wannabe) couple's sex drive is pitted against some seriously savage aggression. With Darcy's propensity to "hate everybody" and Elizabeth's "to willfully misunderstand them,"[17] their love collides with hostile urgency, but again superego gives id a beat-down as Elizabeth manages to refrain from her violent impulses when socially unbefitting: "In spite of her deeply rooted bloodlust, she could not be insensible to the compliment of such a man's affection, and though her intention of killing him did not vary for an instant, she was somewhat sorry for the pain he was to receive. . . ."[18] Eventually realizing her prejudice, Elizabeth regrets her hatred and is "ashamed of ever wishing to drink the blood from [Darcy's] severed head."[19] She feels guilty.

The Seven Cuts of Shame

Superego metes out guilt when the rules are not followed, and if ego is having a day off, the guilt can become disproportionate and all-consuming. Of course, "rules" have different contexts. Zombie-slaying-Elizabeth lives by a warrior code taught to her by Pei Liu of Shaolin, where she received her training in the deadly arts. But when it comes to Darcy, Elizabeth contravenes a "personal code"—a set of ethics that passes judgment over her misinformed prejudice toward poor Darcy, and Elizabeth's ensuing guilt is something very real. After reading Darcy's "letter of revelation," absolving him from his perceived crimes, Lizzy longs for justice—to be punished for her unfairness: "Had she her dagger, Elizabeth would have dropped to her knees the seven cuts of dishonor without a moment's hesitation. 'How despicably I have acted!' she cried: 'I. Who prided myself on my discernment! . . . Oh! Were my master here to bloody my back with wet bamboo!'"[20]

On another occasion Elizabeth feels "anew the justice of Mr. Darcy's objections" and with all pleasure lost in pain "never had she been so happy to open the scabs of her seven cuts."[21] When Lizzy learns of Darcy's involvement in restoring Lydia's character and meting out just deserts upon Wickham, she longs "to see her seven scabs open and bleeding once more."[22] And in final emphasis of self-loathing (and guilt) Elizabeth "would, at times, have given anything to leap onto the table and administer the seven cuts of shame in front of Mr. Darcy—to see her pitiful blood drip onto his plate; atonement for her many prejudices against him."[23] Elizabeth wishes to inflict violent pain upon herself as penance for her sins against Darcy—this, in itself, a form of catharsis. The guilt that is repressed by order of society manifests in an attack on her physical person, which smacks of "displacement"—another defense mechanism articulated by Freud. Displacement is similar to sublimation in that it also refers to satisfying an impulse (like aggression) with a substitute object, although in this case, it's not done in a socially acceptable manner. Elizabeth's self-harm, which exists as both reality and fantasy, is a way to purge subjugated emotion, which in "normal society" would not be considered acceptable behavior although one might argue that in the zombie apocalypse, self-harm is part of the warrior code and thus a worthy punishment for shame, in which case sublimation would be more correctly applied.

Elizabeth's self-loathing is not likely a trait of character, but rather something contextual, a result of repressed emotional angst associated with her mistreatment of Darcy. Her reaction is extreme, even within the conscripts of the "Shaolin code," but perhaps this is horror's way of implying the extent of Lizzy's love for Darcy. She has not maltreated *just anyone*; she has maltreated her soul mate—and that's huge. Violence is how Elizabeth deals; it's a symptom of living in an apocalyptic era. At one point the heroine even acknowledges, "If only words were capable of beheading a zombie,"[24] but they're not; violence—fighting skill—is a necessary evil required for survival, and it has become an integral part of her identity.

She Is as Ferocious as She Is Fetching

Jane Austen describes marriage as fundamental to a Regency woman's sense of worth—her identity—but when "legions of Satan's slaves"[25] overrun the world, skill in the deadly arts is invaluable to the sustainability of life and thus "self"—it's not a substitute for wealth (or class), but it adds another dynamic to identity. Darcy describes an accomplished woman as one who has a "thorough knowledge of music, singing, drawing and dancing, and the modern languages; she must be well trained in the fighting styles of the Kyoto masters and the modern tactics and weaponry of Europe."[26] Knowing how to fight imbues a Regency gal with maximum street cred, and Elizabeth has spent many a long day within the confines of the Shaolin Temple in Henan Province being trained to endure "all manner of discomfort"[27]— "the pain of Maser Liu's glowing brand searing her flesh; the sparring matches with her sisters atop a beam no wider than their swords, as pikes waited to punish an ill-placed foot below."[28] She wields a blade with "uncommon skill" and is described as "ferocious as she is fetching."[29] So even without a husband, Elizabeth is afforded value because of her skill in the deadly arts, and in fact, she happily admits that it is a large part of the reason Darcy falls for her:

> you were sick of civility, deference, of officious attention. You were disgusted with the women who were always speaking, and looking, and thinking for your approbation alone. I roused, and interested you, because I was so unlike them. I knew the joy of standing over a vanquished foe; of painting my face and arms with their blood, yet warm, and screaming to the heavens—begging, nay daring, God to send me more enemies to kill. The gentle ladies who so assiduously courted you knew nothing of this joy, and therefore, could never offer you true happiness.[30]

Elizabeth stands in direct contrast to women like Caroline Bingley, who avoids any sort of cathartic gratification and thus remains quite dull. Elizabeth notices Miss Bingley's true feelings toward her, saying, "Oh! How she must long to strike at me with her clumsy, untrained fists"[31]—but of course she doesn't, not only because she *won't* (for propriety's sake), but because she doesn't know how.

Elizabeth is imbued with a self-awareness that informs her identity and the violence she wreaks, although enjoyable (especially when in cohort with the man of her dreams) is necessary. With every deadhead she dislocates Elizabeth does her part to rid the world of zombie infestation, and yet there is the unavoidable truth that this unmentionable, man-masticating force was once human. She's a warrior imbued with an innate compassion for her enemy.

I Am Because *You Are* . . . Zombie

Fumbling around in a mindless, ravenous hunger for flesh; groaning and grunting without point or purpose; void of intellect, passion, power, psychosis, sexuality, romance, reason, method or madness, zombies are defined by the populace of Seth Grahame-Smith's bastardized Regency "romance" as "Other": as beings that stand in opposition to the self. The zombie others are a mirror for the living, an exposition of mankind at its most degenerate. One cannot perceive the "Other" without integrating the resulting opinion or understanding into an awareness of self. When walking in the woods with her sisters one day, Elizabeth and her crew stumble upon a zombie infant; Lizzy lifts her musket to blast the creature to smithereens and as she does so, Jane calls on her to remember her oath. Lizzy doesn't pull the trigger, recognizing a feeling from her earliest days—before she first traveled to Shaolin: "it was a curious feeling; it was something akin to shame but without the dishonor of defeat—a shame that demanded no vengeance. 'Could there be honor in mercy?'"[32] It's as if, through the once-upon-a-time innocence of the zombie child, Elizabeth comes face-to-face with the humanness of the "Other" and takes pity on it.

The philosophical implication of "otherness" is fundamental to the satire that pervades Grahame-Smith's zombie adaptation. French philosopher Emmanuel Levinas (1906–1995) spent much of his life contemplating the ethics of the "Other," which is understood as the entity in contrast to which identity is constructed. Otherness implies the ability to distinguish between the self and not-self—the "Other." For Levinas, ethical responsibility for the "Other" was the foundation of his philosophical analyses. He articulated the "Other" as inextricably linked to the self because the self is possible only with its recognition of the "Other"—I am *me* because you are *you*. What Levinas was getting at is that as individuals in society, we locate our identity in reference to that which is around us; that which is "Other" to us—I know who *I* am because I know who *you* are. *Except* . . . I don't *really* know who you are, do I? I name *you*, who is "Other" to me, according to the language that represents my own sense of self, a process that makes my version of you subjective and thus not entirely reliable. Levinas took it one step further; he claimed that the "Other" is unknowable and that by inflicting our own mental processes on the "Other" in an attempt to "know" it (and in turn ourselves), a metaphorical murder takes place. When Elizabeth Bennet is named a "bride of man"[33] after her union with Darcy, everything else that Elizabeth is—sister, daughter, warrior, intellect—is eradicated from her identity, and so part of her objective "self" dies. Of course, Elizabeth can be all those things, but through the act of "naming" they are excluded, even if for a brief moment. Regency society's literal murder of the zombie "Other" echoes the violent relationship that exists between the self and the "Other."

Levinas sought to break what he termed "the obstinacy of being"[34] by showing that we owe our very existence to the "Other," and that we are therefore irrevocably responsible for the "Other." He emphasized a relationship of respect and responsibility for the other person rather than a relationship of mutuality and dialogue—because through dialogue, the self subjugates the other with words in a desire to "name" and thus "know." The fact that the zombies in Grahame-Smith's adaptation are called "unmentionables" alludes to the individual's need to "know" through "naming," but to define them as "unspeakable" is also an acknowledgment of the "Other's" alterity—something that, in essence, is irreducibly different. And yet the zombie "Other" looks like us . . . but we want to kill it; it's a real dilemma—how then does a kick-ass heroine like Elizabeth Bennet exercise her responsibility? The only thing that she can really do is act with compassion and intelligence.

American philosopher Judith Butler (born in 1956) combines Levinasian insights about the primacy of the "Other" with psychoanalytic insights about the intersubjective formation of human beings. A psychoanalytic understanding of Levinasian ethics reminds us that the "Other" dwells within the self—through the unconscious and even through our bodily drives.[35] The zombie "Other" is a part of Elizabeth Bennet, not only in that it has shaped her identity, but in that it is a part thereof—the rot and horror lurking within her subconscious, waiting, *itching*, for release. Butler puts it:

> I am confounded by you, then you are already of me, and I am nowhere without you. I cannot muster the "we" except by finding the way in which I am tied to "you," by trying to translate but finding my own language must break up and yield if I am to know you. You are what I gain through this disorientation and loss. This is how the human comes into being, again and again, as that which we have yet to know.[36]

Butler's theory is extreme in that it implies that there is nothing about our being that can be separated from the "Other," which means that we are overwhelmed by the "Other," rather than enabled. In *Pride and Prejudice and Zombies*, Seth Grahame-Smith offers us either/or, the chance to be overwhelmed or enabled.

Elizabeth Bennet is *enabled*. The zombie "Other" offers Lizzy the chance to manipulate her identity in a way that Regency society never *ever* would. In response to the otherness of her zombie foe, Elizabeth turns herself into a zombie assassin and exists as the embodiment of cathartic expulsion. Without the "Other," Elizabeth is doomed to a mediocrity imposed by the constructs of civilized society. Her identity is bonded to the "Other" and as a result, polite society's "delightful array of tarts, exotic fruits, and pies" is "sadly soiled by blood, brains and the unusable"[37]; Elizabeth insults the conservativism demanded by the culture of her time.

In an astute commentary on *Pride and Prejudice*, D. W. Harding describes Austen's work as resonating a "regulated hatred" for many aspects of the society with which she is so closely identified.[38] Unfortunately, Ms. Austen didn't have the luxury of a zombie apocalypse to allow for an ablution of soul. Her outlet was art, and by invoking ourselves as participants through reading, we too, as Aristotle suggested, purge a little pain along the way.

Notes

1. Jane Austen and Seth Grahame-Smith, *Pride and Prejudice and Zombies* (Philadelphia: Quirk Books, 2009), 8.

2. Jane Austen, *Pride and Prejudice* (Great Britain: Wordsworth Editions, 1999), 9.

3. Grahame-Smith, *Zombies*, 13–14.

4. Austen, *Pride and Prejudice*, viii.

5. Austen, *Pride and Prejudice*, 85.

6. Austen, *Pride and Prejudice*, 85, 93.

7. Grahame-Smith, *Zombies*, 71.

8. Grahame-Smith, *Zombies*, 99.

9. Grahame-Smith, *Zombies*, 120–22, 142.

10. Austen, *Pride and Prejudice*, 239.

11. Grahame-Smith, *Zombies*, 151.

12. Grahame-Smith, *Zombies*, 146.

13. Grahame-Smith, *Zombies*, 58.

14. Grahame-Smith, *Zombies*, 44.

15. Grahame-Smith, *Zombies*, 204.

16. Grahame-Smith, *Zombies*, 138.

17. Grahame-Smith, *Zombies*, 47.

18. Grahame-Smith, *Zombies*, 149.

19. Grahame-Smith, *Zombies*, 212.

20. Grahame-Smith, *Zombies*, 165.

21. Grahame-Smith, *Zombies*, 184.

22. Grahame-Smith, *Zombies*, 263.

23. Grahame-Smith, *Zombies*, 274.

24. Grahame-Smith, *Zombies*, 43.

25. Grahame-Smith, *Zombies*, 286.

26. Grahame-Smith, *Zombies*, 34.

27. Grahame-Smith, *Zombies*, 37.

28. Grahame-Smith, *Zombies*, 75.

29. Grahame-Smith, *Zombies*, 20, 74.

30. Grahame-Smith, *Zombies*, 311.

31. Grahame-Smith, *Zombies*, 311.

32. Grahame-Smith, *Zombies*, 92.

33. Grahame-Smith, *Zombies*, 317.

34. Mari Ruti, *Between Levinas and Lacan: Self, Other, Ethics* (New York: Bloomsbury, 2015), 40.

35. Ruti, *Between Levinas and Lacan*, 40.

36. Ruti, *Between Levinas and Lacan*, 41.

37. Grahame-Smith, *Zombies*, 80.

38. Austen, *Pride and Prejudice*, xii.

CHAPTER EIGHTEEN

"Till This Moment I Never Knew Myself"

On Identities and Zombies

A. G. HOLDIER

It is a truth nearly universally acknowledged that . . . a story with an opening line such as this one is anything but novel. In the two centuries since her career came to an end, the works of Jane Austen have found such a welcome home in the public consciousness that, like Shakespeare, Dickens, Doyle, and Greek myth before her, the stories in the Austen canon, peppered with witticisms and memorable phrases, are now their own springboard for new tales, ranging from lengthy BBC dramatizations of Austen's original narratives to updated, reimagined adventures of heroines like Bridget Jones and *Clueless*'s Cher Horowitz.

In particular, a flood of authors has thought themselves worthy to resume, retell, and reimagine the story of Elizabeth Bennet and her family from Austen's beloved *Pride and Prejudice*,[1] spinning new stories of family embarrassments, returning to old tales from the perspective of other characters, and adding new elements to the narrative to entertain new audiences. Even without considering the half dozen star-studded cinematic adaptations of Austen's original story, recent twists have seen Mr. Darcy busy solving murders or drinking the blood of the living, leaving Elizabeth to either farm in northwest India or develop her zombie-killing skills to some acclaim.

But with such a large number of "Elizabeth Bennets" and "Fitzwilliam

Darcys" occupying contemporary bookshelves, the question of a character's identity becomes complicated: when a reader thinks of "Elizabeth Bennet," must she imagine only Austen's original character? If so, how should the identically named characters (with near-identical personalities) in P. D. James's sequel *Death Comes to Pemberley*[2] or Seth Grahame-Smith's parody *Pride and Prejudice and Zombies*[3] be considered, given that they ostensibly describe the "same" character in different circumstances? It was hard enough for the original Elizabeth to come to know herself—a challenge no less formidable for readers today faced with a multiplicity of candidates vying for attention.

Much to Miss Bennet's chagrin (however familiar she might be with the experience), we have on hand two suitors from the twentieth century who each offer valuable insight into solving this problem of character identity: philosophers Paul Ricoeur and David Lewis. Hailing from France, Ricoeur's two-part framework for understanding existential questions about the self takes care to differentiate between a subject's internal personality and her external situation—what Ricoeur calls the "*ipse/idem*" distinction—and will help to differentiate between various Elizabeths. The American Lewis can offer an explanation of "possible world semantics"—a tool philosophers use to understand different-yet-similar sets of circumstances in imagined scenarios—to help explain how these different characters are yet related. By bringing these two ideas into conversation, we can not only gain wisdom into so-called "counterpart solutions" about character identities, but will come to see just how it is that all three of these different Elizabeth Bennets can, in fact, be worthy of the name.

"You Must Learn Some of My Philosophy"

Imagine, then, a ball whose magnificence would impress even Kitty Bennet, with attendees not only from everywhere between Hertfordshire and Derbyshire, but from *alternative versions* of those English countrysides found in stories written by authors other than Jane Austen. The hostess of this interdimensional ball is Austen's own Elizabeth Bennet, newly Elizabeth Darcy at the end of the original novel and now mistress of the great house Pemberley. This "Elizabeth-A" is she whose story of courtship and family embarrassments launched a thousand other imaginations.

Also in attendance at this imaginary ball is the Elizabeth Darcy from P. D. James's ostensible continuation of Austen's tale in the 2011 novel *Death Comes to Pemberley*. This Elizabeth has grown into a happy wife, mother, and talented manager of the noble Pemberley over the course of her six years of marriage to Mr. Darcy when her sister Lydia (and her disgraced brother-in-law George Wickham) upsets her peaceful life with a murder investigation. As James's Darcy looks into the accusations against the scoundrel Wickham (and eventually testifies in court on his behalf), this "Elizabeth-J" investigates the history of her onetime suitor on her own as she learns how to best protect her family.

Finally, stumbling into this cross-dimensional ball is the Elizabeth Bennet from Seth Grahame-Smith's 2009 *Pride and Prejudice and Zombies*, a parodic retelling of what Austen's story would have been like if a plague of zombies had infested England during the events of the original tale. This "Elizabeth-G" is a war-torn fighter, hardened by years of training and experience on the battlefield with the undead. Still, when Grahame-Smith's Elizabeth meets the zombie-hunting Mr. Darcy, she follows a familiar series of events that does eventually lead to their marriage, but not without her (unsuccessfully) trying to first decapitate him.

Indeed, the differences between the three Elizabeths—maiden, mother, and monster killer—are clear; no one familiar with each story would confuse one character for the other. Yet, at the same time, these three characters seem more closely related to each other than three characters chosen simply at random—that is, they seem to have some part of their identities in common with each other. This is puzzling, for the primary thing that all three Elizabeths seem to share is their name (or, at least the fact that at some point in their respective histories they shared the same name). Though their individual personalities are similar, Elizabeth-A lacks important knowledge and attitudinal responses to scenarios that Elizabeth-J and Elizabeth-G would find quite familiar (and likewise in both cases). However, it seems plausible to say that any one of these Elizabeths *could* have turned out to be the same as any of her counterparts were she to have been placed into those alternative circumstances all along—but is this right?

More importantly, is that enough to grant that these three Elizabeths are the "same"? How can these different characters truly be distinguished?

"I Had Hoped to Pass Myself Off with Some Degree of Credit"

The first order of business is to understand what is meant by calling any of the three Elizabeths a "character" or "person." Since Europe's Enlightenment period, the common Western impulse is to adopt the perspective of the seventeenth-century Frenchman René Descartes and assume that a person is comprised of a duality of body and soul, with one's identity, character, or personality being a rationalistic property of the latter. Because Descartes believed it possible to doubt everything in one's own experience beyond the experience of doubt itself, his famous declaration "I think, therefore I am"— the so-called cogito—necessarily divorces the thinking part of a person from the rest of the world around her. Consequently, on this view, "Elizabeth" becomes simply the spiritual ego of the individual character that drives her physical body much like an operator inside a vehicle; the body itself could be any number of imagined options—trained warrior or untrained wit. The differences between the three Elizabeths, then, would boil down entirely to circumstances in their three external worlds—for instance, whether they include zombies or not—for the internal element of the soul-based personality is the same in each case.

It is at this point that our own Frenchman, Paul Ricoeur, would begin to criticize the Cartesian framework: whereas Descartes settles on the "soul" as the basest foundation for his philosophy of mind, Ricoeur takes a more radical step by splitting the concept into even more fundamental pieces. In his 1992 work *Oneself as Another*,[4] Ricoeur points out that we can draw a further distinction between a thought and a thinker *thinking* that thought, so the cogito can be shattered by simply asking "who is thinking"? Though his critical tongue is somewhat more gentle than Elizabeth-A's when aimed at the hapless Darcy, Ricoeur insists that Descartes actually answers the wrong question: focusing not on *who* was thinking but on what sort of thing was doing the thinking—namely, a "thinking thing," or, to Descartes, a "soul." In contrast, Ricoeur wants to focus on the more personal question: Who exists and what is that person like?

Relying on two Latin terms to keep his thoughts as clear as Mrs. Bennet's matchmaking intentions, Ricoeur explains that a person's identity is the result of the interplay between two different forms of identity: the *ipse* and the *idem*, or the "self" and "the sameness" of how that self remains what it is over time. The *ipse* identity is the self, or a subject doing something in the flash of a moment, whereas the *idem* identity is the sameness of that subject that does not change despite the many other changes that the subject undergoes through time. Ricoeur's favorite illustration of this dialectical relationship is how a character in a novel is recognizable despite undergoing change; Elizabeth-A learns several valuable lessons and makes a number of important choices over the course of her story as her *ipse* identity repeatedly responds to her circumstances; the sum total of those choices when viewed externally from any individual choice is the *idem* identity of which fans think when they imagine Austen's "Elizabeth Bennet."

This is why Ricoeur describes personal identity as always encapsulating a narrative: to consider any person, fictional or not, is to think of an individual who has experienced change over time (or "undergone plot development"), but who is still substantially the same person. Consequently, to use another of Ricoeur's favorite practical examples, humans can make and keep promises to each other: when Mr. Darcy's father promised George Wickham a living on the Darcy estate, this was sealed in good faith that, despite how either Darcy or Wickham would change in the future (due to shifts in their respective *ipse* identities), the overarching responsibility of "caring for Wickham" would be grounded in the prediction of how their *idem* identities would eventually read (when considered in retrospect as a whole). The full concept of identity to Ricoeur is one's *ipse* becoming *idem* as a subject grows and changes into how the person will be remembered; much like how a sewing pattern limits how a seamstress will work, a person's moment-to-moment identity (*ipse*) is predicted by that person's comprehensive identity (*idem*), even as that person's *idem* is simultaneously and constantly created as the person continually develops his or her *ipse* while living life. This explains why Wickham's decision to force the breaking of the elder Darcy's promise by cashing out his curacy with a simple lump settlement significantly changes Elizabeth-A's opinion of the scoundrel once she learns the truth of his history: his narrative was intended to have been different—he broke the sewing pattern.

Though it uses complicated terminology, Ricoeur's two-part framework for understanding personal identity ends up being far more valuable than Descartes' simplified cogito-option: because the Cartesian version emphasizes the thinking ego so strongly, it essentially ignores the role of the circumstances that shape the ego as it grows and develops over time. Differentiating between Elizabeth-J and Elizabeth-G, for example, becomes very difficult: for Descartes, the substance of their souls could indeed be identical, but that would fail to explain the unique elements of their experiences as housewife or zombie killer—facets of their characters that are easily assumed to be parts of their personal identities.

Instead, a Ricoeurian perspective could posit that all three Elizabeths share the same *ipse* identity, with all of the personality traits and attitudinal responses that characterize "Elizabeth Bennet/Darcy," but because of the drastically different circumstances of each of their lives, that shared *ipse* ends up expressing significantly different *idem* identities by the end of each story. Not only does this give credit to the formative effect of a person's context on the person herself and therefore allows for an honest treatment of, for example, Elizabeth-G's character in light of her unique supernatural situation, but it also helpfully answers other questions that would otherwise be more complicated. The age gap between Elizabeth-A and Elizabeth-J, for example, can be bridged by Ricoeur in a way that fully bypasses political debates surrounding the "authenticity" or "propriety" of the appropriation of one author's characters by another writer. A subsequent author (in this case, James) might well borrow the *ipse* identity of a previous author's character (Austen's Elizabeth), but she will unavoidably place that *ipse* into her own new narrative, thereby necessarily creating a brand-new *idem*. Ricoeur's philosophy of mind helps to simplify some of the conceptual complexities of derivative works of fiction.

However, as described here, Ricoeur was focused on single individuals coming to understand themselves; this comparative projection of one Elizabeth variant next to another is a somewhat different concept than what the French philosopher was discussing. Instead, it is an American that can offer further insight into the nature of the different dimensional Elizabeths in question (what Ricoeur's *idem* identity has been discussing) and how they can be compared.

"The More I See of the World, the More I Am Dissatisfied with It"

In one sense, this sort of comparison is based heavily on the natural intuition that the similarities between Elizabeth-A and Elizabeth-G are sufficient not only to outweigh whatever differences they share, but to highlight those two specific characters as being more closely related than, say, Elizabeth-A and the suicidal Mr. Collins found in Grahame-Smith's work. The twentieth-century American philosopher David Lewis has done a great deal to advance this intuitive conclusion in a more rigorous manner by adapting the language of possible world semantics to reach what he calls a "counterpart" solution to these sorts of questions about identity.

In short, a "possible world" is simply an alternative way that the world could be if different cosmic circumstances had led to different facts becoming true. Lewis's 1986 *On the Plurality of Worlds*[5] explains how imagining "the ways things might have been" is not only a very natural method for solving philosophical puzzles, but has offered a foundation for many of the most popular science fiction tales in recent memory. By playing with sentences in the subjunctive mood—those that do not state "how things *are*" but instead are concerned with "how things *would be if*"—possible world semantics leverages the imaginative power of counterfactual statements to offer a near-infinite mental playground for philosophical gymnastics. Moreover, it provides a launchpad for a wide variety of stories, as any fantasy or science fiction fan familiar with "alternate universe" tales (like "what *Pride and Prejudice* would be like if set in the middle of a zombie outbreak") can attest.

And while imagining counterfactual possibilities has been done by philosophers for centuries, Lewis's unique contribution to the methodology was to suggest that each and every possible world is not simply a fictional construct in a thinker's mind, but actually exists concretely within some spatiotemporal framework. That is to say that the intuition that the real world is a privileged possible world (in that it is not only a possible set of circumstances, but is an actualized set of circumstances) is false: instead, our "real world" only seems especially real to us, but is simply one more of the infinite "possible world" options for every other person in every other possible world. All possible worlds and all inhabitants of all possible worlds (including a wildly different world where zombies exist, for example) are, to Lewis, equally real.

Another way to imagine this is to consider the idea of being "here"—a concept whose referent is necessarily relative to the speaker. When Elizabeth-J receives a letter from her husband saying that he has "arrived here" for Wickham's trial, "here" means "London," for that is where her Darcy is; however, if Elizabeth-J were to ask her sister-in-law Georgiana to come "here," then she would not be referring to "London," but to a particular room of Pemberley—most likely, whatever room in which Elizabeth-J was sitting. This does not mean that the word "here" is useless, but that it is *indexical* to whomever is speaking; in much the same way, Lewis would say that the phrase "real world" is likewise relative to the speaker, with no "real world" being more or less existent than any given "here."

The interesting thing for Lewis is the possibility of comparing possible worlds along a metric of "closeness," where worlds that are "closer" to each other are those which resemble each other more than they resemble other worlds that are "farther away." The world of Elizabeth-A, for example, is certainly closer to the world of Elizabeth-J than that of Elizabeth-G, since [A] and [J] share more true statements (such as "Elizabeth is stubborn" and "Zombies do not exist") than do [A] and [G] (which agree on the former statement, but not the latter). Again, this intuitive conclusion might seem obvious, but the methodology offers a philosophical toolbox for explaining a variety of other puzzles.

To return to the primary question of this chapter, the Lewisian understanding of a character's identity is necessarily restricted to a single possible world—what Lewis calls being "world-bound." Because each possible world is equally real, they are each fully populated with inhabitants who each live out their own unique lives: it would not make sense to say that Elizabeth-A is exactly the same person as Elizabeth-J, for they each simultaneously exist with the other and act in different ways in different possible worlds. Much like in a science fiction story revolving around "parallel universes," the different Elizabeths might be mistaken for twins or triplets if they were to meet at our earlier imaginary ball (there's no telling which is the "evil" one, though). However, instead of twins, Lewis suggests that each Elizabeth is a *counterpart* of the other, which means that they are sufficiently similar to be uniquely compared to each other across worlds without being absolutely identical (even closer to each other metaphysically than twins are biologically). To be a counterpart of a person in another possible world allows for statements about what a character *would be* like to be considered true given that they *are* true for at least one of the character's counterparts.

Consequently, the three Elizabeths are freed from the confusing expectation of being absolutely identical to each other: instead, they are but three of the many different counterfactually based counterpart options for "Elizabeth Bennet/Darcy" that exist within the infinite panoply of the possible parallel-world compendium. Their many similarities (both in their intrinsic, personality-based properties, as well as their relational properties to their respective worlds) grant them unique comparability, despite the clear differences in their unique situations. Further away on the metric system of Lewis's modal realism about possible worlds might even sit the titular character from *Bridget Jones's Diary*, though she would likely be far less "close" than would even Elizabeth-G, who has devoted her life to hunting the undead. The important thing, though, is that each shares certain familiar, if vaguely described, properties.

"Till This Moment I Never Knew Myself"

To Lewis, those vagaries of identity theories based on counterparts are a strength, for it allows them to be flexible to a wider variety of conceptual concerns. In this case, it allows for Ricoeur's double-sided definition of character identity to be mapped onto the evident differences between the three Elizabeth counterparts in question. In short, Austen's Elizabeth Bennet, James's Elizabeth Darcy, and Grahame-Smith's Elizabeth Bennet (zombie killer extraordinaire) may appear to share a similar sort of consciousness (Ricoeur's *ipse* identity) though they are placed in considerably different possible worlds (which help form Ricoeur's *idem* identity). Jumping in, Lewis would say that these similarities with differences make them counterparts who are not actually identical with each other, despite sharing many of the same qualities, but who can still be compared relative to each other.

Consequently, the question that began this chapter—"When a reader thinks of 'Elizabeth Bennet,' must she imagine only Austen's original character?"—will have a different answer depending on what the questioner means by "Elizabeth Bennet." If the reader is imagining a character with a proclivity for responding to a given scenario "as Elizabeth Bennet would," then the reader must be imagining the *ipse* identity that Austen first created: the answer would then be "yes." However, if the reader is instead thinking of the overall narrative that one of many Elizabeth counterparts have been placed into, then any number of those *idem* scenarios might be equally valid: the answer would have to be "no."

If there was one lesson that the first Elizabeth learned over the course of Austen's original novel, it is that first impressions and simple questions often have far more complicated answers than we would like. That is not to say that exploring the truth is unimportant, but merely that it can be difficult, and we might not always like what we find. Coming to understand yourself is never easy—for Elizabeth Bennet, copied and translated into the cornucopia of stories in which she now finds herself, the task is exponentially more complicated, but that only makes the eventual payoff that much more rewarding. Not only does this Austen industry offer readers greater opportunities to rediscover beloved characters, but it presents ever-increasing foils to better understand the narratives of our own real lives.

Because, if Lewis is right, then all of these Elizabeths (and more) might be just as real as you and I; and if Ricoeur is right, then our own lives are simply stories in the process of being written. So, if all of these Elizabeths can come to know themselves, then we can hope to do so as well.

Notes

1. Jane Austen, *Pride and Prejudice* (New York: Dover, 1995).
2. P. D. James, *Death Comes to Pemberley* (New York: Alfred A. Knopf, 2011).
3. Seth Grahame-Smith and Jane Austen, *Pride and Prejudice and Zombies: The Classic*

Regency Romance—now with Ultraviolent Zombie Mayhem (Philadelphia: Quirk Books, 2009).

4. Paul Ricoeur, *Oneself as Another*, trans. by Kathleen Blamey (Chicago: University of Chicago Press, 1994).

5. David K. Lewis, *On the Plurality of Worlds* (Malden, MA: Blackwell Publishers, 2001).

Index

Fictional characters appear alphabetically by their first names or titles; viz.: "Admiral Croft"; "Anna Weston."

~

About the Contributors

Charles Bane has lived in numerous places all over the country, working variously as a country music disc jockey, an oil refinery demolition specialist, a movie critic, a television producer, an eighth-grade English teacher, and a college professor. Along the way, he managed to earn various degrees including a PhD in literature, film, and theory from LSU. He is the coauthor of *A Primer of the Novel*, and his articles have appeared in *Stephen King and Philosophy*, *Hollywood's America: Twentieth-Century America Through Film*, *Stanley Kubrick: Essays on his Films and Legacy*, and *Papa, PhD: Essays on Fatherhood by Men in the Academy*. Currently, he is an assistant professor of film and literature at Harding University in Arkansas, where he lives with his wife, the poet Paulette Guerin, and their three children and three cats.

Vittorio Bufacchi is head of the Department of Philosophy at University College Cork, Ireland. He earned his undergraduate degree from the University of Sussex (UK), and his MA and PhD from the London School of Economics (UK), where he worked with Professor Brian Barry. He has held visiting positions at Yale, University of Colorado (Boulder), and Dartmouth College. He is the author of *Social Injustice: Essays in Political Philosophy* (2012) and *Violence and Social Justice* (2007), and edited three volumes on philosophy and violence, including *Violence: A Philosophical Anthology* (2012). He is editor of the Palgrave Philosophy Today book series. His work has been translated into Spanish, Chinese, and Italian.

Nancy Marck Cantwell is associate professor and chair of the English department at Daemen College in Amherst, New York, where she teaches British literature. Her scholarly work investigates texts produced by nineteenth-century novelists from England, Scotland, and Ireland. Recent publications include an article on Thackeray's *Vanity Fair* in *Nineteenth-Century Gender Studies*, as well as a chapter in *The Contemporary Irish Detective Novel* (2015); current essays treat gothic narrative elements in Maria Edgeworth's *Castle Rackrent* and subversive tourism in novels by Edgeworth and Susan Ferrier. Her current book project is a study of nineteenth-century women novelists and nationalism.

E. M. Dadlez has a PhD in philosophy from Syracuse University and is professor of philosophy at the University of Central Oklahoma. Her work is mainly on the philosophy of art and literature, and on topics at the intersection (sometimes, more accurately, the collision) of aesthetics, ethics, and epistemology. She is the author of various articles on aesthetics and applied ethics, as well as *What's Hecuba to Him? Fictional Events and Actual Emotions* and *Mirrors to One Another: Emotion and Value in Jane Austen and David Hume*. She is also a feminist ethics dilettante.

Kathleen Poorman Dougherty believes in true love but is grateful to make her own fortune without having to marry for it. She is even more grateful making her fortune doing something she loves. She holds a PhD in philosophy from the University of Oklahoma and currently serves as the dean of the School of Humanities, Social Sciences, and Education at Mount Mary University. Her philosophical work is in virtue ethics, focusing on the development of character and the moral importance of self-knowledge. Though her chosen profession does not permit a grand estate or a barouche, it makes for a satisfying and stimulating life. She does, however, continue to keep her eyes open for her own Mr. Darcy and hopes that she will judge him charitably when he crosses her path.

Keith Dromm is associate professor of philosophy in the Louisiana Scholars' College at Northwestern State University. He has written *Wittgenstein on Rules and Nature* (2008) and *Sexual Harassment: An Introduction to the Conceptual and Ethical Issues* (2012), and coedited with Heather Salter *The Catcher in the Rye and Philosophy* (2012). He has also published articles on other subjects, such as the philosophy of film. Alas, to his continuing regret, none of this has yet to earn him an entry in the *Baronetage*.

Suzie Gibson teaches literature at Charles Sturt University, Australia. She has published widely across the disciplines of literature and philosophy. For example, her articles in the journals *Philosophy and Literature* and *Philosophy Today* reveal her interest in examining interrelationships between these important areas of research. Her past contribution to *James Bond and Philosophy: Questions are Forever* is another example of her interest in connections between philosophy, literature, and popular culture.

Richard Gilmore is professor and chair of the philosophy department at Concordia College, in Moorhead, Minnesota. He is the author of *Philosophical Health: Wittgenstein's Method in Philosophical Investigations, Doing Philosophy at the Movies,* and *Postmodern Movies: Neo-Comic Tragedies, Neo-Noirs, Neo-Westerns.*

A. G. Holdier is currently the program director for Idaho's Minidoka Christian Education Association, as well as an instructor for Colorado Technical University. His research interests lie at the intersection of philosophy, theology, and aesthetics with a focus on the ontology of creativity and the function of stories as cultural artifacts, themes he has developed in publications on the problem of evil, animal ethics, and the philosophy of forgiveness (forthcoming), as well as for several volumes of Open Court's *Pop Culture and Philosophy* series. He holds an MA in the philosophy of religion from Denver Seminary but prays that he is found to be far more interesting than Mr. Collins.

Christopher Ketcham has an earned doctorate from the University of Texas at Austin and is an adjunct professor of risk management and ethics at the University of Houston Downtown College of Business. His research interests are in risk management, applied ethics, social justice, comparative philosophy, including Emmanuel Levinas and Buddhism. He also is a frequent contributor to philosophical projects involving popular culture. Living right next door to Wilmington, Delaware, one cannot avoid seeing the wealth and influence of the DuPont family even as it has been distributed across many generations since 1802. DuPont is what Austen began to see, that industry and not land would become the new wealth generator.

David LaRocca, PhD, is visiting scholar in the Department of English at Cornell University; lecturer in screen studies for the program in cinema and photography in the Department of Media Arts, Sciences, and Studies at the Roy H. Park School of Communications at Ithaca College; and lecturer in value theory and film in the Department of Philosophy at the College at

Cortland, State University of New York. Educated at Buffalo, Berkeley, Vanderbilt, and Harvard, he is the editor of *The Philosophy of Charlie Kaufman* (2011) and *The Philosophy of War Films* (2014). He is also the editor of Stanley Cavell's *Emerson's Transcendental Etudes* (2003); and his coedited volume, *A Power to Translate the World*, focusing on transnational representation and cultural translation appears in Donald Pease's "Re-mapping the Transnational" series for Dartmouth College Press (2015). His most recent monograph, *Emerson's English Traits and the Natural History of Metaphor* (2013); was researched, in part, while he served as Harvard's Sinclair Kennedy Fellow in the United Kingdom. A father of two daughters, he is caught up by the expression and exercise of *paideia* (παιδεα) by women, and contributed an essay on HBO's *Girls* to that effect (2015). Austen's novels are another source of fascination, since the minds, morals, and metaphysical commitments of the girls and women in her books constitute interventions into the habits of millennia-old misogynies, including the very lexicon of thought: after all, a παῖς is a boy!

William A. Lindenmuth is associate professor of philosophy at Shoreline College. He received his MA in philosophy in New York City from the New School for Social Research, and his BA in English from Saint Mary's College in California. He's had success in getting students to ask questions like "What does God need with a starship?" in New York, Las Vegas, Seattle, and Rome, Italy. He specializes in normative ethics and moral psychology, particularly through the mediums of literature and film, arguing that our stories show us both who we are and who we'd like to be. Regarding the motion picture, he has contributed to *The Ultimate Star Wars and Philosophy*, and the forthcoming *The Philosophy of Christopher Nolan*, and *The Ultimate Star Trek and Philosophy*. He will be presenting on film at the SWPACA and National ACA/PCA conference in 2016.

Mimi Marinucci is a professor at Eastern Washington University with a joint appointment in philosophy and women's and gender studies. She is interested in the role of popular culture in the production and distribution of knowledge, particularly knowledge about gender and sexuality. In addition to numerous published articles, Marinucci is also the author of *Feminism is Queer: The Intimate Connection Between Queer and Feminist Theory*, a second edition of which will be available in 2016. While she is not convinced that anything is an actual truth, let alone a truth universally acknowledged, she nevertheless expends a great deal of effort attempting to sway others to her way of thinking.

Rita J. Dashwood is a second-year PhD student of English and comparative literary studies at the University of Warwick. Her thesis, "Women in Residence—Forms of Belonging in Jane Austen," investigates the various kinds of relationships between women and houses in Jane Austen's novels. In 2013, she graduated with an MA in English literature from the same university. Her main research interests include Jane Austen, eighteenth-century literature, and gender studies. When she is not procrastinating by memorizing all the lines from the 1995 *Pride and Prejudice*, she is dreaming of such mythical creatures as tenure and funded postdocs, thinking about how great it would be to have dinner with Jane Austen, or succumbing to her addiction to Disney movies.

Elizabeth Olson lives and works in Minneapolis, Minnesota, and is an avid follower of all things Austen. She holds her BA in English and economics from Oberlin College, and she also managed to pick up an MBA at the Wharton School several years ago. With Charles Taliaferro, she has co-authored several articles on philosophy and classic or popular literature. Despite her current gig in finance, Elizabeth lives for *Pride and Prejudice* marathons and has been known to enter spirited debates regarding whether Mr. Darcy or Mr. Knightley would make the better romantic partner. (Turns out that if Mr. Darcy looks like Colin Firth, and Mr. Knightley looks like Jeremy Northam, neither side wins.)

Handsome and clever **Janelle Pötzsch** is unfortunately far from being rich. To divert herself from this distressing thought, she obtained degrees in philosophy and English and wrote a dissertation on business ethics. She has contributed chapters to *Roald Dahl and Philosophy*, *Frankenstein and Philosophy*, and *The Big Bang Theory and Philosophy*, among others. And due to her penchant for British literature, she couldn't resist coediting *Dracula and Philosophy*. Does that make her think a little too well of herself? Probably yes.

Amanda Riter is a PhD student studying adaptations at De Montfort University in Leicester, England. Her research interests include transmedia adaptations, pop culture, and contemporary storytelling—and not just because that means she can play video games and watch TV shows as part of her research.

Thus far her work has been published in *Interdisciplinary Humanities*, and she is currently writing her dissertation on Jane Austen and the mashup phenomenon.

Heather Salter, of Northwestern State University, in Louisiana, is an English instructor who, for her own amusement, took up many books. There she found occupation for idle hours and wrote "Sincerity and Bad Faith in Zelda Fitzgerald's *Save Me the Waltz*" for *New Approaches to the Jazz Age* (forthcoming); "*The Awakening* as Fairytale?" for *Louisiana Folklife*; "Kitchen Slaves and Bologna Tacos: Food Codes in Sandra Cisneros's *Caramelo*," for *Postnational Appetites: Food in Chicano/a Literature*; and "Calling Salinger Up" with Keith Dromm for *Philosophy and The Catcher in the Rye*, of which she was also coeditor.

Charles Taliaferro, chair of the Department of Philosophy, St. Olaf College, is the author, coauthor, or editor of more than twenty books including *Turning Images* and *The Image in Mind*. Prior to their contribution to this volume, Charles has coauthored published essays with Elizabeth Olson on *Alice in Wonderland*, *Catcher in the Rye*, and *Princess Bride*. Friends, including Elizabeth, doubt that Charles has ever been quite as irresponsible and dangerously reckless as Edmund in *Mansfield Park*, but virtually everyone who knows Charles is relieved that he has someone in his life like Ms. Fanny Price, who has helped him weather through more than a few tempests.

Sally Winkle is professor of German and women's and gender studies at Eastern Washington University. She teaches German language, literature, culture, and film as well as women's and gender studies courses, and has been at EWU for ages. Her research specialties have evolved over the years from the image of women in eighteenth-century German literature to German films about the Nazi past and gender in contemporary German cinema. She is author of *Woman as Bourgeois Ideal* and coeditor of *The Nazi Germany Sourcebook: An Anthology*. She loves Jane Austen and is fascinated with life in the eighteenth century but would not like to travel there by time machine. No indoor plumbing.

Andrea Zanin likes zombies. She's never met one but figures that the best place for an apocalyptic zombie attack would be London—it's overpopulated and has a history of plague-like infestation. So there she waits; writing, editing, and pondering Jane Austen . . . hoping that one day she'll be able to plant a roundhouse kick on the soggy head of at least one living dead—*Elizabeth Bennet style*. She is also a cum laude English honors graduate (with a random law degree to boot) from the University of Johannesburg, South Africa, as well as the author of pop-culture blog Rantchick.com. A part-time philosopher with expertise in discourse analysis, Andrea has contributed chapters to *Sons of Anarchy and Philosophy* (2013) and *Hannibal Lecter and Philosophy* (2016).